pay inequity

public affairs administration
(editor: James S. Bowman)
vol. 16

Garland reference library
of social science
vol. 373

the public affairs and administration
series: James S. Bowman, editor

pay inequity
a guide to research on social influences

Eliot R. Hammer

Garland Publishing, Inc. • New York & London
1986

Library of Congress Cataloging-in-Publication Data

Hammer, Eliot R.
  Pay inequity.

  (Public affairs and administration ; vol. 16)
(Garland reference library of social science ; vol. 373)
  Includes index.
    1. Pay equity—United States—Abstracts.   2. Pay
equity—United States—Bibliography.   I. Title.
II. Series: Public affairs and administration series ;
16.   III. Series: Garland reference library of social
science ; v. 373.
HD6061.2.U6H36   1986   016.3312′1   86-19540
ISBN 0-8240-9919-2 (alk. paper)

Cover design by Alison Lew

Printed on acid-free, 250-year-life paper
Manufactured in the United States of America

contents

acknowledgments

As noted in the introductory section, an aim of this volume is to present material not only of use to social scientists, but also to academic professionals and private/public researchers in the fields of administration. This aim could not have been achieved without the assistance of James S. Bowman of the Florida State University Public Administration Department, as well as that of Marc J. Wallace, Jr. and Stephen E. Werling of the University of Kentucky Business Administration program. Gratitude is therefore expressed to these three people for their editorial advice and recognition of the collection's value to a broad range of academic disciplines. My thanks are also accorded to Jim Bowman, as Garland's Public Affairs series editor, and to Pamela Chergotis, managing editor of Garland, for providing the forum by which this research information could be made available.

                                                    Eliot R. Hammer
                                                    Lexington, KY

series foreword

The twentieth century has seen public administration come of age as a field of study and practice. This decade, in fact, marks the one hundredth anniversary of the profession. As a result of the dramatic growth in government, and the accompanying information explosion, many individuals—managers, academicians and their students, researchers—in organizations feel that they do not have ready access to important information. In an increasingly complex world, more and more people need published material to help solve problems.

The scope of the field and the lack of a comprehensive information system has frustrated users, disseminators, and generators of knowledge in public administration. While there have been some initiatives in recent years, the documentation and control of the literature have been generally neglected. Indeed, major gaps in the development of the literature, the bibliographic structure of the discipline, have evolved.

Garland Publishing, Inc., has inaugurated the present series as an authoritative guide to information sources in public administration. It seeks to consolidate the gains made in the growth and maturation of the profession.

The Series consists of three tiers:
1. core volumes keyed to the major subfields in public administration such as personnel management, public budgeting, and intergovernmental relations;
2. bibliographies focusing on substantive areas of administration such as community health; and
3. titles on topical issues in the profession.

Each book will be compiled by one or more specialists in the area. The authors—practitioners and scholars—are selected in open competition from across the country. They design their work to include an introductory essay, a wide variety of biblio-

graphic materials, and, where appropriate, an information resource section. Thus each contribution in the collection
provides a systematic basis for managers and researchers
to make informed judgments in the course of their work.

Since no single volume can adequately encompass such a
broad, interdisciplinary subject, the Series is intended as a
continuous project that will incorporate new bodies of literature as needed. Its titles represent the initial building blocks in
an operating information system for public affairs and administration. As an open-ended endeavor, it is hoped that not only
will the Series serve to summarize knowledge in the field but
also will contribute to its advancement.

This collection of book-length bibliographies is the product
of considerable collaboration on the part of many people. Special appreciation is extended to the editors and staff of Garland Publishing, Inc., to the individual contributors in the Public
Affairs and Administration Series, and to the anonymous re-
viewers of each of the volumes. Inquiries should be made to
the Series Editor.

James S. Bowman
Department of Public Administration
Florida State University

introduction

Compensation and the Sociology of Pay Equity

The administration of new legislation frequently creates a basis for debate over the merits of legal policy, both for society and specific subgroups of it. Such debate is no stranger to the history of civil rights legislation, in general, and to "pay equity" in particular. As a discourse on issues surrounding equity vs. inequity, the concern of this book is with actual and/or perceived discrimination in pay. This concern is shared across several disciplines. For example, writers borrow from economics, when making the distinction between "internal" and "external" forms of inequity. The former relates to the "value" or "worth" placed on various jobs within an organization. The latter relates to how any job value or worth becomes defined by the "market"; i.e., external inequity or the inadequacy of using market exchange rates to discern job value when comparing different categories of occupations.[1]

At the levels of legislative interpretation and administration, concern over matters of external inequity, in particular, has contributed to what Remick labels the "comparable worth controversy." In describing this controversy, she remarks that "few issues have generated as much as heat and as little light..." as the matter of what constitutes pay equity when comparing skills across occupational categories.[2] A review of the literature on internal equity suggests that the Remick disclaimer is no less a concern for internal equity.[3] The problem is that, whether the value of jobs being assessed is based on internal judgments about worth or on external market exchange rates, it is difficult to discern agreement on a baseline definition of what is and is not "equitable" when comparing wages across occupations.[4]

Lack of agreement over what can be considered "equitable" is reflected in such empirical issues as: how variant perceptions about equity might be described; how such perceptions might vary by quality of intraorganizational and interorganizational interactive processes; how such perceptions might be affected by changes in law; and, whether changing opinions about pay equity compromise economic explanations for why inequity occurs. These issues derive from that psychological, legal, and economic literature which influences most work on pay equity in business and public administration.[5]

However, such issues only open the door to broader inquiry into attitude formation and expressed behavior. Exemplifying such inquiry are questions like these: why perceptions vary; why interactive patterns develop and change as they do; why legal changes affect the quality of perceptions as they do; and, if economics does not offer a satisfactory explanation as to the "why" of attitudinal/behavioral phenomena, what is there that exists as an alternative to such economic thought? What is being called for, therefore, by this latter line of inquiry is a more comprehensive examination of social contextual, social structural, and demographic effects than that found in most contemporary management literature. Such questions are currently being addressed predominantly in the sociology literature.

The Value of Sociological Inquiry

Internal equity assessments. This broader line of inquiry into the "why" of attitude formation and expressed behavior is of potential value to management scholars and compensation administrators when evaluating internal job worth. For example, in their review of the role played by "compensation" in social life, Wallace and Fay note:

> Money cannot buy happiness, but it will soothe the nerves.... Many employees come to view their level of compensation (relative and absolute) as a symbol of their accomplishment and value to their employer. In sum, compensation is not merely pay for hours

worked: it influences employee reactions to their employment in a variety of fashions.[6]

From a sociological perspective, what Wallace and Fay are saying is that compensation is a "social force" that can affect employee perceptions of behavior on the job. By further arguing that compensation represents a "symbol of accomplishment and value," they suggest that compensation has "social meaning" attached to it. Compensation as a social force that can be given variant social meaning has been well examined in sociology.[7] However, Wallace and Fay note how it is incomplete to examine pay as a social force that affects behavior without addressing the broader social context in which compensation values are formed in the first place.

The perception of inequity *per se* is an isssue often called "individual" equity analysis. A more complete assessment of the broader social context, from which values and perceptions derive, is what also makes the analysis important from the standpoint of "internal" equity. For example, when evaluating the internal worth of jobs, a manager might want to assign different weights on the basis of "responsibility required." The organization's social structure might impact on employees in certain ways, such that the occupants of one position can be expected to place a greater "value" on the assumption of some form of responsibility than those of another position. The values placed by employees not only on pay, but also responsibility, are very much a part of the development of variant "social meaning."

As Douglas points out, social meanings can be viewed in a heterogenous context across cultures and subcultures, as well as across time.[8] As a result, such writers as Merton and Williams[9] prefer to: (a) accent contextual/cultural factors (within and beyond employment boundaries) that affect the development of compensation social meanings; and, (b) look at the resultant social force, pay, not only as a factor that affects on-the-job behavior, but also off-the-job behavior. These writers, therefore, recognize the dynamics of social interaction on and off the job, that contribute to ongoing changes in social meanings about the relationship between compensation and such social values as accomplishment and equity of reward. Several of the articles, annotated in this collection not only discuss, but also offer "measurement" for the effects of social structure on both individual and internal equity considerations.

External equity assessments. The majority of annotated articles that focus on external equity issues do not use the label, "comparable worth," nor do they deal with legal and/or administrative aspects surrounding the determination/assessment of market exchange rates. As a consequence, the reader new to sociological literature might (at first glance) feel that these articles have little relevance to the ongoing comparable worth debate. Yet the information contained in many of the articles is of central importance to that debate, as one of the more important external equity issues today. For example, in their discourse on problems associated with the determination of external equity, Wallace and Fay reflect on the difficulties associated with defining labor markets and the fact that "employers face a series of rather discontinuous or segmented labor markets...", when having to assess the applicability of market exchange rates.[10] An entire section (Part C) looks at this issue of "segmentation" from a sociological perspective; and, several selections in other parts of the book borrow from the segmentation literature when constructing arguments that broaden into other concerns.

One value of such sociological discourse is what it means to potential "resolution" of the comparable worth "controversy." The particular definitional problem over what is and is not equitable is only enhanced by disagreement among scholars, managers, and attorneys/judges over what constitutes a "non-arbitrary" means of comparable worth evaluation.[11] The end result, from a legal point of view, has been variant interpretations of the law and reversals of court decisions upon appeal.[12] The point is that changing definitions that, in turn, result in variant legal interpretations/court reversals do not occur in cultural and temporal vacuum. Rather, such variations in "definition" or "social meaning" can be more fully understood through detailed examination of social structure and context. Perhaps, by doing this, management practitioners and scholars can better anticipate and plan for changes in the nature and interpretations of law.

The Book's Purpose

The apparent neglect of sociological influence on an otherwise interdisciplinary mix affecting compensation administrative writing appears strange. It does not appear that sociological information is "unwelcome," as such administrative writers as Remick and Mahoney have called for increased examination of sociological issues in the compensation literature.[13] So, this task is approached here. The result is to present an examination of that research and theory on pay published primarily in sociology forums.

Consequently, beyond the presentation of a literature review for sociologists, this volume provides the management scholar with information on the sociology of pay equity and what remains to be done in this area. Therefore, the book is a research tool for those with an interest in examining social factors that contribute to actual and/or perceived inequity. It is hoped that, as a result, compensation administrative writing will increasingly entertain sociological analyses in the interdisciplinary flow of critical thinking about pay equity and comparable worth.

The relevance to the sociologist of that which is published in managerial forums—as well as that in psychological, legal, and economic forums—cannot be over-emphasized. The sociologist knows that s/he cannot adequately address "why" attitudes are formed/behavior occurs, unless that scholar understands "how" attitudinal and behavioral change transpires and "what" features of the legal and economic policy environment are interacting to create a basis for such change. Consequently, much of the literature found in non-sociological publishing forums, which nevertheless borders on sociological interests, is brought to the reader's attention.

The Style of Presentation

Like all books in this series, this volume represents a collection of annotations. The approach taken here, however, is to provide something more than descriptive information, because the content of much writing on equity seems to "beg" fundamental sociological questions. Attempts to address certain questions have a way of generating even more questions. Consequently, beyond a baseline presentation of theory, methods, and findings, commentaries are made, in most of the entries, on what additions/shortcomings appear evident in the selections. In doing this, an attempt is made to establish "linkages" among the findings reported and the conclusions drawn by the various authors. The annotations, then, take on a critical analytical quality. While much of the commentary/referencing occurs within the text of the annotations, some of this discussion is found in footnotes to the annotations.

Annotated entries are grouped into five parts (labeled A-E), which are described below. Given the rather substantial amount of cross-referencing done within the text and the resultant need for ease of movement among entries, listings appear alphabetically within each part of the volume. References to entries, listed elsewhere in this collection, include the name of the author(s) plus an identification code. So, for example, Adams (A-1) means that this reference to Adams represents the first selection in Part A.

The Scope of the Collection

The emphasis placed on thoroughness of review has prohibited the assembling of an exhaustive volume. The book's scope is primarily limited to journal publishing in academic sociology and in management fields from 1971 to 1985. The procedure began with a search of the following journals over the 15-year period:

ACADEMY OF MANAGEMENT JOURNAL *PUBLIC ADMINISTRATION REVIEW*
ACADEMY OF MANAGEMENT REVIEW *PUBLIC PERSONNEL MANAGEMENT*
ADMINISTRATIVE SCIENCE QUARTERLY *SEX ROLES*
AMERICAN JOURNAL OF SOCIOLOGY *SOCIAL FORCES*
AMERICAN SOCIOLOGICAL REVIEW *SOCIAL SCIENCE QUARTERLY*
AMERICAN SOCIOLOGIST *SOCIAL SCIENCE RESEARCH*
INDUSTRIAL RELATIONS *SOCIOLOGY AND SOCIAL RESEARCH*
PERSONNEL JOURNAL *WORK AND OCCUPATIONS*

While these journals do not exhaust the total number available, they are major publications in their respective fields. By starting with a complete search of these journals and then "working back" to articles from other journals (cited in the articles selected from the above list), a comprehensive representation of what has been published was obtained. A limitation of the collection is that perspectives on social factors affecting the specific job evaluation decision-making process might have been more broadly represented; however, some of the articles do deal with this issue and offer references to more complete reading elsewhere (e.g., Stolzenberg, C-16; Remick, E-8).

The reader is advised that most of the journals listed contain a large number of articles of interest to the student of pay equity; indeed, one might wonder why certain ones (beyond the acknowledged omission of those on the job evaluation decision-making) were not annotated. Three categories of articles that offer potential relevance to pay equity issues are not generally included:

(1) Excluded are those articles that do not directly bear on the question of *pay* equity so much as they bear on such broader interests as occupational status differentials and equality of hiring/promoting practices.

(2) Since entries are restricted to those that discuss the application of sociological theory and method to the analysis, descriptive pieces that are restricted to demographic statistics or judgments about what must be "sociological" (without citing much that is sociological) have been excluded.

(3) Generally speaking, articles that focus on issues of conceptual and/or methodological debate have not been included. The primary focus of this collection is on those presentations with a pronounced emphasis on demonstrating the empirical relationship *per se* between elements of social structure/context and actual/perceived pay inequity.

Where articles excluded for any of the above reasons nevertheless appear potentially relevant to one's total understanding of relevant issues are cited (with explanation) in notes to appropriate annotations.

It needs to be acknowledged that there are a few exceptions to the indicated rules. On occasion, a predominantly "descriptive" article has been annotated because it presents some important data that demonstrably contradicts what has been found in a more "analytical" annotated article (e.g., Asher and Popkin, D-1). On other rare occasions, articles have been included that do not directly bear on pay equity or are more conceptual in scope (e.g., Kaufman, et al., C-10). This is because of some pronounced and unique contributions that such articles make to the field. The reader can, however, assume that the vast majority of annotated articles: (1) directly bear on pay equity issues; (2) involve fundamental citing of sociology literature; and, (3) emphasize the testing of relationships between structure and equity.

Where there appears to be a "glut" of articles from sociology journals and a "dearth" of articles from management journals, it is because of the weight of "social influence" literature (defined by these inclusion criteria) published in sociological forums. Indeed, no annotations appear at all from some of the administrative journals, because none were found that fulfilled the criteria.

Beyond the matter of time that could be expended on this search, there is a reason for stopping the work of thorough annotation at 15 years of publication. Much of the sociological literature before 1971 is dated, due to a reliance on old data sets, less sophisticated methodologies, and/or the fact that knowledge about pay equity laws was still very much in its infancy. Nevertheless, the reader might want to review some of the pre-1971 literature in order to gain a broader historical overview of thinking and research on social factors affecting pay inequity. As a consequence, some of the pre-1971 literature (both of journal and non-journal format) that appears particularly germane to the issues discussed in this volume is cited in notes to the annotations (for example, see the notes to Szymanski, D-30).

Many of the cited authors are also writers of contemporary books on social factors affecting inequity. In the articles, they have a tendency to cite and summarize not only their own books, but books authored by others as well (cf., Fligstein, et

al., C-5; Wright, D-35; Wright and Perrone, B-7). Consequently, the reader will find a wealth of information on the
content of books in the articles. In many (if not most) cases,
the books written by these authors offer extended theoretical
and methodological presentations; and, in some cases, they
provide a more comprehensive presentation of the findings
reported in the articles. Where certain works appear to be
particularly germane to extended study, they are cited and
discussed in the notes to annotations.

Finally, while time constraints precluded in-depth search of
the psychology, economics, and legal literature, the literature
reviewed in journals that were searched, plus the strong input
of these other fields to management publishing, reveals that a
considerable portion of the thought generated by these other
disciplines was evident in the articles reviewed. This writer
has made note of the cited articles from psychology, economics, and law journals and has read many of them. Where it has
been found that their content still makes fundamental contributions to one's overall knowledge of the issues at hand, the
articles are cited (with explanation) in the notes to appropriate
annotations.

The Use of Notes to an Annotation

Summarizing the above discussion, notes to an annotation
are primarily used to cite and analyze non-annotated literature
which appears to have some relevance to the subject at hand
and which can be said to have substantial bearing on the article being annotated. This literature primarily falls into three
groups: contemporary journal articles, which (because they do
not fulfill all criteria for inclusion) have a more indirect bearing
on the focal interest of this book; journal articles published
before 1971; and, manuscripts appearing in non-journal format
(books, readings from books, dissertations). Notes are num-
bered consecutively within each annotated entry and listed at
the end of each entry.

As indicated earlier, the notes are also used to facilitate
commentary on article content, as well as "linkage" among

various articles in the collection. However, the major discussion of this type is done within the body of the annotation.

Parts of the Volume

Part A is reserved mainly for the benefit of new readers to equity literature, inasmuch as it annotates entries that review basic concepts in the field. Because a good amount of this literature has been published in early non-journal formats, an exception has been made here to include a few readings from edited books, some of which were published before 1971. Some of these selections are considered to be of "seminal" quality, from the standpoint of offering initial operationalization of concepts. Most Part A entries raise questions about the validity of certain economic theories, in general, and what is often referred to as the "human capital" approach to explaining pay inequity, specifically.

Many of the basic ideas and derived concepts, initiated in Part A, are expanded upon in Part B. The selections in Part B act to "bridge" the content of Part A with Parts C-E. Several of the Part B authors present a broader range of thinking and empirical study than that provided in Part A entries. Thus, Part B authors more saliently attempt to answer the question of "why" perceived/actual pay inequity occurs than do those cited in Part A.

The entries in Part C relate to what is the most fundamental challenge to human capital theory and research, i.e., work done on the relationship between "economic segmentation" and wage variation. An emphasis is placed, in several of these studies, on how broader aspects of social "structure" and "context" condition any relationship between "personal" characteristics (many of which are demographic in quality) and pay variation.

Two personal characteristics, race and sex, appear to receive greater attention in the literature than do others, perhaps due to a public policy interest in race and sex-based pay discrimination. Part D presents annotations of that literature, focusing on perceived/actual pay inequity by race and/or sex. It includes: literature concentrating on analysis of pay differences by race (not controlling for sex differences); literature which focuses its analytical attention on pay differences by sex (not controlling for the effects of race); and, literature which controls for *both* race and sex effects on pay variation. Some of these studies consider the contributions of other variables (e.g., age, education, veteran's status, occupational status); and, the reader will also find some of the writers in Part D offering additional contributions to the debate over economic segmentation vs. human capital theory (the predominant concern in Part C). Nevertheless, a judgment has been made that the primary focus is on the nature of differential earnings/income by race and/or sex.

Because of a substantial degree of "overlap" among the articles contained in Part D, a decision was made to group these articles together, rather than to separate them into three parts. For the benefit of the reader with more specific research needs than this, a key is presented at the beginning of Part D, identifying those articles with race-exclusive, sex-exclusive, and combined race and sex analytical focuses.

Another research theme, derivative from economic segmentation literature in Part C, is differential allocation into occupational categories that are or are not represented by unions. While there exist many articles that focus on pay differences by union status *per se* there exist few articles that definitively deal with what aspects of social structure contribute to such differences. Among the studies that do deal with broader aspects of social structure, some discuss the impact of other variables than just union status (e.g., education, sex, race, etc.). Nevertheless, judgment was made that the predominant interest of such articles remains on what socially conditions the effects of union status and/or the unionization process. The articles of this type are included in Part E.

Annotations on the effects of unionization constitute only one portion of those in Part E. This part has been labeled "pay inequity potpourri," since it annotates articles, which have interests that do not fit neatly into Parts A-D, but which do have something to say about social factors contributing to perceived/actual inequity. The articles are grouped together into this one part, since (at best) there exist only three articles per subject area. In addition to the effects of union status, entries reflect: EEO policy effects on inequity; what lies behind comparable worth policy formation; factors contributing to managerial and subordinate strategic decisions toward potential restoration of equity; and, what contributes to pay structures across societies. A key is provided at the beginning of Part E, identifying the entries by areas of substantive interest.

Indexes/Keys/Resource Section

In addition to those keys provided to facilitate identification of articles by more specific content focus (in Parts D and E), other keys/indexes are found in this book. First, given the degree of substantive overlap among entries in Part C, as well as among those in Part D, some readers may prefer to review the entries in each of those sections chronologically. Inasmuch as there are a relatively large number of articles annotated in each of these parts, chronological keys are presented at the front of Parts C and D.

Immediately following this introductory section, the user will find the main index. There all annotations are listed (complete with author and title) in the manner assembled in this book. At the back of the volume is one other general index, an alphabetical author listing of all entries.

Preceding the author index is a resource guide. This section provides information on major legislation and court cases, as well as organizations from which more information on pay equity issues might be obtained.

Toward Enhanced Theoretical Integration

While macro/sociological literature is primarily annotated in this volume, it is again emphasized that the contributions of writers in micro/psychological areas, on matters of pay inequity, cannot be ignored.

As an example, Katz wrote an early essay regarding the need for closer scrutiny of what it takes to bring about "internalization" of organizational goals and values (emphasizing more intrinsically rewarding pay administrative practice). Further, Mahoney reminds readers that any assessment of the potential for change in compensation practice must be considered within the broader context of how changing societal values affect organizational control.[14] The emphasis by Katz on what it takes to "motivate" the employee might be argued to be a more microbehavioral issue, while the Mahoney disclaimer on needing to account for broader social system (societal/organizational) impacts might be argued to be more macrobehavioral in context. Writers, such as Remick (E-8), suggest that some work is being done on merging these concerns with respect to such issues as job evaluation decision-making.

Nevertheless, the present writer suggests that there is room for more work in such areas as this. The reason is due to questions posed by such writers as Krupp and Perrow on whether any truly fundamental change in managerial practice can occur. Krupp and Perrow raise the issue, given what they regard as the rigidity of underlying organizational control of decision-making premises and the apparent societal sanctioning of such control. Indeed, these writers are suggesting that supposedly intrinsically rewarding/"motivating" experiences can be thought of as little more than tools that facilitate such premise control.[15]

Yet another example of potential merger between more micro and more macro levels of interest lies in a suggestion by such writers as Crosby that it is not always the case that "actual" inequity translates into "perceived" inequity.[16] Most of the annotated entries here use *either* actual inequity or perceived inequity as the dependent variable—either assuming that one form of inequity translates into the other form or not addressing the issue at all. The point is that writers such as Spilerman (C-14) and Major and Konar (D-20) infer that many of the social factors (contextual, structural, and/or demographic), discussed in these annotations, could help explain discrepancies between what is "actual" and what is "perceived," when it comes to pay inequity. It would, therefore, appear that there exists room for future work, which would serve to integrate the more macro/sociological with more micro/psychological literature on such matters as explaining variation between what is perceived and what is actual, in terms of pay inequity.

Notes

[1] The definitional distinction between internal and external equity is largely derived from M. Wallace and C. Fay, COMPENSATION THEORY AND PRACTICE (Boston: Kent Publishing Co., 1983).

[2] The reference is to H. Remick, "The Comparable Worth Controversy." PUBLIC PERSONNEL MANAGEMENT 10(1981):371–383 (quotation taken from p. 371). The Remick article is annotated in this collection (entry E-8). Writers, such as Wallace and Fay (re: note #1), define comparable worth as largely an external equity issue, since legal decisions on the matter, to date, have primarily focused on the quality of market exchange rates as job worth criteria.

[3] This statement is largely derived from information contained in Wallace and Fay (re: note #1).

[4] The matter of debate over "proper" definition is discussed by a number of authors in this area. Wallace and Fay (re: note #1) provide references to several sources that view the issue from the standpoint of both internal and external equity. Additional references are cited in the Remick annotation (E-8).

[5] For reviews of the literature that demonstrate this to be the case, see: J. Campbell and R. Pritchard, "Motivation Theory in Industrial and Organizational Psychology." In M. Dunnette, HANDBOOK OF INDUSTRIAL PSYCHOLOGY (Chicago: Rand McNally, 1976); P. Goodman and A. Friedman, "An Examination of Adams' Theory of Inequity." ADMINISTRATIVE SCIENCE QUARTERLY 16(1971): 271–288; J. Martin, "Relative Deprivation: A Theory of Distributive Justice for an Era of Shrinking Resources." In L. Cummings and B. Staw, RESEARCH IN ORGANIZATIONAL BEHAVIOR, Vol. 3 (Greenwich, CT: JAI Press, 1981); F. Crosby, "Relative Deprivation in Organizational Settings." In B. Staw and L. Cummings, RESEARCH IN ORGANIZATIONAL BEHAVIOR, Vol. 6 (Greenwich, CT: JAI Press, 1984).

[6] Wallace and Fay (re: note #1), p. 14.

[7] Reviews of this literature can be found in such texts as: J. Douglas, AMERICAN SOCIAL ORDER: SOCIAL RULES IN A PLURALISTIC SOCIETY (New York: The Free Press, 1971); R. Merton, SOCIAL THEORY AND SOCIAL STRUCTURE (New York: The Free Press, 1968); D. Miller and W. Form, INDUSTRIAL SOCIOLOGY: WORK IN ORGANIZATIONAL LIFE (New York: Harper and Row, 1980); R. Williams, AMERICAN SOCIETY: A SOCIOLOGICAL INTERPRETATION (New York: Alfred A. Knopf, 1970).

[8] Reference is to the Douglas listing at the beginning of note #7.

[9] Reference is to the Merton and Williams listings in note #7.

[10] Wallace and Fay (re: note #1), p. 26.

[11] For reviews of the controversy surrounding what constitute "nonarbitrary" evaluation methods, see: E.R. Livernash, COMPARABLE WORTH: ISSUES AND ALTERNATIVES (Washington, DC: Equal Employment Advisory Council, 1980); D. Miller and W. Form, INDUSTRIAL SOCIOLOGY (referenced in note #7).

[12] An excellent review of such matters can be found in D. Treiman and H. Hartman, WOMEN, WORK, AND WAGES: EQUAL PAY FOR JOBS OF EQUAL VALUE (Washington, DC: National Academy Press, 1981). Perhaps the most recent major example of judicial reversal on the question involves the case of AFSCME v. State of Washington. More information on this case and where to read about it can be found in the Resource Guide at the back of this book.

[13] The reference is to the Remick entry (E-8), as well as to publications authored by Mahoney. Examples of the latter include: an article by Mahoney that is annotated in this collection (entry A-4); and, T. Mahoney, COMPENSATION AND REWARD PERSPECTIVES (Homewood, IL: Irwin, 1979).

[14] References are to: D. Katz, "The Motivational Basis of Organizational Behavior." BEHAVIORAL SCIENCE 9(1964):131–146; T. Mahoney, "Toward an Integrated Theory of Compensation." In T. Mahoney, COMPENSATION AND REWARD PERSPECTIVES (listed in note #13).

[15] Reference is being made to arguments by S. Krupp, PATTERN IN ORGANIZATIONAL ANALYSIS: A CRITICAL EXAMINATION (New York: Holt, Rinehart and Winston, 1961); C. Perrow, COMPLEX ORGANIZATIONS: A CRITICAL ESSAY (New York: Random House, 1986). Extended discussion by these authors does not infer such an "absolute" quality to the impact of premise control that fundamental change cannot, at least from a theoretical point of view, occur. Much depends, for example, on the general nature of power relationships, the quality of organization set/network coupling, etc.

[16] Reference is to the Crosby listing at the end of note #5.

pay inequity

CONTENT INDEX OF ANNOTATIONS

CONTENT INDEX OF ANNOTATIONS

Part A: Basic Concepts

Part B: Extended Development/ Testing of Basic Concepts

6   PAY INEQUITY

Part B (continued)

Part C: Economic Segmentation

Part C (continued)

Part C (continued)

Part D: Specific Studies on Race/Sex Effects

Part D (continued)

Part D (continued)

Part E: Pay Inequity Potpourri

PART A: BASIC CONCEPTS

PART A: BASIC CONCEPTS

Annotated Entries

A-1

Adams, J. Stacy
1965 "Inequity in Social Exchange." In L. Ber-
kowitz, ADVANCES IN EXPERIMENTAL PSYCHOL-
OGY, Vol. 2. New York: Academic Press.

Adams uses the concept "social comparison" to
describe the type pay comparison made between a focal employee and his/her significant other(s)/ref-
erence group(s). The Adams essay offers more detail, than does that of Thurow (A-6) on the nature
of perceived "relative deprivation" (i.e., perceived
focal employee underpayment, due to the quality of
any social comparison). The resolution of relative
deprivation is part of what Adams calls "distributive justice"(1). However, distributive justice
can also connote the resolution of any perceived
overpayment. This particular essay concentrates
on the nature of perceived underpayment/overpayment,
while only providing brief attention to the issue
of what means might be employed to resolve such
perceptions, thus bringing about perceived "justice"(2).
    Writers, such as Livernash (A-3), tend to fo-
cus on pay inequity that can evolve from differences in "job content." However, from the standpoint of social factors that may contribute to such
inequity, Adams goes beyond this more general Livernash thinking by specifying the nature of compared "outcome-input" ratios. Such ratios, argues
Adams, form the basis of perceived inequity vs. distributive justice. Succinctly, Adams argues that,
within the context of work setting social interaction, individual employees compare their own "in-

A-1 (continued)

puts" to a job (relative to their own pay "outcomes") with similar ratios of significant others,
while accounting for the following qualities associated with level of "input": skill, seniority, education, expended effort, incurred risk, physical
fitness, age, and sex. With respect to the last
variable, for example, Adams suggests that, if a
female employee feels that a greater quality of
"input" is expected (by her superiors) of male employees, then the woman will not feel as if she is
treated inequitably, when receiving a lower pay outcome than do her male counterparts. This observa-
tion leads Adams to offer a quotation from Homans
that seems to capture the general theme of his article: "Justice is a curious mixture of equality
within inequality"(3).

Notes

(1) As alluded to, in the the introductory remarks to this volume, Part A annotations are included for the sole purpose of introducing the reader, new to the general subject matter of equity, to
such basic concepts as "social comparison," "distributive justice," etc. Over the years, there has
been no small amount of empirical examination of
the Adams thinking in particular--some of which
supports his theory, some of which does not. Two
of the more widespread reviews of the equity research, in general, and the Adams research, in particular, include: P. Goodman and A. Friedman, "An
Examination of Adams' Theory of Inequity." ADMIN-
ISTRATIVE SCIENCE QUARTERLY 16(1971):271-289; J.
Campbell and R. Pritchard, "Motivation Theory in
Industrial and Organizational Psychology." In M.
Dunnette, HANDBOOK OF INDUSTRIAL AND ORGANIZATION-
AL PSYCHOLOGY (Chicago: Rand-McNally, 1976). Also,
fairly comprehensive reviews of this research tra-
dition can be found in several textbooks, such as:
J. Miner, THEORIES OF ORGANIZATIONAL BEHAVIOR (Hins-
dale, IL: Dryden, 1981); D. Organ and W. Hamner,
ORGANIZATIONAL BEHAVIOR: AN APPLIED PSYCHOLOGICAL
APPROACH (Plano, TX: Business Publications, 1982).
     More advanced conceptual/methodological com-
mentary and debate, relevant to the social compar-

A-1 (continued)

ison process, has evolved over the years. Some of
this is discussed in the above-noted references,
as well as in several of the empirical annotations,
listed elsewhere in this collection. For even more
broad-based commentary of this type, the reader
with an interest in such conceptual and/or methodological debate, per se, might wish to more exten-
sively consult the microbehavioral literature. Some
suggestions, in this respect, include: P. Goodman,
"An Examination of Referents Used in the Evaluation
of Pay." ORGANIZATIONAL BEHAVIOR AND HUMAN PERFORM-
ANCE 12(1974):170-195; F. Hills, "The Relevant Other in Pay Comparisons." INDUSTRIAL RELATIONS 19
(1980):345-351; R. Coser and D. Dalton, "Equity
Theory and Time: A Reformulation." ACADEMY OF MAN-
AGEMENT REVIEW 8(1980):311-319; P. Varadarajan and
C. Futrell, "Factors Affecting Perceptions of Smallest Meaningful Pay Increases." INDUSTRIAL RELATIONS
23(1984):278-286.
      While there are several similarities between
the literature on "relative deprivation" and that
on "inequity," there remain certain rather salient
differences that have evolved in research over the
years. Two rather excellent reviews, demonstrating
the nature of the differences between inequity and
relative deprivation research, are: J. Martin, "Relative Deprivation: A Theory of Distributive Justice
for an Era of Shrinking Resources"; and, F. Crosby,
"Relative Deprivation in Organizational Settings."
These readings can be found, respectively, in Vol.
3 (1981) and Vol. 6 (1984) of RESEARCH IN ORGANIZA-
TIONAL BEHAVIOR (Greenwich, CT: JAI Press). Co-
editors of the volumes are B. Staw and L. Cummings.

      (2) Methods to resolve perceived inequity have
been discussed, at some length, in other sources.
Perhaps, the most definitive discussion by Adams of
this type is presented in an unpublished work, en-
titled "Wages Inequities in a Clerical Task" (New
York: General Electric Company, 1961). Readers,
who do not have access to this study, will find
fairly comprehensive summaries in several of the
references provided in note #1, especially the
Campbell and Pritchard, Goodman and Friedman, Miner, and Organ and Hamner references.

A-1 (continued)

(3) G. Homans, SOCIAL BEHAVIOR: ITS ELEMENTA-
RY FORMS (New York: Harcourt, Brace, 1961, p. 244).

A-2

Jacques, Elliott
1979   "Equitable Payment." In T.A. Mahoney,
        COMPENSATION AND REWARD PERSPECTIVES.
        Homewood, IL: Irwin.

This essay, which is excerpted from Jacques'
1961 book of same title, reports on the results of
a study at the Glacier Metals Company. The structure of the study departs from the suggestions of
such writers as Adams (A-1) and Thurow (A-6), in
three fundamental respects:

(1) Jacques relies on comparison against absolute
     standards, rather than on social comparison,
     to determine degree of pay inequity.

(2) Jacques uses "time" as a variable to distin-
     guish differential job content and to thus
     form the basis for the absolute standards.

(3) Adams and Thurow note that employees, who use
     social comparison, are often criticized for
     attempting such comparisons "externally" (due
     to differences across firms, industries, etc.).
     Jacques, however, argues for the generaliza-
     bility of his absolute standards across firms
     and thus argues for the very real potential
     for valid external (not just internal) wage
     comparisons.

     The use of the "time" variable is specifical-
ly operationalized by Jacques as "time span of discretion." This means that the quality of some job
might allow for a greater length of time (and,
therefore, greater individual employee latitude
for judgment or "discretion") in between supervisory inspection/evaluation, than is the case for
other jobs. According to Jacques, individuals sub-
scribe to certain "norms of equity," surrounding a

A-2 (continued)

certain level of pay attached to various jobs of
similar time span of discretion. Jacques indicates
that, within an actual pay range of plus or minus
three percent of the perceived equity norm, employees tend to regard their wage levels as "fair."
From the standpoint of macro-level research, however, an apparent drawback of the Jacques study is
that it does not specify what type social factors
(through cultural transmission, internal comparisons, external comparisons, or whatever) might lead
to the formation of such equity norms.

A-3

Livernash, E. Robert
    1957 "The Internal Wage Structure." In G.W. Tay-
          lor and F.C. Pierson, NEW CONCEPTS IN WAGE
          DETERMINATION. New York: McGraw-Hill.

    The general purpose of this qualitative essay
is to go somewhat beyond "economic" analysis, when
discussing those elements of compensation policy
(within an organization) that can be expected to
contribute to pay inequity. The particular "non-
economic" criteria that Livernash discusses are
couched in terms of "internal" and "external" wage
comparisons. It is Livernash's intent to establish
criteria for specific use in job evaluation.
    From the standpoint of internal comparisons,
the author provides detail on that variation in job
content contributing to differential pay rates within firms. From the standpoint of external comparisons, Livernash discusses how variation in the content of seemingly "similar" jobs can exist, due to
differences in the importance placed on said jobs
(across firms) by different groups of managers(1).
Also discussed as impacting on pay rate variation,
from the standpoint of external comparison, are differences in operating costs across geographical locales and differences among firms in the manners by
which "inequity grievances" are managed. In addition, Livernash acknowledges that more specific
analysis is needed (than he provides) on the re-

A-3 (continued)

lationship between collective bargaining and the
existence of wage variation.

Note

(1) This particular reason why external comparison is difficult, as well as some of the other
reasons brought up by Livernash, are expanded upon,
in more detail, among annotations listed elsewhere
in this collection. As an example, the reader is
directed to Grandjean (B-3).

A-4

Mahoney, Thomas A.
1975 "Justice and Equity: A Recurring Theme in
Compensation." PERSONNEL 52:60-66.

Mahoney reviews the history of literature on
the issue of distributive justice, from the standpoint of how different definitions of the issue
(reflecting different perspectives on what constitutes pay equity) derive from changes in social
values. For example, Mahoney traces the historical transformation of definitions of a "just" wage,
in different eras and societies--where religious
values influenced such definitions, at one point
in time, and variant economic values influenced
such definitions at other times.
A contemporary reliance, in the United States,
on certain classical economic principles(1), argues
Mahoney, derives from a social value that "exchange
value" is the "true measure of social justice."
The author argues that this translates into a reliance on marginal productivity theory, whereby (unlike a Marxist point of view) the use value of labor is determined to be equivalent to exchange value. Mahoney provides examples of how, in concert
with this line of thinking, both management and labor (in any collective bargaining exchange) rely on
"market-based" statistics to negotiate wages.
The thrust of the Mahoney article is to outline that literature, which the author sees as

A-4 (continued)

presently challenging the reliance on marginal productivity theory. Mahoney argues that, by doing
such, a social basis can be discerned, explaining
why inequity/equity perceptions are formed. Mahoney begins by outlining the nature of "distortions"
in the market exchange model that derive from such
things as government subsidies and the nature of
defense spending. One gets the impression, from
the flow of the author's argument, that perceptions
of such "distortions" are what contribute (from Mahoney's point of view) to questions about pay equity under a system based on exchange value. Specifically, Mahoney discusses how certain select groups
(based on sex, race, etc.) might have perceived a
particular "lack of justice," due to distortions in
exchange value application.
    Mahoney infers that the exchange value distor-
tions invalidate marginal productivity assumptions
surrounding the value of competitive markets and
long-run equilibrium in the determination of wages.
The distortions, argue Mahoney, offer no potential
for fairness of market-based wages, since "dual labor markets" result from the distortions. On the
one hand, there exist labor market concerns (expressed "external" to the firm) about such issues
as general black vs. white or male vs. female wage
comparisons. The other market concern, as Mahoney
sees it, surrounds issues of "within firm" (i.e.,
"internal") wage differentials. The author argues
that, to redress external market concerns, new
(entry-level) employees might be initially paid
according to market-set rates; but, once in the
firm (as their careers progress), wage levels for
such employees are set not by market comparisons
but by administrative rules. Such rules, as Mahoney sees it, are designed to redress internal pay
discrepancies; such discrepancies, in turn, are
perceived (due to externally changed social values)
to be inequitable.
    One assumes, based on the above presentation,
that Mahoney fundamentally disagrees with the assumption of Adams (A-1) that there currently exists
some value-based "acceptance" of differential pay,
due to non-merit related factors. However, Mahoney only infers that distortions in the application
of market-based wage setting might contribute to

A-4 (continued)

changes in social values--without really addressing
the detailed dynamics of how those values might be
changed. Specifically, the reader will not find
extensive discussion about the nature of shifting
forms of social interaction (educational, religious,
familial, political, etc.) that might contribute to
the type "value" changes that Mahoney sees as affecting compensation policy(2). On the other hand,
some other writers do attempt to describe the nature of such shifting forms of social interaction
in a bit more detail. As examples, the reader is
directed to: Stolzenberg (C-15); Talbert and Bose
(C-17); Spilerman (C-14).

Notes

(1) The reader will find some of the classical
economic principles, being outlined by Mahoney, to
be shared by adherents to "human capital" theory--
particularly, the assumption of homogeneity of
market-set wages. For more specific information
on the human capital approach, the reader is directed to the work of Fligstein, et al. (C-5),
Fogel (C-6), and Spilerman (C-14).

(2) Some of the thought, being generated in
this paper, is brought up to date by this selection's author--in T. Mahoney, "Approaches to the
Definition of Comparable Worth." ACADEMY OF MAN-
AGEMENT REVIEW 8(1983):14-22. In the later article, Mahoney still does not develop detail on the
forms of interaction that might contribute to value
changes; however, he does offer a somewhat more
thorough consideration of the problems associated
with the interpretation of value (and consequent
norm) formation. The paradox, which Mahoney addresses a bit more thoroughly in the later paper,
is that interpreted "societal" consensus on norms
may conflict with the norms of selected smaller
social systems (industries, firms, work groups)--
making more complex the process by which inequity
is perceived.

A-5

Mahoney, Thomas A.
   1979 "Organizational Hierarchy and Position
         Worth." ACADEMY OF MANAGEMENT JOURNAL
         22:726-737.

   In another entry, Mahoney (A-4) comments on
how perceptions of pay inequity are partly formed
on the basis of social conditions within a firm.
In this paper, Mahoney concentrates on one aspect
of such internal social conditions--the nature of
hierarchical relationships among managerial employees. The author tests for the relationship between
management organizational hierarchy and compensation structure.
   Mahoney offers a review of literature that
has consistently found compensation differentials
between any two managerial ranks to be perceived
by the managers involved as "equitable." Mahoney
is interested in determining the amount of compensation differential, from one vertically adjacent
rank to the next, that is (indeed) perceived as
equitable. To achieve this end, the author uses
a technique of weighting the survey data of other
writers on the subject; and, he then proceeds to
compare the acceptable differentials found in the
various studies by one another. The results of the
analysis are that a pay differential, between adjacent ranks, of about 30-40 percent is perceived to
be equitable(1).
   From the standpoint of macro-level interest,
the article can be said to be providing some information on the relevance of hierarchical structure to perceptions of equity--at least, in this
case, among managers. However, no further empirical information is provided as to what social factors might be impacting on the relationship. Mahoney suggests, along these lines, that investigation be made into differences in the "quality of
perceptions" across the samples used in the different surveys. For example, some of the studies,
analyzed by Mahoney, tested for the views of compensation administrators, while others tested for
the views of management students. As the author
notes, the variant experiences, among different
types of samples, could have led to differences
in social norms surrounding the ratings. As a re-

A-5 (continued)

sult, such normative differences could have contributed to variation in the precise amount of acceptable compensation differential.
    Mahoney also reflects on the need to more
rigorously account for perceived differences in job
content. Beyond similarities in perception of "time
span of discretion" (re: Jacques, A-2), no other
"job content" variables (e.g., skill, ability, education, etc.) are found by the author to influence
wage differentials. Thus, Mahoney concludes that
some "unknown" job content variables might be influencing pay variance. One presumes that it could
also have something to do with the way the job content variables are operationalized; however, definitive conclusions of this type cannot be derived
from the information provided in this article.
    Finally, in an earlier piece, Mahoney (A-4)
emphasized the potential influence of such factors,
as sex and race differences, on equity perceptions.
Consequently, it is a bit surprising that the author does not acknowledge, let alone test for, the
potential influence of these variables on the variant managerial perceptions reported in this article.

                        Note

    (1) Issues of what constitute acceptable pay
differentials, as well as what constitute acceptable levels of pay increase, appear to have some
relevance (in a more psychological sense) to knowledge about comparative inputs/outcomes, in social
comparison, as well as to variant "preference mixes"
(cf., Cook, B-2; Freedman, E-4; Spilerman, C-14).
For a more contemporary review of literature on some
psychological dynamics surrounding perceived accept-
ability, the reader is directed to P. Varadarajan
and C. Futrell, "Factors Affecting Perceptions of
Smallest Meaningful Pay Increases." INDUSTRIAL
RELATIONS 23(1984):278-286.

A-6

Thurow, Lester C.
1979 "The Sociology of Wage Determination." In
      T.A. Mahoney, COMPENSATION AND REWARD PER-
      SPECTIVES. Homewood, IL: Irwin.

      This essay is excerpted from Thurow's book,
GENERATING INEQUALITY (New York: Basic Books, 1975).
The author begins by challenging certain economic
assumptions made by others. For example, whereas
some writers might (rather exclusively) argue that
individual employees have highly marketable skills
that they can sell in a labor market (and will sell
if dissatisfied with earnings), Thurow points out
that dissatisfied employees can behave in yet another manner--by lowering productivity. Of interest, however, are the reasons why pay dissatisfac-
tion might exist in the first place; and, Thurow
focuses on those aspects of social interaction within a firm that contribute to perceptions of relative
deprivation.
      Specifically, Thurow argues that all employees
identify certain reference group(s) with which they
will make pay comparisons. Thurow suggests that the
broader the reference group used in any comparison,
the greater the potential for perceived relative
deprivation--as there exists the potential for employees to compare across jobs of different content
inside the organization. In brief, therefore, Thurow argues that pay inequity results from the quality
of relative deprivation that derives from reference
group-based wage comparisons. For a more specific
theoretical application of this line of thinking,
see Adams (A-1)(1).

                        Note

      (1) While Thurow rather loosely uses "relative
deprivation" in conjunction with "inequity," from
an operational standpoint, the concepts are not exactly the same. Contemporary research on relative
deprivation tends only to account for comparisons
among outcomes. As noted in the Adams annotation,
the tradition of equity research has been to emphasize comparisons among both inputs and outcomes.
For definitive review of the variant operational

A-6 (continued)

quality and application of the two concepts, see
the articles by J. Martin and by F. Crosby in RE-
SEARCH IN ORGANIZATIONAL BEHAVIOR (Volumes 3 and 6).
Complete references to these articles can be found
in note #1 to the Adams entry, as well as in note #5
to this volume's introduction.

PART B: EXTENDED DEVELOPMENT AND/ OR TESTING OF BASIC CONCEPTS

PART B: EXTENDED DEVELOPMENT AND/
OR TESTING OF BASIC CONCEPTS

Annotated Entries

B-1

Bailey, William R. and Albert E. Schwenk
 1980 "Wage Rate Variation by Size of Establish-
       ment." INDUSTRIAL RELATIONS 19:192-198.

       Bailey and Schwenk review literature that dem-
onstrates a direct relationship between organizational size and wage level, as well as literature
that offers three alternatives to such a direct
relationship:

(1)   That what really creates the variation in wage
       level is degree of unionization; greater or-
       ganizational size, therefore, is related to
       higher wages, only because larger organiza-
       tions are more inclined to have unions.

(2)   That what really creates any variation in wage
       level is the absence vs. presence of incentive
       pay systems; greater organizational size leads
       to higher pay, only because larger organiza-
       tions can better afford incentive systems.

(3)   That what really creates variations in wage
       level is the size of the geographical "area"
       (i.e., "labor market"); greater organization
       size contributes to higher wages, only because
       larger organizations are more inclined to lo-
       cate in larger market areas.

       The authors analyze data, based on Bureau of
Labor Statistics. They find that, in most circumstances, none of the above explanations for wage

31

B-1 (continued)

variation hold. Increased organizational size does
not directly contribute to higher wages, uniformly
among industries nor across occupations within any
given industry. Furthermore, in those cases where
size is found to contribute to wage differentials,
it is found to do so independent of the effects of
company union status, incentive system, and area
size. Bailey and Schwenk suggest that, perhaps, some
other variables might serve to better explain why
earnings vary by size in some industries, but not
in others. Along these lines, the reader is referred to the specific presentation of Hodson (C-8)
on how sex differences moderate the effects of size
on earnings, as well as the work of Hodson, Beck,
et al. (C-1), and Stolzenberg (C-16) on: (1) how
the nature of markets define the organizational/
industry structure in terms of a more complex array
of factors other than size; and, (2) how size can
be considered more or less important, as a variable,
depending on whether measurement is done at the company or industry level.

B-2

Cook, Karen S.
    1975 "Expectations, Evaluations, and Equity."
          AMERICAN SOCIOLOGICAL REVIEW 40:372-388.

    As a preface to his discourse on the nature of
pay equity research, Mahoney (A-4) states that work
in the subject area is in a state of disarray. Cook
concurs with this assessment. She suggests, however, that the reason for such disarray is very simple. Theories on distributive justice assume that
focal employees possess knowledge about two items:
(1) what their significant others (in a circumstance
of social comparison) are earning; and (2) whether
any organizational "distribution rules" (for example, that pay discrimination for comparable work
will not occur on the basis of race) are being violated. However, when such distributive justice
theories are tested, they are, at times, not supported. Cook argues that the reason why this oc-

B-2 (continued)

curs is that, in reality, focal employees may not
be aware of whether distribution rules are being
violated and, thus, may not "perceive" inequity--
when such "actually" exists.
     A study, conducted by Cook, manipulates con-
ditions by which clearly defined circumstances of
equity/inequity are presented at one phase and lack
of clear definitions of such are presented at another. Results are as predicted; i.e., the less
knowledgeable subjects are about violations of distribution rules, the less that they perceive inequity. This particular study, which is done by means
of lab experimentation (N=20), focuses solely on
the question of degree of awareness; however, from
a macro-level standpoint, Cook infers that future
research questions might be asked about what social
structural conditions contribute to variations in
awareness.

B-3

Grandjean, Burke D.
   1975   "The Economic Analysis of the Davis-Moore
           Theory of Stratification." SOCIAL FORCES
           53:543-552.

     Writers, such as Adams (A-1), Livernash (A-3),
and Thurow (A-6), suggest that one of the problems
with external social comparisons (that result in
perceived inequity), is that differences exist in
economic conditions, from one geographical locale
to the next. Consequently, the argument goes, it
is not always fair to assume the need for compara-
bility across such geographical boundaries. At a
more specific level of analysis, the logic relates,
in part, to an economic principle surrounding elas-
ticity of labor demand--that wage levels vary by
the amount of demand for labor. In other words,
in areas where demand is greater, wage levels for
comparable jobs will, arguably, be higher than in
areas where the demand is less. Grandjean reviews
the nature of a social stratification theory, developed by Davis and Moore(1)--which is based closely on the above and other economic principles.

B-3 (continued)

        Davis and Moore apparently concluded that, from
one geographical area to another, certain occupations would be regarded as more or less "functionally important," depending on how "functionally
unique" the positions were (i.e., to what extent
circumstances existed where no other positions, than
those labeled "unique," could satisfactorily perform
needed tasks). In this essay, Grandjean attempts
to summarize centrality of thought toward the an-
swering of three lines of questioning:

(1) If the job situation is such that a particular
     position is "functionally unique," to what ex-
     tent can it be said that this creates a circum-
     stance of demand inelasticity with respect to
     the position in question? If it is the case
     that such demand inelasticity exists for a po-
     sition, regardless of the geographical locale
     where the work must be done, can it then be
     argued that external social comparisons are
     more valid?

(2) Grandjean introduces a matter, not considered
     by Davis and Moore, surrounding "talent and
     training requirements." The essential ques-
     tion to be considered is this: If variation
     occurs, across localities, with respect to
     talent/training requirements (for the perform-
     ance of the duties attached to a given posi-
     tion), might that not influence differential
     demand circumstances and consequent structur-
     ally-induced differences in pay levels?

(3) Can differences, across geographical areas
     (with respect to the functional uniqueness
     of jobs or the ability/training needed to do
     jobs), be considered a viable measure of "func-
     tional importance" (i.e., the importance of
     the jobs)?

        Based on the reviewed literature, Grandjean
concludes that neither functional uniqueness nor
ability/talent requirements have been found to be
consistently valid operational measures of functional importance. Grandjean, therefore, concludes
that the Davis-Moore usage of "functional impor-

B-3 (continued)

tance" is questionable. On the other hand, the literature reviewed by Grandjean does not debunk the
reality of functional uniqueness, per se, nor differential talent/ability requirements for similar
positions, per se. Consequently, it might be assumed that these are social structural conditions
of some potential value, when assessing the validity of perceived pay inequity, based on external social comparison.

Note

    <1> K. Davis and W.E. Moore, "Some Principles
of Stratification." AMERICAN SOCIOLOGICAL REVIEW
10(1945):242-249.

B-4

Jasso, Guillermina and Peter H. Rossi
    1977 "Distributive Justice and Earned Income."
          AMERICAN SOCIOLOGICAL REVIEW 42:639-651.

        Some writers, such as Mahoney (A-4), argue that
certain "value criteria" (or "personal characteristics")--race, sex, education, etc.--enter into assessments of perceived fairness of pay. However,
Mahoney, in particular, does not empirically test
for the relevance of such value criteria to focal
individuals, when the latter engage in social comparisons. Jasso and Rossi do empirically test for
the relevance of five such criteria: formal educational attainment, occupational attainment, sex,
marital status, and knowledge of family earnings.
The Jasso and Rossi analysis is based on data collected from a sample of 200; all five criteria are
found to influence earnings patterns and to thus be
important in the social comparison process.
        The Jasso and Rossi description of sampling
technique reveals some care taken toward stratification based on the relevant criteria (for example,
to provide a sufficient number of males and females
in the sample, such that meaningful sex comparisons
could be made). However, the authors restrict their

B-4 (continued)

analysis to measurement of the direct relationship
between personal characteristics and wage variation.
The reader will find that such writers as Beck,
et al. (C-1), Hodson (C-7), and Parker (C-12) find
it to be more informative to only entertain such a
relationship within the context of broader social
structural conditions, such as the impact of economic segmentation differences(1).

Note

(1) While the Jasso and Rossi presentation
seems to "fall short" of what these and other economic segmentation theorists (reviewed in Part C)
have in mind, there does exist one quite recent article that attempts to make the case for the superiority of some direct personal characteristic effects measurement over the more indirect type relationship preferred by economic segmentation theory.
The article is: D. Jacobs, "Unequal Organizations
or Unequal Attainments? An Empirical Comparison of
Sectoral and Individualistic Explanations for Aggregate Inequality." AMERICAN SOCIOLOGICAL REVIEW
50 (1985):166-180. For a bit more information on
the content of the Jacobs article, see note #6 in
the Ward and Mueller (D-34) entry.

B-5

Spaeth, Joe L.
    1979   "Vertical Differentiation Among Occupa-
           tions." AMERICAN SOCIOLOGICAL REVIEW 44:
           746-762.

        Mahoney (A-5) comments on the importance of ac-
counting for the nature of "hierarchy"--as a structural condition potentially affecting wage differentials. However, a literature review by Stolzenberg (C-16) reveals that measurement of hierarchy
(or "vertical occupational differentiation") is not
as simple as merely counting the number of levels on
an organizational chart. Spaeth agrees with Stolzenberg on the difficulty of measuring dimensions of

B-5 (continued)

hierarchy. In order to somewhat extend discussion on the matter, he begins by reflecting on that literature which identifies two dimensions of vertical differentiation, "authority" and "complexity." Spaeth, then, definitionally distinguishes these two dimensions of differentiation from a third, occupational "prestige" (or "status"). The definitional distinction among these dimensions is important, because some of the literature, reviewed by Spaeth, reveals variation among hierarchy-wage level relationships, depending on what operational measure of differentiation is used. Specifically, the literature reveals that the use of "complexity" and/or "autonomy" yields different findings, with respect to earnings patterns, than does the use of "prestige."

Spaeth argues that the reason for such variance in results is that prestige refers to a "status" (i.e., an "ascription" or "label"). Such a status can simply be attached to a hierarchical level because some outside observer "thinks it should be there"--but, this does not mean, for example, that the individual with a higher "status" necessarily has more "authority" than some alter person in the organization. It is Spaeth's perspective that the dimensions of authority and complexity relate to "roles" (i.e., "performed behavior") that derive from the nature of the organization's division of labor. Authority and complexity, from the Spaeth point of view, are highly interrelated. For example, as occupations become more specialized, it can be argued that the range of tasks that must be performed in any one occupation become more "complex." At the same time, there exists a need for managerial "authority" to coordinate the work of individual specialists. Spaeth's point is that, while any outside party can capture certain generalities about complexity and authority--and then integrate such into a prestige label-- no such outside observer can fully capture the specific dimensions of such role performance. As a consequence, Spaeth argues that attempts to empirically equate the effects of authority (and/or complexity) with those of prestige leave something to be desired, from the standpoint of enhancing validity.

B-5 (continued)

Spaeth offers a detailed description of how he develops measures of authority, complexity, and prestige, based on a variety of secondary sources of data. Through the application of factor analytical techniques, he demonstrates a degree of difference between authority/complexity, on the one side, and prestige on the other. However, Spaeth notes that the demarcation is not as pronounced as might have been expected, based on the reviewed literature. The author attributes the lack of salient demarcation to the crudity with which he operationalizes his definitions of authority and complexity. He, therefore, proposes alternative forms of operationalizing authority, in particular, in future research.

B-6

Treas, Judith and Robin J. Walther
1978 "Family Structure and the Distribution of
       Family Income." SOCIAL FORCES 56:866-880.

Criteria associated with familial values, such as marital status and family earnings, have been considered potentially important to definitions of wage differentials (cf., Jasso and Rossi, B-4). Treas and Walther engage in an analysis of census data, so as to explore what new knowledge exists about variation in family income, given changes in family structure.

In general, the authors find that income inequalities have declined among single-headed families and individuals who live alone. However, Treas and Walther also find that such decreases in "intragroup" inequality have not translated into a reduction in overall (among-group) wage discrepancies. This leads the authors to conclude that differentiation by such other personal characteristics as sex, age, and occupational status might be important to consider. Treas and Walther also discuss the potential importance of accounting for population shifts, inasmuch as shifts of larger numbers of some family types into lower income categories might have led to greater inequality. In any event, the study seems

B-6 (continued)

to reinforce the need for consideration of a broader array of personal characteristics than just familial variables, when attempting to explain earnings variation.

B-7

Wright, Erik O. and Luca Perrone
    1977   "Marxist Class Categories and Income In-
           equality." AMERICAN SOCIOLOGICAL REVIEW
           42:32-55.

        Wright and Perrone review the body of socio-
logical literature that justifies usage of social
class, as an aspect of social structure[1]. The
authors then proceed to operationalize their definition of class in a Marxist context as "positions
within the social relations of production." The
emphasis on the phrase "social relations" is important to this definition, as it infers a desire by
Wright and Perrone to separate "class" from occupational "status"[2]. In much the same context as
Spaeth (B-5) differentiates the concept "authority"
from the concept "prestige" (i.e., "status"), Wright
and Perrone emphasize the phrase "social relations"
in their definition, so as to inform readers that
their classes are defined in terms of differential
"role performances," not simply in terms of some
artifical labels provided to positions on an organizational chart.
        Reanalyzing the content of Marxian literature,
Wright and Perrone find it to have been a mistaken
impression, by some writers, to have assumed no
"buffer" class between employers and workers. Indeed, the authors establish a case for the presence
of a "managerial" class in the Marxian scheme[3].
Wright and Perrone, then, proceed to operationalize social class on the basis of these three categories: employers, managers, and workers[4].
        A number of research questions are addressed
in this article. With respect to the issue of potential pay inequity, the most crucial question
asked (and the results found) appear to be as follows: What role does education play in condition-

B-7 (continued)

ing the relationship between class and income?
Stolzenberg (C-16), for example, feels that structural variables do not act directly on wage levels
but on relationships between personal characteristics (such as education) and income. Wright and
Perrone find that this is, indeed, the case with
respect to class as a structural variable. Specifically, it is found that the returns to education
are greater for managers than for workers and are
greater for employers than for managers. Of interest is that the authors find these results to
hold, when controlling for the effects of such other personal characteristic variables as sex, race,
age, and job tenure.

In the case of employers enjoying higher returns to education than do managers, Wright and
Perrone suggest that this occurs only because small
businesses are included in their sample (So, for
example, a lawyer in the sample might be expected
to earn more than a shopkeeper.). Had this been a
sample of larger businesses, then the authors feel
that managers could have expected greater returns
to education than employers. The reasoning is that,
under those circumstances, differential employer
salaries would not be directly contingent on level
of education, whereas managerial salaries would.

While social class differences represent an
important part of the social environment that obviously enters into the explanation of why pay inequity exists, a question might be raised as to
whether (based on the use of Marxist classes) perceived pay inequity might result, due to any vertical social comparison. For example, assuming (as
do Wright and Perrone) that education enters into
the mix with status to define the precise nature
of manager-employer pay variation, then a question
might be asked as to whether either party might
perceive the education-status tradeoff that favors
the other to be inequitable. On the other hand,
the reader will find Fligstein, et al. (C-5) suggesting that the issue of unfairness, derivative
from vertical comparison, may not be so much a matter of examining discrepancies "among classes" as
it is to analyze the nature of differences "within
the managerial category." Whether it be a matter
of vertical comparisons among classes or among dif-

B-7 (continued)

ferent sublevels within a class (managerial or otherwise), it would appear to be of some interest to
test conclusions, such as that reached by Mahoney
(A-5)--to the effect that members of adjacent class
categories will not perceive their circumstances as
inequitable, if the pay difference between adjacent
classes does not exceed 30-40 percent.

Finally, Wright and Perrone try to measure for
differences in income on the basis of race and sex,
in a social class context. Among other things, they
find that, within class categories, differences by
sex tend to be more pronounced than are differences
by race(5). However, Wright and Perrone also find
that whatever within-class variation occurs by race
and sex, it is not nearly as pronounced as that
which is found to exist between classes. Wright
and Perrone conclude, therefore, that initial sorting by race and sex into classes might have something more to do with pay inequity than what sorting occurs within class categories. Corresponding-
ly, the authors call for more definitive research
on the nature of social class effects--which would
attempt (in part) to analyze the degree to which
members of particular protected groups are concentrated in one class or another. The reader of this
volume will, in fact, find such an attempt to view
differentials in pay on the basis of race sorting/
allocating into classes in a later article by this
entry's senior author (Wright, D-35)(6); and, a
similar interest with respect to sex sorting/allo-
cating into classes can be found in a later article
by Ward and Mueller (D-34). There does not appear
to be any journal literature, to date, that analyzes the effect of combined class sorting by both
race and sex on pay inequity. However such research
(even from a "within-class" perspective) would appear to be quite relevant, given the following finding, which Wright and Perrone cannot explain: Within
the managerial class, black men tend to earn more
than do white women.

Notes

(1) The consideration of "social class," as an
aspect of social "structure," is not uncommon in
sociology. However, in doing so, the impression is

B-7 (continued)

not necessarily left that all defining characteristics of structure are of similar explanatory quality. Indeed, Fligstein, et al. (C-5) make a broad
distinction between "individual" and "structural"
characteristics; and, given the context of their
definitions, the question is raised, in that annotation, as to whether it is not more appropriate to
label "class" as an "individual" than as a "structural" characteristic. In any event, regardless of
how writers decide to "categorize" class, the argument might be made (as noted in the Fligstein,
et al. annotation) that social class is not of the
same quality of explanatory variable as is, say,
economic segmentation.

(2) Readers, with an interest in the development of this particular theoretical emphasis on
"social relations" will see such discussed in even
greater detail in E. Wright, et al., "The American
Class Structure." AMERICAN SOCIOLOGICAL REVIEW 47
(1982):709-726.

(3) This interpretation, by Wright and Perrone
of the Marxian literature, leading to their inclusion of the "managerial" class, is not without controversy. For more information on the nature of the
theoretical debate, see: R. Robinson and J. Kelley,
"Class as Conceived by Marx and Dahrendorf: Effects
of Income Inequality and Politics in the United
States and Great Britain." AMERICAN SOCIOLOGICAL
REVIEW 44(1979):38-58.

(4) Marx had also included a class of owners,
who do not qualify as employers--the "petit bourgeois." Wright and Perrone choose not to use the
category, since they consider the element of employer to not be of sufficient quality to preclude
combining all owners (petit bourgeois and employers)
in the same category. For a contrasting point of
view on the matter, see Fligstein, et al. (C-5).

(5) The matter of more pronounced sex than
race differences is also found to be the case in a
number of other studies, which do not control for
the effects of social class. For examples, see:
Beck, et al. (D-3); Treiman and Terrell (D-33).

B-7 (continued)

(6) In the later research by Wright (D-35),
the reader will find more definitive analysis,
whereby the author is able to better establish the
quality of "within" and "between" class differences
in pay, by race. Kluegel (D-18) also offers discussion on such "within" vs. "between" class differentiation, by race. The writer of this volume does
not find the Kluegel distinction of "within" vs.
"between" class effects to be as salient as is that
presented by Wright. Nevertheless, it would appear
that Kluegel finds more pronounced within-class pay
differences, by race, than are found either by
Wright and Perrone or by Wright in the later analysis.

PART C: ECONOMIC SEGMENTATION

PART C: ECONOMIC SEGMENTATION

Chronological Key

Entries are listed chronologically by year of publication. Multiple entries, within a year, are listed alphabetically.

Author(s)	Year	Code	Page
Bridges & Berk	1974	C-3	54
Stolzenberg	1975	C-15	84
Bibb & Form	1977	C-2	53
Spilerman	1977	C-14	80
Talbert & Bose	1977	C-17	90
Beck, et al.	1978	C-1	48
Hodson	1978	C-7	65
Stolzenberg	1978	C-16	86
Fogel	1979	C-6	63
Lord & Falk	1980	C-11	75
Tolbert, et al.	1980	C-18	92
Kalleberg, et al.	1981	C-9	71
Kaufman, et al.	1981	C-10	73
Parker	1981	C-12	76
Zucker & Rosenstein	1981	C-19	93
D'amico	1982	C-4	57
Fligstein, et al.	1983	C-5	58
Sørensen	1983	C-13	79
Hodson	1984	C-8	68

Annotated Entries

Beck, E.M., Patrick M. Horan, and Charles M. Tol-
     bert II
   1978 "Stratification in a Dual Economy: A Sec-
        toral Model of Earnings Determination."
        AMERICAN SOCIOLOGICAL REVIEW 43:704-720.

     Several writers, listed elsewhere in this col-
lection, argue for the importance of going beyond
certain economic explanations for pay variation to
a consideration of social structural factors (i.e.,
"social forces") that impact on perceived/actual
earnings patterns (For example, see: Spilerman,
C-14; Stolzenberg, C-15; Talbert and Bose, C-17.).
Beck, et al. purport to provide additional evidence
on the importance of considering structural variables in any analysis of compensation issues.
     The authors, cited in the preceding paragraph,
all seek to conceptually separate "personal characteristics" (such as demographic characteristics)
from social structural characteristics--and then
suggest the potential for empirical association between structural and personal characteristics. Reviewing much of the literature in this area, Beck,
et al. contend that there has been a lack of systematic evidence presented, through actual testing
of structural-personal characteristic relationships.
So, Beck, et al. feel that the relationship deserves
further investigation--such as that which they report on in this particular paper.
     Spilerman (C-14) comments on the importance of
accounting for segmented labor markets and tends to
support a body of literature that dichotomizes "primary" and "secondary" sectors. As Spilerman sees
it, "primary" sector jobs are considered central to
the viability of an organization. Incumbents of
such positions can expect their organizations to
invest heavily in the upgrading of their capabili-
ties and to provide career paths along which continued upward mobility, in the firm, is expected.
"Secondary" sector jobs, however, are not considered of central importance to an organization. Consequently, there is little (if any) investment in
employee development, and upwardly mobile secondary career paths are the exception rather than the
rule(1). Beck, et al. reflect on the perspectives

C-1 (continued)

of Spilerman and other authors about "dual" sector
influences--suggesting that, to account for the influence of social structure, it is more appropriate
to examine the nature of what type "economies" contribute to primary vs. secondary sector jobs, rather
than to simply measure differences in job content,
per se<2>.
      To facilitate comparison at the level of "econ-
omies," Beck, et al. borrow upon the work of Aver-
itt<3> and Bluestone, et al.<4>, whereby a dichot-
omy between "core economy" and "peripheral economy"
is used. The core economy consists of firms noted
for industrial leadership; the peripheral economy
does not. Characteristics of core economic firms
are higher degrees of productivity, profit, capital utilization, monopoly elements, and unionization than can be found in the peripheral economy.
Because of these factors, higher wages have generally been found, report Beck, et al., in the core
rather than in the peripheral economy. Methodolog-
ically, the authors classify industries into one
economic sector or the other in a manner similar
to that of Bibb and Form (C-2).
      The nature of sectoral differences, then, rep-
resent the Beck, et al. measure of social structure.
As noted above, Beck et al. intend to test a relationship between structural and personal characteristics. To measure personal characteristics, the
authors analyze the effects of parental education,
respondent education, parental occupational prestige, age, sex, and race<5>. Beck, et al. also include a series of occupational variables, which (because they constitute market conditions encountered
by individual employees) might also be classified
as "personal" characteristics. These include the
incumbent's current employment status, occupational
prestige, union membership, and work stability. As
Beck, et al. see it, a company's "labor force composition" can be described on the basis of the percentage of employees in these particular personal
characteristic categories.
      Analyzing NORC data<6>, the first research
question that Beck, et al. address is whether there
exist differences in labor force composition or in
earnings patterns, across the different sectors.
Findings reveal that, indeed, differences in both

C-1 (continued)

labor force/personal characteristics and in earnings
exist between core and peripheral sectors. Specifically, core economic earnings are higher than those
found in the peripheral sector; and, among personal
characteristics, the only aspect that is not found
to vary by sector is age. So, in terms of labor
force composition, Beck, et al. find the following.
Core economic employees tend to be white, male, and
employed full time. They tend to be better educated[7] and to have more educated parents, as well
as to occupy and have parents who occupy higher
prestige jobs. In addition, such core workers are
more likely to be union members and to have more
stable work histories.
           Beck, et al. next address the question of whe-
ther sectoral differences in earnings can be explained away by these differences in labor force
composition[8]. Findings reveal that they cannot.
Controlling for potential variation in personal
characteristics, sectoral differences in earnings
persist. The importance of this particular finding, as Beck, et al. see it, is that: (a) it contradicts any "human capital"/"classical economic" assumption that income differentials can be explained
by the behavior of "non-segmented" or "homogeneous"
markets; and, (b) it substantiates the claims made
by several writers that wage level differentials
cannot be adequately explained by personal characteristics alone--independent of more macro-level influences (For example, see: Spilerman, C-14; Stolzenberg, C-15; Stolzenberg, C-16; Talbert and Bose,
C-17.). From the standpoint of external social
comparison, the data, therefore, seems to substan-
tiate an inference made by Livernash (A-3) that
perceived (or, in this case, "actual") pay inequity
might be the result of comparisons made among occupations located in different types of labor markets.

Notes

      [1] Writers, such as Mahoney (A-4), Fogel
(C-6), and Spilerman (C-14), discuss an economic
perspective, often labeled "human capital," that
argues for pay rates set by homogeneous markets,
as a return on organizational investments made in

C-1 (continued)

the development of employee skills, over time. One
of the challenges that economic segmentation or
"sector" theory makes to human capital theory is
hereby revealed. Segmentation theorists are arguing that investment in the development of employee
skill only occurs among primary sector jobs; such
investment is not provided to those employed in secondary sector capacities.

(2) It should be noted that Beck, et al. acknowledge a technical distinction made in the segmentation literature among dual labor markets, dual
labor force segmentation, and dual economies. This
particular technical distinction is of no small importance to writers such as Zucker and Rosenstein
(C-19). However, it is Beck, et al.'s intention to
focus on patterns that "dualistic" thinkers have in
common, rather than focus on what it is about their
conceptualizations that make them different. Zucker
and Rosenstein take the opposite point of view; and,
as a result, they come to different conclusions,
than do Beck, et al., on the merit of segmentation
theories.

(3) R. Averitt, THE DUAL ECONOMY: THE DYNAMICS
OF AMERICAN INDUSTRY STRUCTURE (New York: Horton,
1968).

(4) B. Bluestone, et al., LOW WAGES AND THE
WORKING POOR (Ann Arbor: Institute of Labor and
Industrial Relations, Univ. of Michigan, 1973).

(5) For a theoretical treatise on why personal
characteristic differences correspond with sectoral
differences in pay, the reader is directed to E.
Bonacich, "A Theory of Ethnic Antagonism: The Split
Labor Market." AMERICAN SOCIOLOGICAL REVIEW 37
(1972):547-559.

(6) The Beck, et al. usage of this data has
been questioned. For some initial reading on this
particular commentary and debate, the reader is directed to: R. Hauser, "On Stratification in a Dual
Economy." AMERICAN SOCIOLOGICAL REVIEW 45(1980):
702-712; E. Beck, et al., "Social Stratification in
Industrial Society: Further Evidence for a Struc-

C-1 (continued)

tural Alternative." AMERICAN SOCIOLOGICAL REVIEW 45(1980):712-719.

<7> This is mainly due to education, when measured in terms of "degree of formal certification" (high school, bachelor's, post-graduate). In such a case, a greater relationship is found between education and earnings in the core than in the periphery. However, Beck, et al. also measure education by "number of years of schooling"; and, when using this measure, they find a more pronounced influence of education on earnings in the periphery.

<8> In the literature, the labels "labor force," "individual," "status attainment," or "personal" characteristics, at times, come under the general heading of "human capital" type characteristics. Thus, there is a parallel between the Beck, et al. usage of "labor force" and what some other writers label as "human capital." Some of these other writers have actually attempted to measure for differences between "human capital" and "structural" (i.e., segmentation) models (cf., Bibb and Form, C-2; Lord and Falk, C-11). In a sense, this is what Beck, et al. are doing by examining whether structural effects can be explained away by matters of labor force composition. It need be noted that, while the writers (in this part of the book) tend to share the Beck, et al. contention that preeminent structural explanations are more logical than preeminent human capital explanations, some exception to this line of thought has recently been taken through the work of D. Jacobs (AMERICAN SOCIOLOGICAL REVIEW, Vol. 50, 1985). For brief descriptions of the Jacobs work plus a more complete reference to that work, see note #1 to the Jasso and Rossi (B-4) entry and note #6 to the Ward and Mueller (D-34) entry.

In saying that "personal"/"labor force" characteristics are often equated with "human capital" characteristics, in the literature, this is mainly because both are perceived as being of an "individualistic" (rather than a "social structural") quality. However, some writers will still make a technical distinction between "human capital" and "personal" characteristics (normally labeling the lat-

C-1 (continued)

ter as "status attainment" characteristics). Writers, who do such, claim that "human capital" theory relies on market-based wages, whereas "status
attainment" theory does not. For further information on this technical distinction between personal
characteristics and human capital characteristics,
the reader is referred to such sources as: Fligstein, et al. (C-5); Sørensen (C-13).

C-2

Bibb, Robert and William H. Form
  1977   "The Effects of Industrial, Occupational,
          and Sex Stratification on Wages in Blue
          Collar Markets." SOCIAL FORCES 55:974-996.

     Writers, such as Spilerman (C-14), comment on
the distinction between "human capital" and "dual
market" (i.e., "economic segmentation" or "sectoral") theories; and, indeed some, such as Fogel (C-6)
and Lord and Falk (C-11), have empirically tested
for the relative worthiness of the two models. Bibb
and Form, whose work appeared before that of Fogel
and Lord and Falk, engage in similar empirical analysis. The Bibb and Form method for classifying industries into dual sectors was borrowed upon by such
writers as Beck, et al. (C-1); and, the reader,
therefore, will find Bibb and Form providing more
detail on the nature of this particular classification scheme than is provided in the writing of others who borrow upon the scheme.
     Unlike most other studies, the Bibb and Form
analysis is restricted to "blue collar" workers.
However, their findings are not at variance with
most other studies that rely on more broad-based
employee populations. Specifically, the authors
find sufficient variance in income across economic
sectors to make a case for greater validity of the
"dual market" than the "human capital" point of
view. Bibb and Form appear to only control for
variability in a few personal characteristics (or,
as they label them, "societal variables"). Their
major interest, among these variables, is in sex effects. Their finding, with respect to such effects,

C-2 (continued)

corresponds with that of Beck, et al. (and most other segmentation researchers): A disproportionate percentage of women can be found in the peripheral sector, and, thus, a disproportinate percentage of women earn the lowest of incomes.

C-3

Bridges, William P. and Richard A. Berk
1974   "Determinants of White Collar Income: An Evaluation of Equal Pay for Equal Work." SOCIAL SCIENCE RESEARCH 3:211-233.

Among entries, listed elsewhere in this collection, a number of issues surface with respect to behavioral aspects that affect actual/perceived inequity. For example, writers, such as Mahoney (A-4) and Jasso and Rossi (B-4), argue for the direct effects of personal characteristics (sex, education, etc.); other writers, such as Beck, et. al. (C-1) and Stolzenberg (C-15), argue that inequity patterns can only be accounted for by measuring the impact of broader social structural forces (such as variant labor market conditions) on any personal characteristic-wage level relationship. Still other writers comment on the importance of judging differences in specific "job content," when assessing the worthiness of comparisons made across occupational categories (For example, see the review by Talbert and Bose, C-17.). The above three issues--influence of personal characteristics, influence of broader structural conditions, and influence of job content differences--constitute the three issues of primary concern to Bridges and Berk, in this particular article.
      Bridges and Berk interview 1308 "white collar" employees in Chicago financial institutions. Job content is measured by certain "mean work measures," derived from a cluster analysis on five "work characteristics" (degree of routinization, frequency of supervision, length of training, degree of control over breaks, and degree of task repetitiveness).
      The personal characteristics selected for measurement by the authors include: education, race,

C-3 (continued)

marital status, seniority, and sex. A combined
score is derived from these personal characteristic measures, by cluster analysis, so as to facilitate comparison with the job content and social
structural effects. The effects of each personal
characteristic variable are also tested for in disaggregated fashion.

Social structural conditions are simply measured in terms of company identification. The study
bears a very general theoretical resemblance, in
this regard, to the later thinking of such writers
as Stolzenberg (C-16) and Sørensen (C-13)--to the
effect that research should aim toward being "firm-
specific." However, unlike other writers on this
matter of social structure, Bridges and Berk do not
set out to either empirically test for or critically
comment on the variant impact of economic sectors.
Rather, the authors seem to assume the worthiness of
dual economy/labor market thinking at face value--
and then use that line of theory, after the fact,
to potentially explain differential earnings patterns among firms.

In order to discern a more complete accounting
for the nature of social environmental influences
on earnings variation, the personal (or, as Bridges
and Berk label them, "biographical") variables and
the job content variables are measured within three
contexts: individual differences, differences among
work groups, and differences among occupations.

Among the aggregated variables explaining, at
least, one percent of variation in earnings, Bridges
and Berk find individual personal characteristics
to contribute more than either individual job content or company variables. Therefore, assuming each
aggregated category to be "functionally unique,"
Bridges and Berk conclude that personal characteristics (especially when measured in the context of
"individual differences") are more "functionally
important" to the explanation of earnings variation
than are job content and social structure. However,
the measurement of aggregate effects on earnings,
in this manner, plus interpretations based on "functional importance" have, apparently, been the subject of some controversy in the literature (See
Grandjean, B-3, for a review.).

C-3 (continued)

Most other writers, in this part of the book, do not follow the Bridges and Berk procedure of separately analyzing the effects of structure (i.e., "company") and some aggregated personal characteristic score. Rather, such writers as Beck, et al. (C-1) and Stolzenberg (C-15) argue for analyzing the effects of structure on a relationship between specific personal characteristics and wage levels. While Bridges and Berk do not really engage in this type analysis, as has been noted, they do (after the fact) reach a conclusion similar to that of the other writers--to the effect that economic sectors exist. Bridges and Berk reach this conclusion in the following manner. First of all, they test for the direct effects of disaggregated personal characteristics on wage levels, finding that those employees--who are single, female, black, less educated, and less senior--have lower incomes. Secondly, the authors find that larger proportions of employees in these categories are located in lower-paying companies. Since the literature on economic segmentation often reveals lower earnings among workers in the "peripheral" sector (cf., Beck, et al.; Bibb and Form, C-2), Bridges and Berk conclude that a dual economy must exist, with an overrepresentation of single, female, black, less educated, and less senior employees in the peripheral sector. The authors report that their data reveals the greatest pay segregation of this type to be on the basis of sex.

As noted earlier, the Bridges and Berk study is restricted to white collar workers in Chicago financial institutions. Thus, much the same as Talbert and Bose (C-17), Bridges and Berk restrict their analysis to a specific type of business organization--contributing to criticism by such writers as Stolzenberg (C-16) concerning lack of generalizability to other types of firms. Stolzenberg, among others, also challenges the generalizability of the Bridges and Berk results, for two other reasons. One relates to the selectivity of study locale (Chicago). The other relates to the fact that, like Bibb and Form (C-2), Bridges and Berk limit their analysis to selected (in this case, only "white collar") occupational categories.

<u>C-4</u>

D'amico, Ronald
  1982 "Explaining the Effects of Capital Sector
         for Income Determination." WORK AND OCCU-
         PATIONS 9:411-439.

         D'amico reviews much of the literature on ec-
onomic segmentation, listed elsewhere in this collection, including Beck, et al. (C-1), Bibb and Form
(C-2), and Hodson (C-7). D'amico suggests that the
greater employment "stability," assumed by these authors to be attached to core sector occupations,
does not clarify whether higher wages paid in the
core are due more to greater rates of pay or to the
larger number of annual hours worked, as would be
associated with such assumed greater stability of
employ.
         Through an analysis of National Longitudinal
Surveys of Young Men data, D'amico concludes that
the higher core wages are due more to greater rates
of pay than to a larger number of annual hours
worked; and, he finds this to be the case, when
controlling for race, geographical region, union
status, occupational status, job tenure, labor force
experience, and an interaction between education
and experience. An acknowledged limitation on the
study is the use of a "young" sample (aged 24-34),
thereby not fully controlling for age. Also, by
only analyzing men, D'amico obviously offers no control for sex differences.
         In addition, D'amico finds "that substantial
interindustry variation in mean hourly wages exists
which cannot be explained by the simple sector di-
chotomy alone" (p. 434). The author, therefore,
suggests need for a "supplemental model," other than
economic segmentation, to explain wage variation--
briefly bringing up the matter that, perhaps, dual
"labor markets" (primary vs. secondary) exist within
each sector. This particular line of argumentation
is developed more fully by Ward and Mueller (D-34)
and is important, since other writers (e.g., Hodson,
C-7) seem to infer that primary vs. secondary markets can be used as an indicator of core vs. periphery segmentation.

C-5

Fligstein, Neil, Alexander Hicks, and S. Philip
   Morgan
   1983   "Toward a Theory of Income Determination."
         WORK AND OCCUPATIONS 10:289-306.

   Writers, such as Mahoney (A-4) and Fogel (C-6),
discuss the history of the "human capital" approach
to compensation analysis, which is reliant on certain classical economic assumptions about market-
based pay levels. Mahoney challenges such human
capital assumptions with an argument for behavioral
differentiation based on any number of personal
characteristics (race, sex, education, etc.). At
times, a reliance on personal characteristics in
compensation analysis becomes labeled as measures
of "status attainment"(1). Still other writers argue that, to fully account for non-economic factors
contributing to wage variation, aspects of broader
social structure must be accounted for (cf., Spilerman, C-14; Stolzenberg, C-15; Talbert and Bose,
C-17). Fligstein, et al. refer to those studies
that call for an accounting of broader social structural variables as "structural" analyses of compensation.
   Fligstein, et al. begin this article with a
review of the literature on the "human capital,"
"status attainment," and "structural" approaches,
outlining in some detail the definitional distinctions among and purposes of the three postures, as
well as a number of methodological and theoretical
criticisms that have been directed toward each approach. The authors then proceed to apply some selected elements of these three research traditions
(particularly the status attainment and structural
traditions) in their own empirical analysis of the
reasons behind income variation. To summarize how
this is done, the manner in which Fligstein, et. al.
categorize variables is hereby outlined--followed by
a discussion of how the authors apply the selected
elements.
   Categories of variables. Fligstein, et al.
categorize variables into three groups: Individual,
Sociotechnical, and Social Position. "Individual"
variables include the following status attainment
or personal characteristics: age, education, race,
and sex. "Sociotechnical" measurement involves the

C-5 (continued)

construction of an index that measures "the complexity of task interaction with people, data, and
things" (Fligstein, et al., p. 294). "Social position" measurement involves three items: (1) a measure of economic segmentation; (2) a measure of individual union status; (3) a measure of social class.
Conceptual similarities. The manner in which
Fligstein, et al. categorize "individual" variables
is in concert with similar classification by several
other writers cited in this part of the book (e.g.,
Beck, et al, C-1; Bibb and Form, C-2; Hodson, C-7).
Furthermore, the reader will find some parallel between the Fligstein, et al. "sociotechnical" category and Spaeth's (B-5) usage of "task complexity."
Spaeth argues for the empirical separation of measures of "complexity" from measures of "prestige" (or
"social class"). Fligstein, et al. follow this procedure by separating their sociotechnical and social
class measures.
Conceptual novelty. The category of which
"social class" is a part (what the authors of this
article call "social position") is what clearly separates what Fligstein, et al. are operationalizing
from what many others, cited in Part C of this book,
are doing. For example, Beck, et al. (C-1) and Kalleberg, et al. (C-9) represent writers who argue for
a clear demarcation between personal characteristics
(i.e., individual-level variables) and structural
characteristics (e.g., measures of economic segmentation). While it may be that structural and personal variables interact to explain perceived/actual
pay variation, the point is that these other writers
argue to separately categorize structural and personal characteristics. It is on this matter of
clearly demarcating what is "personal" (or "individual") from what is "structural" that Fligstein,
et al. are departing from mainstream literature,
when using the "social position" concept.
The manner in which the focal authors are de-
viating from much other segmentation literature can
be more specifically illustrated as follows. Fligstein, et al. cite Hodson (C-7) as the source of
their measure of economic segmentation. Hodson uses
"unionization" (the status of any firm and/or industry) as a component of sector differentiation; so,
one assumes that Fligstein, et al. are doing the

C-5 (continued)

same. However, the point is that Fligstein, et al.
have combined this measure of economic segmentation
(including macro-level unionization) in the same
"social position" category with an individual measure of "union status." Most other writers in the
field seem to reflect the perspective of Parker
(C-12) that individual union status should be considered as a personal characteristic, conceptually
separate from the structural consideration of unionization as a segmentation component.

A similar issue can be raised with respect to
the combined inclusion of social class and economic
segmentation in the same general social position
category. Fligstein, et al., as do Kalleberg,
et al. (C-9), suggest that social class is an important variable in any analysis of wage variation,
as it infers the degree of control that individuals
have over factors of production. Kalleberg, et al.
argue, however, that class is an individual-level
construct (what they call a "worker power" variable); and, those authors act to clearly demarcate
social class, conceptually, from broader structural
measures of economic segmentation. It is not clear
whether Fligstein, et al. regard class as an individual or structural concept. However, by theoretically combining class in the same social position
category as they place segmentation, Fligstein,
et al. are, at the very least, offering operationalization that clearly departs from the Kalleberg,
et al. usage.

Fligstein, et al. cite the work of Wright (of
Wright and Perrone, B-7)(2), as the basis for their
analysis of social class, per se, as a variable.
However, the reader will find an operational departure, from the Wright and Perrone treatment, in the
Fligstein, et al. application of class. Specifically, Wright and Perrone reinterpret Marxist categories. Whereas many writers find Marx only outlining
three strata (employers, petit bourgeois, and workers), Wright and Perrone suggest that Marx actually
included a fourth class: managers. Wright and Perrone then proceed to operationally include only
three of the four categories, in their analysis.
They delete the petit bourgeois as a separate class
from employers, arguing that, since both of these
categories constitute "owners," they should more

C-5 (continued)

logically be grouped together. Fligstein, et al.,
agree with Wright and Perrone on the importance of
including a managerial class. However, unlike the
latter authors, Fligstein et al. retain separation
of the petit bourgeois from the employers category.
The Fligstein, et al. argument is that, because the
petit bourgeois includes owners, who do not employ
others, then (as a class) it must be considered separate from that grouping of owners who do employ
others. A degree of ambiguity exists over the Fligstein, et al. usage of the "workers" class. At one
point, the authors state (without providing ration-
ale) a decision to delete the workers stratum from
the data set used in their analysis. However, they
then proceed to report data that supposedly demonstrates an income differential between the employers
category and the workers category, inferring that
such data was not actually deleted.
     Findings. Some of the Fligstein, et al. find-
ings are as follows:

(1)   With respect to sociotechnical measures, there
      is a certain lack of strength to the relation-
      ship between these variables and earnings pat-
      terns. This leads the authors to recommend
      broadened measurement of the sociotechnical
      dimension in future research.

(2)   Utilizing the Hodson (C-7) three-fold segment
      demarcation (core, periphery, and state), Flig-
      stein, et al. find the greatest earnings re-
      turns to the core sector.

(3)   Among individual-level variables, the authors
      report, for example, that greater education and
      being a male constributes to higher earnings,
      but being white does not.

     Writers, such as Stolzenberg (C-15; C-16) and
Beck, et al. (C-1), argue, however, that what direct
effects may be evident between variables and earnings patterns are not nearly as important to explaining pay variation as are interactive effects.
Specifically, these writers argue that the most complete analysis accounts for the effects of variation
in social structure on the relationship between per-

C-5 (continued)

sonal characteristics and earnings. To this end,
Fligstein, et al. do report interactive effects between segmentation and sex-wage/education-wage relationships. They find (for example) that, in spite
of the overall result of core sector earnings ex-
ceeding that of other sectors, state-sector females
earn more than do state-sector males. For reasons
unexplained, Fligstein, et al. appear to restrict
their investigation of segmentation interactive effects to the core and state sectors, not reporting
information on periphery sector effects.

Lord and Falk (C-11) suggest that social class
differences might influence the relationships between certain clearly identifiable personal characteristics (e.g., sex, education) and earnings. The
potential for this type interaction is tested by
Fligstein, et al. Based on a review of the literature, the authors had hypothesized, for example,
that males would earn more than females, regardless
of social stratum. However, this is not found to
be the case within the "managers" class. Fligstein,
et al. suggest that, inasmuch as they do not discriminate among different levels of management within the "managers" category, it might be fruitful to
do so in future research(3). By doing such, argue
the authors, the degree to which sex earnings differences might vary across managerial categories
can be investigated.

Notes

(1) The concept, "status attainment," appears--
from time to time--among articles, listed elsewhere
in this collection, such as that by Sørensen (C-13).
For a rather extensive definitional essay on the use
of this concept, the reader is referred to: P. Horan, "Is Status Attainment Research Atheoretical?"
AMERICAN SOCIOLOGICAL REVIEW, 43(1978):534-541.

(2) The reference by Fligstein, et al. is to
E. Wright, CLASS STRUCTURE AND INCOME DETERMINATION
(New York: Academic Press, 1979).

(3) For an example of, at least, one attempt to
discriminate among different levels of management,
in this type of research, see Wright (D-35).

C-6

Fogel, Walter
  1979 "Occupational Earnings: Market and Insti-
        tutional Influences." INDUSTRIAL AND LABOR
        RELATIONS REVIEW 33:24-35.

    Fogel argues, as does Stolzenberg (C-15), for
the merging of sociological and economic knowledge,
when it comes to making judgments about what contributes to wage variation. Whereas Stolzenberg
approaches matters from somewhat more of a sociological perspective, Fogel from more of an economic perspective, the two writers are in fundamental
agreement on several matters. For example, Fogel
agrees with Stolzenberg that the focal unit of analysis should be "occupations," and he also agrees
with Stolzenberg that pay levels for similar occupations may vary across markets.
    Essentially, Fogel's approach is to test the
"human capital" theoretical assumption that pay
levels do not so vary--that uniform "market rates"
emerge for occupations. The analysis is done on
census-supplied data of full-time employed males.
    Much the same as Beck, et al. (C-1), Fogel re-
jects the human capital assumption, as he finds
structural differences in earnings, across economic
segments (what he refers to as differences in "institutional power").
    Both Beck, et al. (C-1) and Stolzenberg (C-15)
argue, however, that what main effects may exist between aspects of social structure and earnings patterns are not as important to explaining wage variation as is the impact of structure on personal characteristic-wage level relationships. Fogel reports
on the relationship between one personal characteristic (education) and wage levels. While he reports
that his findings hold across all occupations, it
is difficult to discern for sure whether he is also
claiming uniformity of findings across economic segments.
    On the matter of education-wage measurement,
per se, Beck, et al. (C-1) and Stolzenberg (C-16)
report contradictory findings, when using "years of
schooling" as a measure(1). Fogel uses the "years
of schooling" measurement and also reports somewhat
contradictory results. Specifically, he finds a
consistent relationship between level of education

C-6 (continued)

and earnings to hold only among employees with less
than 13 years of schooling. Inconsistencies exist
among those with more education.

Since Fogel only analyzes data for males, no
differences by sex (as a personal characteristic)
are reported. Nevertheless, Fogel does present
findings to the effect that the greater the avail-
ability of a female labor supply in a particular
occupational category, the lower the overall earnings in that occupational category(2).

Spilerman (C-14) suggests that, for some employees, variations in "preference mixes" will contribute to the circumstances where certain non-
income factors (what Fogel calls "non-pecuniary"
factors)--such as job security--compensate for lower levels of pay. Fogel does not find this to be
the case. However, Spilerman argues that such a
result can only be found among "older" employees.
Fogel does not control for the effects of age, as
a personal characteristic; so, whether or not the
Spilerman argument holds cannot be discerned from
the Fogel research.

Notes

(1) Contradictions on the matter of educational effects, both within and between the studies of
Beck, et al. and Stolzenberg, are discussed (in some
detail) in the Stolzenberg (C-16) annotation.

(2) For an example of research that finds the
opposite of this--that female entry into an occupational category does not necessarily lower overall
earnings in that category, see Fox (D-12).

<u>C-7</u>

Hodson, Randy
    1978   "Labor in the Monopoly, Competitive, and
           State Sectors of Production." POLITICS
           AND SOCIETY 8:429-480.

    The tradition of "dualistic" or "economic seg-
mentation" theories have generally centered around
"core" and "peripheral" distinctions, whereby one
of the defining characteristics of each are that the
firms in the core sector are argued to be more "monopolistic," whereas those in the peripheral sector
are argued to be more "competitive" (cf., Beck,
et al., C-1). This particular theme is central to
the Hodson discussion, as he concerns himself with
what factors contribute to variation between the
different sectors and consequent variable impact
on earnings distribution. Hodson simply uses the
labels "monopoly" and "competitive" to refer, respectively, to core and peripheral sectors; and, he
adds to his analysis a third sector, the "state,"
which represents government organizations and such
"quasi-public" entities as utility companies.
    The hypothesized differences that have tradi-
tionally been made between core and peripheral economies (and, which are briefly outlined by such writers, as Beck, et al., C-1, and Bibb and Form, C-2)
are discussed in detail by Hodson. For example,
Hodson hypothesizes that job conditions among sectors are sufficiently different that occupation-
specific earnings vary among the sectors. The
reasoning behind this particular hypothesis is as
follows. Comments made by such writers as Beck,
et al., Spilerman (C-14), and Zucker and Rosenstein
(C-19) suggest that a technical distinction is often made in the dualist literature between "labor
markets" and "economies." The Hodson usage of
"sectors" refers to what Beck, et al. label as
economies--i.e., broad patterns of activity that
delineate the structure of organizations/industries
found in one segment from those found in another.
Such patterns of activity include unionization, capital utilization, monopolization, profitability,
etc. At the same time, Hodson does not dismiss,
as unimportant, the separate quality of "labor markets." Much the same as does Spilerman, Hodson sees
differences among labor markets as reflecting dif-

C-7 (continued)

ferences in the "central importance" companies place
on certain occupations. Consequently, labor markets can be somewhat separately defined (from "economies"), as being dependent on the degree to which
organizations invest in the development of employee
ability to perform certain occupations and become
upwardly mobile. "Primary" labor market jobs are
considered "central" to organizations and are, thus,
characterized by high degrees of organizational investment in employee development. "Secondary" labor
market jobs are not considered central to organizations and are, thus, characterized by low degrees of
organizational investment in development. One way
in which dual "economies" are, therefore, traditionally separated is that core economies are seen as
having a predominance of primary market jobs, while
peripheral economies are seen as having a predominance of secondary market jobs. This, then, translates into an assumption that the better "job conditions" (stability of jobs via career paths and
better paying job categories) exist in the core
than in the peripheral economy. Thus, the difference in predominant job conditions, from one sector
to the next, is hypothesized as translating into
significantly different earnings patterns from one
sector to the next. Hodson tests for occupation
distributions, unemployment/employment patterns,
and earnings trends, across sectors, in order to
judge the worthiness of this particular hypothesis.
        Writers, such as Beck, et al. (C-1) and Stolz-
enberg (C-15), argue that aspects of social structure (such as the over/underrepresentation of occupational categories in one sector or another), not
only impact on earnings patterns, per se, but also
impact on the relationship between certain personal
characteristics and the distribution of earnings.
Thus, dualistic thinkers (including Hodson) do seek
to measure distributions of such factors as race,
sex, age, and education among sectors. The argument, for example, might proceed to the effect that,
comparing core and periphery sectors, males earn
more than do females only because the core economy
is overrepresented by a male work force. Hodson,
therefore, tests for the degree of over/underrepre-
sentation by personal characteristics, across the
sectors. Some of his findings are as follows:

C-7 (continued)

(1) As hypothesized, employees at the extremes of
     age groups (i.e., under 21 and over 65 years)
     are found to be overrepresented in the periph-
     eral sector. This finding follows a body of
     literature (reviewed by Hodson) that argues
     how employees with "weak market positions"
     (presumably due to lack of experience and/or
     proximity to retirement) are "selected out"
     of the core sector--since any organization in
     that sector can "buy whatever labor it chooses"
     (Hodson, p. 435).

(2) A similar line of thinking, regarding the abil-
     ity of the core sector to "select in" whatever
     quality of labor that is desired, led Hodson
     to' hypothesize that less educated individuals
     would be overrepresented in the periphery and
     underrepresented in the core sector. This hy-
     pothesis cannot be confirmed with respect to
     all occupational categories. Hodson seems to
     feel that this may be partly due to his not
     separating one aspect of education (measured
     in terms of "years of schooling") from another
     aspect of education (measured in terms of type
     of degree/certification earned). Some other
     writers in this subject area (e.g., Beck,
     et al., C-1) do separate measures of education
     in this manner. However, still other writers,
     like Hodson, do not; and, they (too) find con-
     tradictory results (cf., Fogel, C-6; Stolzen-
     berg, C-16).

(3) Based on literature reviewed, Hodson hypoth-
     esizes that private sector discrimination
     against blacks and women will be such that an
     overrepresentation of employees in these cat-
     egories will be found in the periphery, where-
     as an overrepresentation of whites and males
     will be found in the core. Hodson also hy-
     pothesizes that, overall, blacks and women will
     be less represented in private sector than in
     public sector (i.e., "state") employ. These
     hypotheses are confirmed.

(4) As is the case for Beck, et al. (C-1), Hodson
     does not find variations in earnings (across

C-7 (continued)

> sectors) to be explained away by the effects
> of personal characteristics. So, any human
> capital/neoclassical economic assumption of
> "homogeneous markets" is again challenged by
> the Hodson findings.

> It need be noted that much of the Hodson anal-
> ysis is not reliant on inferential statistical test-
> ing--but, rather, on the author's interpretation of
> significance--based on the "observed size" of des-
> criptive statistical differences. Indeed, Zucker
> and Rosenstein (C-19) reanalyze the Hodson material,
> using inferential techniques, and find much of it
> not to be statistically significant.

C-8

Hodson, Randy
    1984   "Companies, Industries, and the Measure-
            ment of Economic Segmentation." AMERICAN
            SOCIOLOGICAL REVIEW 49:335-348.

> In an earlier work, Hodson (C-7), like several
> others during the 1970's, defended the validity of
> dualistic approaches to private business economic
> segmentation(1). However, the decade of the 1980's
> brought with it increased criticism of such dual
> sectoral approaches by such writers as Zucker and
> Rosenstein (C-19) and, indeed, even by a group that
> included Hodson himself (Kaufman, et al., C-10).
> Kaufman, et al. actually go beyond critcizing dual-
> istic thinking to offering an alternative frame of
> thought (multiple sectors); and, it is on this
> theme, of offering alternatives to two-sector mod-
> els, to which Hodson is now providing further con-
> sideration.
>   Hodson is specifically concerned, in this par-
> ticular article, with two issues brought up by Zuck-
> er and Rosenstein (C-19): (1) the validity of in-
> formation gained from dual sector (core vs. periph-
> ery) models; and, (2) the validity of interpreta-
> tions made, when comparing models that use differ-
> ent levels of analysis (e.g., firm vs. industry).

C-8 (continued)

As an alternative to the dual sector type model, Hodson offers a "tripartite" model of segments
differentiated primarily on the basis of corporate
power. In more traditional dualistic models, corporate power is one of several variables often used
to demarcate segments, whereby industries that are
more monopolistic in quality constitute the "core"
and those more competitive in quality constitute
the "periphery" (cf., Beck, et al., C-1; Hodson,
C-7). In the tripartite model, Hodson retains a
"monopolistic" sector as one in which companies or
industries exert "national" influence. However, rather than combine all business entities that do not
exert such national influence into one alternative
category (the periphery), the tripartite model sub-
divides "non-monopolistic" business entities into
two sectors, "regional" and "local." The alternative sector in which a business is placed depends
on the extent of its economic influence.
Hodson's initial purpose is to engage in two
types of earnings comparison: industry vs. firm and
dual sector vs. tripartite segmentation. Procedur-
ally, he engages in firm vs. industry comparisons
for each type of segmentation approach (dual and
tripartite) and then analyzes what differences exist
between the dual and tripartite firm vs. industry
comparisons. In general, Hodson finds that, in the
dualistic model, sectoral earnings variation is more
saliently demonstrated based on industry, than on
firm-level, measurement. However, the opposite is
found in the tripartite model: sectoral earnings
variation is more saliently evident at the firm than
at the industry level.
The findings lead Hodson to conclude that it
is unrealistic to argue for either firm-specific or
industry-specific sectoral measurement. Rather, it
is the Hodson conclusion that both forms of measurement have relevance; and, the one having the greatest relevance depends on the type segmentation model
used. Unlike Zucker and Rosenstein (C-19) and even
unlike the earlier stance to which he was party
(Kaufman, et al., C-10), Hodson thus appears reluctant, in this particular paper, to reject the dualistic model outright. In part, this is due to his
finding an overall greater degree of consistency of
relationship between industry-level variables and

C-8 (continued)

earnings than between firm-level variables and earnings.
        In any event, accepting some value of measur-
ing at both company and industry levels, Hodson
finds that--among indicators of sectoral differen-
tiation--organizational size (measured in terms of
number of employees) offers the best explanation
for company-level earnings, while capital intensity
(measured as assets per employee) offers the best
explanation for industry-level earnings. These
findings lead Hodson to conclude that "distinct
roles" exist for company and industry segmentation
models and that firm-level and industry-level segmentation, therefore, each "deserves conceptuali-
zation in its own right" (p. 335).
        Segmentation studies traditionally do not rely,
however, on direct relationships between sectoral
differences (as aspects of social structure) and
earnings. Rather, such studies often look at the
impact of social structure on a relationship between
personal characteristics and earnings. As an example, Stolzenberg (C-16) argues that size (as a
structural characteristic) influences a relationship between the personal characteristic, education,
and earnings. The Stolzenberg study exemplifies
research that tests for the relationships between
personal characteristics and earnings, holding
structural factors constant. Other research has
demonstrated the relevance of measuring for the relationship between structural characteristics and
earnings, holding personal characteristics constant
(cf., Beck, et al., C-1)(2). It is the latter procedure that Hodson employs in this particular paper.
        The major personal characteristic, in which
Hodson has an interest is sex; and, given the above-
noted importance of organizational size and capital
intensity indicators of structure, in Hodson's research, the author finds the relationships between
these two sectoral indicators and earnings to vary
by sex. Specifically, Hodson finds that any positive effect of size on earnings is more pronounced
for females, while any positive effect of capital
intensity on earnings is more pronounced for males.
Hodson (p. 346) suggests the following, as possible
explanations for these results:

C-8 (continued)

For women, in the labor force, the bureaucratic rules associated with large
company size ... provide a degree of
protection from some discriminatory wage
and earnings practices.... For men in
the labor force, the heightened productivity and responsibility associated with
[capital intensity] ... offer substantial opportunities for securing higher
earnings opportunities that do not provide equivalent advantages for women.

Notes

(1) In his earlier work, Hodson (C-7) included
a third, "state" or "government" sector. His interest, in this paper, is solely on private business;
so, only his two previously cited business sectors,
core and periphery, are discussed in this paper.

(2) Beck, et al. actually measure the relationship among structure, personal characteristics, and
earnings both ways—holding structural variables
constant and holding personal characteristics constant.

C-9

Kalleberg, Arne L., Michael Wallace, and Robert P.
   Althauser
   1981 "Economic Segmentation, Worker Power, and
        Income Inequality." AMERICAN JOURNAL OF
        SOCIOLOGY 87:651-681.

Writers on the nature of factors contributing
to economic segmentation have, at times, listed concentration, economic scale, government intervention,
capital intensity, and organization size as important defining criteria (See Kaufman, et al., C-10,
for a review.). Kalleberg, et al. also consider
these to be relevant criteria that define segmentation; however, their research on sectoral effects
offers a departure from what is reflected in other

C-9 (continued)

sources. Most of these sources engage in two-sector
("dualistic") type analyses (cf., Beck, et al., C-1;
Bibb and Form, C-2; Lord and Falk, C-11; Tolbert,
et al., C-18). An exception to this rule is the
work of Kaufman, et al., who outline a paradigm
based on 16 sectors. However, Kalleberg, et al.
offer a further deviation from the segmentation
tradition. They point out that, regardless of the
number of sectors that are proposed (be it two,
sixteen, or whatever), the use of such defined segments, per se, only offers the potential for discrete measurement of sectoral effects. In order to
facilitate the measurement of some effects, which
might not be captured by such discrete measurement,
Kalleberg, et al. propose continuous measurement of
segmentation variables. In doing such, the authors
suggest that researchers need not be concerned about
which discrete sectors industries or firms can be
classified in.
        Based on a review of discrete sector-type re-
search, much of which is annotated elsewhere in this
book, Kalleberg, et al. recognize the importance of
not just measuring for the effect of segmentation on
wage variation, per se--but, rather for the effect
of segmentation on a relationship between certain
personal characteristics and wage variation. Among
the characteristics, utilized by Kalleberg, et al.,
are: union membership, occupational skill and li-
censing, tenure with an employer, and class position
(i.e., degree of individual control over production
and other work activities). Kalleberg, et al. label these personal characteristics as "worker power"
characteristics. In addition to the worker power
characteristics, the authors also measure for the
effects of education, sex, and race as personal
characteristics.
        It is the Kalleberg, et al. contention that a
reliance on continuous measurement of segmentation
allows for the highlighting of complexities (in results) that cannot be so recognized through discrete
measurement. For example, Kalleberg, et al. find
that education (measured by "years of schooling")
interacts with some segmentation dimensions, in such
a way, that there results a negative effect on the
income of females. Although such "discrete sector"
researchers as Beck, et al. (C-1) find variation

C-9 (continued)

in education effects (whereby one sector reports
stronger education-income patterns than does the
other sector), these "discrete" researchers find
that some degree of positive relationship between
level of education and income exists, regardless
of sex, in any sector. Therefore, the Kalleberg,
et al. usage of continuous segmentation measurement
appears to add a dimension of knowledge to the nature of structure-education-income relationships
that is not evident from the discrete category type
research. Furthermore, Kalleberg, et al. report
relationships between segmentation and some worker
power characteristics. This is a finding comparable
to that reported in more discrete-level studies, as
well; however, by using continuous measures of segmentation, Kalleberg, et al. are able to discern the
degree to which segmentation varies with different
forms of power--a feature which cannot be determined, argue the authors, based on discrete measurement alone.
     The matter of whether firms or industries
should be used as units of analysis has been debated by several segmentation writers, such as
Kaufman, et al. (C-10) and Zucker and Rosenstein
(C-19). The reader will find what is, perhaps, the
most thorough presentation of this debate in the
Kalleberg, et al. review of relevant literature.
While Kalleberg, et al. recognize a number of both
costs and benefits associated with firm-based and
industry-based analysis, they conduct their own research at the industry level.

C-10

Kaufman, Robert L., Randy Hodson, and Neil D. Flig-
     stein
   1981 "Defrocking Dualism: A New Approach to De-
          fining Industrial Sectors." SOCIAL SCIENCE
          RESEARCH 10:1-31.

     Writers, such as Sørensen (C-13) and Zucker and
Rosenstein (C-19), direct criticisms toward "dualistic" approaches to explaining social structural
variation. The nature of the critical commentary

C-10 (continued)

has led Zucker and Rosenstein, in particular, to
suggest "reformulation" of approaches to economic
segmentation; and, it is such a reformulation that
Kaufman, et al. argue for in this particular article. It is not the Kaufman, et al. purpose to present any type linkage between structure and actual/
perceived pay inequity. However, the proposed model
does represent a rather marked departure from the
two-sector models of a number of other writers, such
as Beck, et al. (C-1), Bibb and Form (C-2), Lord
and Falk (C-11), Parker (C-12), and Tolbert, et al.
(C-18). Consequently, this article is annotated,
given its contribution toward broadening thinking
about the nature of social structural influence(1).
    Kaufman, et al. begin by reviewing some of the
criticisms that have been directed toward dualistic
research: (1) the difficulty over deciding whether
analysis should be done at the level of industry or
firm; (2) the mixing of criteria, used for grouping
in sectors (some of which is firm-specific, others
of which are more applicable to industries); (3) the
insufficient accounting, in some studies, for size
as a variable; and, (4) the propensity of some writers to not separate measurement of dual labor markets from dual economies.
    Kaufman, et al. then proceed to argue for the
worthiness of measurement at the industry level;
and, based on a review of organization theory literature, they conclude that 10 variables should be
used to determine which sectors industries should
be grouped into. The 10 variables are: Degree of
economic concentration; size (based on a measure of
total economic activity); capital intensity (level
of technology employed); degree of involvement of
American producers in foreign markets; degree of
government control over an industry; profit; autonomy (independence of firms in one industry from
those in another industry); productivity; unionization; and, growth (measured in terms of changes in
economic activity).
    Based on a combination of factor and cluster
analyses, industries are grouped into 16 sectors.
Kaufman, et al. provide detail on what mix of values, attributed to the 10 defining variables, constitute inclusion in each sector.

C-10 (continued)

Note

(1) For further reading on theoretical/methodological discussion and debate, surrounding the merits of "dual" sector models (independent of the direct effect that such thinking about structure has on wage variation), the reader is directed to the following references: J. Baron and W. Bielby, "Bringing the Firms Back In: Stratification, Segmentation, and the Organization of Work." AMERICAN SOCIOLOGICAL REVIEW 45(1980):737-765; R. Hodson and R. Kaufman, "Economic Dualism: A Critical Review." AMERICAN SOCIOLOGICAL REVIEW 47(1982):727-739; J. Jacobs, "Industrial Sector and Career Mobility Reconsidered" AMERICAN SOCIOLOGICAL REVIEW 48(1983): 415-421.

C-11

Lord, George E. and William W. Falk
1980 "An Exploratory Analysis of Individualist Versus Structuralist Explanations of Income." SOCIAL FORCES 59:376-391.

Lord and Falk attempt to replicate the work of Beck, et al. (C-1) and Bibb and Form (C-2), on the importance of dual segmentation, while at the same time integrating a social class typology discussed by Wright and Perrone (B-7).
Similar to the work of Beck, et al. (C-1), Lord and Falk analyze NORC data per the establishment of core and peripheral sectors; and, similar to Bibb and Form (C-2), the authors measure for the relative viability of a dual economy vs. a human capital approach to explaining wage patterns. Specifically, Lord and Falk analyze the effects of such variables as "specific vocational preparation" that flow from the human capital management tradition. In general, the authors find (as do Bibb and Form) that the dual sector model explains more variance in income than does the human capital model. Although the findings are not quite as salient as they are for Beck, et al. and Bibb and Form, when con-

C-11 (continued)

trolling for the effect of sex, Lord and Falk still
find males earning a good deal more than do females.
By including the measures of social class in
the analysis, Lord and Falk reach some preliminary
conclusions on the extent to which the above-noted
sex differences might have been conditioned by over/
underrepresentation in a particular class; however,
the authors recommend that more work be done on the
matter, before any definitive conclusions can be
reached. For reading on at least two attempts to
further test for class effect on sex-based earnings,
the reader is directed to the work of Fligstein,
et al. (C-5) and Ward and Mueller (D-34).

C-12

Parker, Robert N.
    1981 "Structural Constraints and Individual
          Career Earnings Patterns." AMERICAN
          SOCIOLOGICAL REVIEW 46:884-892.

    Among entries, listed elsewhere in this col-
lection: Bornschier and Ballmer-Cao (E-2) take note
of how important it is to account for the "total
context" of social environmental influences on pay
discrepancies--including the political environment
in which organizations must operate; Grandjean (B-3)
reminds readers that another aspect of that total
context are economic forces; and, Stolzenberg (C-15)
argues that, from the standpoint of structure, it is
important to attempt empirical integration of both
economic and social forces. It is from this general
tradition of writing that Parker attempts to establish a relationship between the larger "economic
order" (which he considers to be an important element of the total social context) and wage variation. It is not Parker's intention to analyze pay
variation at any one point in time; rather, commen-
surate with a desire to consider the impact of economic fluctuations over time, his purpose is to
analyze resultant career patterns in pay equity/in-
equity. In a sense, this approach appears to somewhat correspond with the Spilerman (C-14) interest

C-12 (continued)

In assessing career earnings/achievement patterns.
Whereas Spilerman, however, provides a qualitative
essay on the matter, Parker provides empirical
analysis.

Specifically, Parker presents a time-series
analysis, whereby he measures temporal economic
changes by unemployment rates. Parker seems to assume a certain validity to economic segmentation
theory--and, indeed, he appears to model his measure of social structure after that of Beck, et al.
(C-1). Basically, Parker is interested in assessing whether variation in unemployment rates affect
employee earnings any differently across core and
periphery sectors. In brief, he concludes that the
impact of variable unemployment rate is different
between sectors. Specifically, he finds that the
earnings among peripheral workers are more closely
tied to unemployment rate changes than are the earnings among core workers. Parker argues that this
accounts for greater fluctuations, over time, in
peripheral than in core earnings patterns.

Parker agrees with such writers as Beck, et al.
(C-1) that it is important to not so much look at
the impact of structure on earnings, per se, as to
look at the impact of structure on the relationship between personal characteristics and earnings.
Three personal characteristics are measured: education, union status, and race. In general, Parker
finds that increases in education and union membership contribute to a decrease in temporal earnings
fluctuations; and, since the core economy is overrepresented by more educated employees, who hold
union membership, Parker assumes that this may be
part of the reason why less earnings fluctuations
occur in the core than in the periphery. On the
other hand, Parker does not find that race makes a
difference. Specifically, whites do not appear to
be any more protected from earnings fluctuations
than do blacks. Thus, any reasoning for less core
than peripheral fluctuation in earnings cannot be
explained (based on Parker's data) in terms of an
overrepresenation of whites in the core segment.

Parker mentions that his study does not account
for all possible economic variables that might contribute to earnings fluctuations--and that such variables as types of goods produced, money supply,

C-12 (continued)

etc. should possibly be accounted for in future research. He also recognizes the limited array of
personal characteristics selected and suggests that
future research account for such variables as sex
and age.

The issue of measuring for differentiation on
the basis of sex would appear to be of no small importance, given the work of such writers as Rosenfeld (D-24), on how different patterns of career-
wage relationships exist by sex, due to the variant
sex composition of labor markets. Indeed, the importance of the issue is enhanced, due to a history
of more general research on segmentation and career
patterns (not directly tied to wage differentials),
that is restricted to an analysis of males only(1).

The issue of measuring for variation in age is
acknowledged by Parker to be important, since the
average age of his sample is about 39. The inference is that a sample this "young" prevents his ob-
taining the most definitive information on total
career patterns. It is for this reason that some
of the more recent research on segmentation and career patterns (re: note #1) relies on older cohorts.
On the other hand, Spilerman (C-14) suggests that a
similar problem exists, due to exclusive reliance
on older cohorts as is the case with sole reliance
on a younger sample. The issue is this: Parker is
interested in measuring actual pay variability
across sectors. While controlling for age differentiation might enhance explanation of such "actual"
variability, still some information on actual variation can be discerned, by simply gaining information on the earnings history of each sample member.
The real problem of not controlling for age differentiation appears to be at the level of gauging
perceived pay equity/inequity. The reason, suggests Spilerman, is that "perceptions" of what is
fair/unfair often change, over time, as people come
to adopt different job feature "preference mixes"--
depending on their ages. Unlike wage history data,
such changed perceptual data cannot be obtained,
short of controlling for age in the research design.

C-12 (continued)

Note

(1) For examples of this research, see: C. Tolbert II, "Industrial Segmentation and Men's Career
Mobility." AMERICAN SOCIOLOGICAL REVIEW 47(1982):
457-477; R. Wanner and L. Lewis, "Economic Segmentation and the Course of the Occupational Career."
WORK AND OCCUPATIONS 10(1983):307-324.

C-13

Sørensen, Aage B.
  1983   "Sociological Research on the Labor Market:
          Conceptual and Methodological Issues." WORK
          AND OCCUPATIONS 10:261-287.

     Several other articles have dealt with the dif-
ference between the use of "structural" (i.e., economic segmentation) and "individualistic" (i.e.,
status attainment/human capital) approaches to explaining pay inequity (cf., Beck, et al., C-1; Bibb
and Form, C-2; Fligstein, et al., C-5; Fogel, C-6;
Lord and Falk, C-11; Spilerman, C-14; Zucker and
Rosenstein, C-19). This tradition of research is
discussed in Sørensen's essay. The author reviews
problems of operational definition and quantitative
measurement, in particular, while highlighting areas
where various studies appear to be in contradiction.
     Much the same as Zucker and Rosenstein (C-19),
Sørensen is especially critical of the "dualistic"
explanations for earnings variation. The author,
for example, joins Zucker and Rosenstein by criti-
cizing the "dual sector" research tradition for
measuring at the "industry" level of analysis--and,
thus, for not entertaining the possibility of differences among firms. However, Sørensen extends
his criticism of sectoral research, beyond that of
Zucker and Rosenstein, in two respects:

(1)   He does not believe that enough emphasis is
      placed on analyzing the relationship between
      union status and earnings differentials.

C-13 (continued)

(2) He criticizes such studies for not measuring
     the effects of job mobility, across economic
     segments, over time.

     With respect to the latter criticism, Sørensen
discusses a number of methodological difficulties,
not the least of which would be to somehow empirically separate the effects of movement among sectors, per se, from patterns of career status attainment. In this case, the inference seems to be that
not all mobility between sectors occurs due to progression through a particular career; and, the effects of career progressive mobility on earnings
variation might be different than the effects of
non-career progressive mobility on earnings variation.

C-14

Spilerman, Seymour
   1977 "Careers, Labor Market Structure, and So-
         cioeconomic Achievement." AMERICAN JOURNAL
         OF SOCIOLOGY 83:551-593.

     Presentations by such authors as Stolzenberg
(C-15) and Talbert and Bose (C-17) provide specific illustrations of the nature of "social force"
influence on potential changes in social values--
thereby providing information about the dynamics of
social interaction that contribute to such changes.
Spilerman extends information, on this particular
subject, through an essay on the importance of variables associated with "career line structures."
Specifically, Spilerman is concerned with how the
"linkages" between jobs (in a total "work history"),
from one employee to the next, shapes actual variation in earnings. These career line structures,
argues Spilerman, further affect the formation of
variable social values held by different groups of
people; and, these values contribute, in turn, to
variable perceptions as to what constitutes equitable compensation.
     Outlining the presentation in a bit more de-
tail, Spilerman argues that the literature, to date,

C-14 (continued)

is reliant on "ideal-type" specifications of career
lines, thus not capturing the full thrust of variation among career line structures(1). Specifically
Spilerman suggests that a social force contributing
to actual/perceived pay inequity might be variations
within career lines that transverse the organizational units in a labor market. A number of examples are provided that demonstrate how, in some occupations, career earnings are enhanced by "staying"
with a given organization, whereas in others such
earnings are enhanced by "moving" among organizations. Spilerman also infers that, similarly,
"staying" vs. "moving"--with respect to specific
occupations--is important toward determining the
degree to which career earnings are enhanced; and,
such would seem to be greatly contingent on what
labor market(s) one was "staying" in or "moving"
among, given the Stolzenberg (C-15) conclusions
about occupational variability by markets. As Spilerman summarizes the case, industries and organizations vary by such things as social organization
(e.g., unionized quality), promotion rules, rate of
employment growth, demographic composition, etc.--
all of which are factors which weigh on decisions
to "stay" or "move."

Some demographic characteristics have been
listed by others as "personal" characteristics (age,
sex, education, race, etc.); and, writers, such as
Stolzenberg (C-15), infer that differentially held
social values reflect variable relationships between
such personal characteristics and wage levels. Two
such personal characteristics are discussed, at some
length, within the context of the Spilerman discourse: education and age. Education is not really
discussed, per se, in terms of the latitude it affords in particular career lines; however, it is
discussed within the context of its interaction with
age. For example, Spilerman reports on findings to
the effect that the more highly educated one is, the
longer that individual can expect (across a lifetime) to retain an earnings increase, before such
wages peak and then decline.

Age is a variable that Spilerman discusses in
other contexts, as well. For example, he reports
on how the physical difficulty of a task and job
security become more important issues, as one be-

C-14 (continued)

comes older. Spilerman points out that it can,
thus, be concluded that employees of different ages
will have variable "preference mixes" for job features. The inference is that level of pay may not
be as important (among the totality of job features)
for older than for younger workers. One might further infer, therefore, that perceptions of pay inequity, from the standpoint of social comparison,
vary by age. The logic of the Spilerman argument
is that an older focal employee might not consider
it "inequitable" for a younger comparison other to
be paid more, if that younger employee has, say,
less job security(2).

Beyond discussion on the importance of movement among organizations and occupations, as well
as the differential perspectives on equity that
might emerge from age and education variation, Spilerman spends some time on the matter of how interpretations of variant earnings potential depend on
whether one assumes a "dual labor market" or a "human capital" perspective. According to Spilerman,
the latter perspective insists that wage differentials among employees of similar skill narrow, over
time, since employers invest in employee skill-
enhancement only as much as is necessary, and employees change jobs if not paid enough. The end
product of this type activity is argued to be a
"market wage." On the other hand, the dual labor
market perspective suggests that wage differentials
do not necessarily narrow, over time, for "primary"
sector employees. This is because (as Spilerman
argues the case) a company continues to invest in
upgrading the ability of such employees (who are
bound to the firm by seniority provisions). Primary sector employees, therefore, are argued to be
"insulated" from the effects of outside (i.e., "external") competition for promotion and salary; so,
wage differentials can remain(3).

Notes

(1) Spilerman is interested in both turnover
patterns ("staying"/"moving") and personal (i.e.,
demographic) characteristics, when assessing the
potential for variant returns to career line pat-

C-14 (continued)

terns. For a recent empirical study that stops
short of analyzing social structural influences,
but which (nevertheless) describes the nature of
such differential returns based on variant turnover patterns and personal characteristics, see:
G. Borjas, "Race, Turnover, and Male Earnings."
INDUSTRIAL RELATIONS 23(1984):73-89. The two personal characteristics, in which Borjas has an interest, are age and race. In brief, he finds that,
among younger men, the earnings returns to a turnover event (quit, layoff, or staying on the job)
are greater for whites than for blacks. Among older workers, Borjas finds that whites have greater
returns to staying on the job than do blacks; however, no racial differences, in returns to quitting
or being laid off, can be found among such older
males.

(2) There has been additional research, suggesting that a number of variables, other than age,
condition variant "preference mixes." For example,
Hudis (D-16) notes that level of familial income
conditions the degree to which female employees have
variant commitment to the monetary aspects of work.
Since blacks, generally, have lower incomes than do
whites, Hudis suggests that, as a variable, level
of familial income helps explain racial differences
in preference for monetary rewards. Still other research has suggested that certain cultural factors
(attributed to different races), variant levels of
education, differential nature of occupations, and
variant values placed on leisure time, all influence
the quality of "preference mixes." For further information on the subject, the reader is directed to
Shapiro (D-26) and to F. Best and J. Wright, "Effects of Work Scheduling on Time-Income Tradeoffs."
SOCIAL FORCES 57(1978):136-153.

(3) The "dual" labor markets are labeled as
"primary" and "secondary." For more information on
the Spilerman presentation of primary vs. secondary
market distinctions, the reader is directed to the
Beck, et al. (C-1) annotation. A question, not addressed by Spilerman, is whether any change in employ, over the course of a career (affected or not
by the strength of primary market career develop-

C-14 (continued)

ment) involves movement among broad occupational
classes or movement within the same occupational
class. Readers with an interest in this issue
might consult R. D'amico, "The Effects of Career
Origins on Subsequent Socioeconomic Attainments."
WORK AND OCCUPATIONS 12(1985):329-356. While D'amico finds one's "industry of first job" to strongly
affect that person's career development, he appears
to also infer that the manifestations of such an
effect are more complex than to simply assume the
strength of "primary" career development to affect
career patterns over time.

C-15

Stolzenberg, Ross M.
    1975   "Occupations, Labor Markets, and the Process
           of Wage Attainment." AMERICAN SOCIOLOGICAL
           REVIEW 40:645-665.

        Mahoney (A-4) attempts to build a case against
the validity of distributive justice theories based
on classical economic principles. He argues that
it is more relevant to view distributive justice
within the context of variation in "occupational
content," as well as within the context of variations in "value perceptions"--resultant from differential skill, ability, education, age, race, sex,
etc. Stolzenberg considers this concern for job
content and value perceptions to be a sociological
concern; yet, he feels that to truly understand why
wage variation exists, this sociological concern
must be somewhat combined with the traditional economic concern for labor market conditions.
        In general, the effect of combining economic
and sociological perspectives, as Stolzenberg defines them, results in an abandonment of any classical economic assumptions about perfectly competitive markets united along occupational lines. Rather, the quality of changing social values is such
that markets are argued by Stolzenberg to be "frag-
mented" along occupational lines. Thus, to use the
author's language, an "occupation by market" approach to analysis is adopted.

C-15 (continued)

Based on a review of existing literature, as
well as empirical analysis of census data, Stolzenberg points out that an "occupation by market"
approach means that variation exists, among occupations, as to the processes governing wage attainment. One might conclude from this finding, alone,
that social comparison, among relevant others in
different occupational categories, might be suspect.
Nevertheless, Stolzenberg concludes that existent
variation in wage attainment processes can be best
explained/predicted on the basis of knowledge about
those social forces contributing to the "occupational segmentation of labor markets."

For example, in a circumstance of social comparison, a focal employee might not feel that he is
receiving equitable payment, relative to some comparison other. The employee may feel that this is
due to age discrimination, since this represents the
only difference that the focal employee perceives
between the comparison other and him. In such a
circumstance, the focal employee is concluding that
wage variation is the direct result of the impact of
differentiation in one "value criterion" (or "personal characteristic")--age. Stolzenberg argues
that such an assessment is a shallow one, inasmuch
as any personal characteristic-wage level assessment can only be explained within a larger social
context. For example, Stolzenberg presents evidence
that any differences in the relationship between age
and earnings can be explained within the context of
at least two social forces that contribute to the
occupational segmentation of markets: the physical
demands of a given occupation's tasks and the social
organization of incumbents with respect to unionization. Consequently, if, in the hypothetical example given, the performed occupation was labeled
the same for both parties to the social comparison--
but, that occupation carried with it a greater quality of physical demands and/or a different wage allocation setting (union vs. non-union) for one of
the comparison parties, then that might be considered a more logical explanation for the wage variance than age and might, as a consequence, diminish
the validity of any focal employee complaint about
age discrimination.

C-15 (continued)

The emphasis placed by Stolzenberg on how certain social forces influence differential wage-level
relationships infers that changes in such social
forces might influence changes in "social values,"
surrounding the nature of relationships between personal characteristics and wage levels, over time.
If this be the case, then it adds a dimension to
the thinking of Mahoney (A-4). Mahoney generally
argues for the importance of changing social values
but does not specify the nature of social forces
(i.e., interactive or social structural conditions)
that facilitate the continued change in values, over
time.

C-16

Stolzenberg, Ross M.
    1978   "Bringing the Boss Back In: Employer Size,
           Employee Schooling, and Socioeconomic
           Achievement." AMERICAN SOCIOLOGICAL REVIEW
           43:813-828.

A number of writers have suggested the importance of considering something of a "contingency"
approach to the understanding of wage variation--
such that differences in personal characteristics
can be found to influence pay variance, contingent
on the quality of social force (or social structural) variability (cf., Beck, et al., C-1; Stolzenberg, C-15; Talbert and Bose, C-17).
    With respect to the use of personal character-
istics, Beck, et al. (C-1) represent those writers
who have taken an interest in the effects of "education." Indeed, Stolzenberg has decided, in this
article, to concentrate attention on educational
effects, since he finds such to be a "central part"
of just about all behavioral research on variables
that influence earnings patterns.
    As far as the social structural variables that
potentially impact on any relationship between education and earnings, the critical concern for Stolzenberg, in this particular article, is with variability in "size." In his conclusion, Stolzenberg
states that he had reviewed (in this article) a

C-16 (continued)

"wide body" of literature suggesting that size could
alter the effect of education on earnings. Actually, based on the content of that literature (as
Stolzenberg presents it), it would appear that the
literature suggests no such thing. Some of the literature suggests that size influences earnings, independent of educational effects. Other literature
suggests that size influences the degree of "standardization" of organizational activities--and standardization, in turn, influences the nature of relationships in organizations. In the latter case,
however, Stolzenberg presents no previous literature
that empirically demonstrates a relationship between
standardization and earnings. The author only infers from the literature that standardization might
influence degree of occupational achievement and,
therefore, the amount of earnings tied to level of
achievement (or "status level"). So, based on the
previous research being reported by Stolzenberg, it
would appear that his study actually constitutes one
of the first, if not the first, attempt to empirically establish the contingent nature of a relationship between degree of standardization (as a function of size), level of education, and amount of
earnings. This would appear to be a most worthy
endeavor, since writers (such as Talbert and Bose,
C-17) discuss the importance of size in such a contingency arrangement, but do not appear to measure
for such effects.
      In general, Stolzenberg develops hypotheses
according to the following line of reasoning. The
greater the size of an organization, the more that
organization must rely on standardized evaluation
methods that measure achievement and form a basis
for the discerning of compensation awards commen-
surate with the level of achievement. "Level of
education" represents a conveniently available, low
cost, body of standardized data that employers can
apply to the achievement evaluation and consequent
award allocation processes. So, the greater the
size of an organization, the more it can be expected
to rely on the thinking that higher levels of education contribute to higher levels of occupational
status achievement and consequent earnings.
      The suggestion of a greater propensity by lar-
ger organizations to use education level as a means

C-16 (continued)

to evaluate achievement/award compensation is supported by the Stolzenberg empirical analysis of
Univ. of Michigan SRC data. The author does not
test for, but nevertheless suggests three possible
lines of explanation for his findings:

(1)   In line with larger organizations needing a
        convenient standardized means to determine
        wages, the structure of larger organizations
        create "conditions which make it especially
        convenient for them to act as if schooling
        were relevant to job performance, whether or
        not [such] a relationship ... exists" (Stolz-
        enberg, pp. 825-826).

(2)   There could exist a "widespread belief" (not
        necessarily empirically validated) that more
        education is needed to perform tasks in larger
        organizations than in smaller ones.

(3)   More education could, indeed, be more strongly
        related to job performance in larger than in
        smaller organizations.

        In any event, the Stolzenberg findings may lend
further credibility to the thinking of such writers
as Beck, et al. (C-1)--to the effect that wage differentials might exist, depending on the type sector
in which occupations are being performed. Assuming
(for the sake of argument) validity to the distinction between core and periphery sectors and, assuming that the practice of more closely aligning educational attainment with achievement contributes to
earnings differences between larger and smaller organizations, then the literature reviewed by Stolzenberg would imply sectoral differences in earnings.
The reason is that the literature in question suggests that only larger organizations command the
resources needed to operate in a core economy.
        There is, however, a certain difference be-
tween the findings of Stolzenberg and those of Beck,
et al. (C-1). Stolzenberg concludes that the relationship between education and earnings levels is
more pronounced in larger organizations (that are
more characteristically found in core economies).
In this case, Stolzenberg is measuring education

C-16 (continued)

In terms of "years of schooling." Using this particular measure, Beck, et al. actually find more
pronounced effects of education on earnings in the
periphery. Beck, et al. do find a more pronounced
effect of education on earnings in the core economy, when using a different measure for education--
"increases in formal levels of certification." Assuming (as does Stolzenberg) that larger organizations are to be found in the core economy, a question thus arises as to why the use of "years of
schooling" yields different results between the two
studies. One possible reason is that Beck, et al.
really do not measure for the influence of size as
a variable. Beck, et al. simply categorize firms(1)
into sectors based on levels of wage payments, investment activity, etc., in order to draw "either-
or" conclusions (such as: "either" education has a
more pronounced effect in the core "or" it has a
more pronounced effect in the periphery). In his
analysis, Stolzenberg does not include a core vs.
periphery demarcation; indeed, he only infers to
that demarcation after his data has been analyzed.
Actually, Stolzenberg's variable is size, per se.
Furthermore, for Stolzenberg, size is not necessarily an "either-or" ("large" vs. "small") measure;
he uses five categories of size. Consequently, it
is possibly the case that this greater variation
assumed to the size variable, by Stolzenberg, contributes to different findings about the relationship between education and earnings than is the
case when writers (such as Beck, et al.) assume
"large vs. small" demarcations.

Note

(1) The Beck, et al. "categorization" is based
on the theory/empirical work of others. In some
later research by Beck and colleagues (Tolbert,
et al., C-18), categorization is based on their own
research, in which case, they find (as inferred by
Stolzenberg), more pronounced effects of "years of
schooling" on earnings in the core.

C-17

Talbert, Joan and Christine E. Bose
  1977 "Wage-Attainment Processes: The Retail Clerk
       Case." AMERICAN JOURNAL OF SOCIOLOGY 83:403-
       424.

     Writers, such as Stolzenberg (C-15), attempt
to empirically establish the importance for joint
consideration of "sociological" (i.e., occupational
content and personal characteristics) and "economic"
(labor market) influences on wage variation. Talbert and Bose, to a certain extent, attempt to extend upon this particular research tradition. For
example, with respect to an issue brought up by
Stolzenberg, Talbert and Bose suggest that it is
insufficient to simply engage in "occupation by market" analysis, whereby it is assumed that labor market variables (such as wage setting processes) vary
across occupational categories. Rather, Talbert and
Bose review literature that argues for variance in
defined job content, plant size, and other "organizational" characteristics--across occupational categories. The importance of these organizational
characteristics, argue Talbert and Bose, is that
they contribute to the type social forces that
Stolzenberg suggests affect variant relationships
between personal characteristics and pay levels.
Illustrating their point, Talbert and Bose argue
that size, as a characteristic, can contribute to
variance in the level of job routinization and/or
the level of effective rank and file bargaining
power--both of which constitute social forces affecting levels of pay.
     Talbert and Bose agree with Stolzenberg (C-15)
that any social forces affecting wage variation actually are affecting differential relationships between personal characteristics and wage levels--a
point concurred upon by several other writers, as
well (cf., Beck, et al., C-1; Bibb and Form, C-2;
Hodson, C-7). In this particular research, Talbert
and Bose test for the applicability of six personal
characteristics: sex, marital status, years of sel-
ling at current store, years of schooling, father's
occupation, and age. Of these six characteristics,
only two (sex and marital status) are found to significantly contribute to wage variance.

C-17 (continued)

Analysis of the interaction between social forces attached to "organizational characteristics" and
variance among personal characteristic-wage level
relationships produces the following results:

(1) Wages are greater for clerks who sell in spe-
     cialty stores (i.e., clerk "location in retail
     organization", as a variable, is important).
     Since more men than women are located in spe-
     cialty stores, the clerk location (as a social
     force) is found to influence the reality of
     wage variation by sex.

(2) Wages are greater for married men than for un-
     married men. Since more married than unmarried
     men are found to receive preferential job as-
     signments, it is assumed that a greater access
     that married men have to the choice of store
     location (as a social force) influences the
     reality of wage variation by marital status.

Talbert and Bose comment on several potential
reasons why patterns of sex segregation, in particular, appear to be perpetuated by the organizations
in their sample. One reason surrounds the existence of "dual reward structures," whereby certain
"sex-specific labor market dynamics" are dominant.
In such a circumstance, it is argued that women are
"locked into" jobs in less desirable locales, which
contributes to lower overall female pay. Another
explanation provided by the authors is that (reflec-
tive of an argument made by Cook, B-2) women might
be unaware of the different wage structure operating for men and might, therefore, not experience
inequity.

C-18

Tolbert, Charles II, Patrick M. Horan, and E.M. Beck
1980   "The Structure of Economic Segmentation: A
       Dual Economy Approach." AMERICAN JOURNAL OF
       SOCIOLOGY 85:1095-1116.

     In previous analysis by these authors (Beck,
et al., C-1), industries were grouped into dual economic segments based on the theory and/or empirical work of others. In this study, Tolbert, et al.
factor analyze census data to determine, for themselves, which industries should be grouped in core
vs. periphery sectors. The first part of the article is devoted to a report on the results of this
categorization. The authors do find some industries
to have been "misclassified" in the Beck, et al.
analysis; but, about 67 percent are classified the
same in both studies.
     The second part of the article is devoted to
determining the distribution of personal characteristics across sectors, as well as what effect the
dual economic structure has on the relationship between personal characteristics and earnings. Only
four of the original Beck, et al. (C-1) personal
characteristics are tested for by the authors this
time around: sex, race, education (years of schooling), and current occupational prestige. By sector,
the distribution of these four characteristics corresponds with the distribution in the Beck, et al.
study; i.e., in general, core employees are found
to be white, male, more educated, and located in
current occupations of higher prestige. In general,
these four characteristics are also found to be positively associated with earnings levels. Tolbert,
et al. also test for the effect of a variable, "work
experience," which appears to involve some adjusted
index of employee age by years of schooling. This
particular variable is also found to be positively
associated with earnings.
     Commensurate with the work of Beck, et al.
(C-1), however, Tolbert, et al. consider the key
issue to be whether variation in earnings by personal characteristics can be explained by sector
location. The authors find that it can; and, in
general concert with the Beck, et al. research,
higher employee earnings, regardless of personal
characteristic, are found to be more pronounced in

C-18 (continued)

the core than in the periphery. The only difference between the Beck, et al. study and this more
recent endeavor appears to be with the effect of
the dimension, "years of schooling." Beck, et al.
found a more pronounced effect between this variable and earnings in the periphery; Tolbert, et al.
appear to find a more pronounced effect in the core.
     Zucker and Rosenstein (C-19) criticize the work
of Beck, et al. (C-1) and Tolbert, et al. for not
conceptually separating dual "economies" from dual
"labor markets." This conceptual issue, as well as
a number of methodological issues, are debated in a
commentary and rejoinder that bear on the research
done by Tolbert, et al.[1]

Note

     [1] The commentary is by R. Hodson and R. Kauf-
man, "Circularity in the Dual Economy: Comment on
Tolbert, Horan, and Beck." AMERICAN JOURNAL OF SO-
CIOLOGY 86(1981):881-886. The rejoinder is by P.
Horan, et al., "The Circle Has No Close." AMERICAN
JOURNAL OF SOCIOLOGY 86(1981):886-894.

C-19

Zucker, Lynne G. and Carolyn Rosenstein
    1981   "Taxonomies of Institutional Structure:
           Dual Economy Reconsidered." AMERICAN
           SOCIOLOGICAL REVIEW 46:869-884.

     Several writers, listed elsewhere in this col-
lection, have either compared economic segmentation
schemes with human capital theory or have tested,
unilaterally, for the utility of the segmentation
approach, as an important addition to our knowledge
about structural factors which influence pay inequity. Beck, et al. (C-1), for example, test for the
relevance of a sectoral model. While Beck, et al.
acknowledge certain differences among "dual economy," "dual labor market," and "dual labor force"
perspectives on segmentation, they (nevertheless)
see much more that such perspectives have in common

C-19 (continued)

than make them different. Beck, et al. choose,
therefore, to concentrate on patterns of similarity among the sectoral perspectives, when designing
their own research. A contrasting point of view is
posited by Zucker and Rosenstein. It is their pos-
ture that what makes sectoral perspectives different
is most important; and, as a consequence, they cannot dismiss what they perceive to be the importance
of those differences.

Zucker and Rosenstein imply that part of the
confusion over attempting to separate different
forms of segmentation perspective (economy, labor
market, labor force) from one another is that labels often become so interchanged that, at an operational level, what one author uses, say, to measure
dual labor market variation is what another uses to,
perhaps, measure dual economic variation. Zucker
and Rosenstein, in fact, do not particularly help
matters, when, in the midst of attempting to conceptually separate one perspective from another, they
proceed to lump all three together, as deriving from
the "dual economy tradition."

It is because of the difficulty of interchang-
ing labels that Zucker and Rosenstein suggest that
the perspectives be separated, based on the type
variables that they consider most important; and,
the authors do spend some time isolating the different types of variables utilized by the different
perspectives. In brief, Zucker and Rosenstein suggest three categories of variables that writers on
sectoral theory tend to consider of primary importance. One set of variables centers around the
"industry," as a unit of analysis; another set centers around the "firm," as a unit of analysis; and,
a third set cannot be thought of as industry-specific or firm-specific. This third set of variables
surround certain individual "worker characteristics"
that are contingent on the entire process by which
income is distributed and attained[1].

Actually, Zucker and Rosenstein list only one
"firm-specific" variable that they find identified
as being of primary importance--"degree of economic
control over a market." The authors then proceed to
discuss difficulties that have been outlined in the
literature over how best to operationalize the variable, claiming (for example) that such measures of

C-19 (continued)

"market control" as concentration, size, and profit
are generally not very highly correlated or show
"inconsistent patterns of relationship."
    Most of the empirical work of segmentation wri-
ters, argue Zucker and Rosenstein, has either been
at the level of "industry" or at the level of "individual worker." The authors find unemployment
levels and degree of unionization to be two of the
more common industry-level variables that are used.
What have been labeled throughout this book as "personal" characteristics (e.g., demographic characteristics) constitute what Zucker and Rosenstein
label as individual worker characteristics.
    The authors proceed to compare the four oper-
ational definitions of sector, posited by Beck,
et al. (C-1), Bibb and Form (C-2), Hodson (C-7),
and Tolbert, et al. (C-18). Contrary to a Beck,
et al. contention that "consensus" exists on the
sectoral classification of most industries, Zucker
and Rosenstein find "considerable variation" among
the four studies in question(2). As one of many
conclusions that they draw, for example, level of
education (measured in terms of degree of certification) is found by Beck, et al. to be higher in
the core economy; on the other hand, the Zucker
and Rosenstein analysis reveals that Bibb and Form
find such level of education to be higher in the
peripheral economy. Upon relating education and
other variables to earnings--and, then attempting
to compare such relationships across sectors, Zucker and Rosenstein do not find evidence of as much
sectoral differentiation as is claimed by the four
studies in question; and, where sectoral differences
do occur, Zucker and Rosenstein find a considerable
degree of inconsistency among the studies. As a
consequence the authors conclude that the current
thinking on economic segmentation needs to be reconsidered and reformulated.
    In the more general formal organizational
literature, there has been an amount of recent criticism of segmentation research, much of which substantiates, clarifies, and/or expands upon the Zucker and Rosenstein point of view. For example, some
of these articles argue for more "firm-specific"
type measures and comparisons. Others support
abandonment of "dual" sector models, in favor of

C-19 (continued)

approaches that can account of "shades of gray" between the extremes of core and periphery (See Kalleberg, et al., C-9, and Kaufman, et al., C-10, for
examples of what several of these more general writers have in mind.). Further reference on the general organizational literature of this type can be
found in the Kaufman, et al. annotation.

Notes

(1) The reader will find a similar concern over
interchangeable usage among dual segmentation labels
being expressed by Ward and Mueller (D-34). Ward
and Mueller offer a resolution that is somewhat similar to the Zucker and Rosenstein suggestion of
"firm" vs. "industry" demarcation; and, the reader
is directed to the Ward and Mueller annotation for
more information on how those authors conceptually
develop much of what Zucker and Rosenstein have in
mind.

(2) "Considerable variation," as Zucker and
Rosenstein interpret it, derives from the following: (1) Variation in the grouping of industries
as core or peripheral (for example, the level of
agreement that the authors find between Hodson and
Beck, et al. is about 57 percent); (2) some variation in the distribution of personal characteristics
between sectors; (3) some variable findings on the
relationship between personal characteristics and
income; (4) variation on the impact that sectoral
differences have on personal characteristic-wage
level relationships.

PART D: SPECIFIC STUDIES ON RACE AND/OR SEX EFFECTS

PART D: SPECIFIC STUDIES ON
RACE AND/OR SEX EFFECTS

Chronological and Content Key

Entries are listed, chronologically, by year of publication. Multiple entries, within a given year, are listed alphabetically. Content is noted under the "control" column, as follows: R = race effect control only; S = sex effect control only; R&S = control for both race and sex effects.

Author(s)	Year	Code	Control	Page
LaSorte	1971	D-19	S	146
Browning, et al.	1973	D-5	R	110
Ferber & Loeb	1973	D-11	S	122
Suter & Miller	1973	D-29	S	172
Cutright	1974	D-7	R	115
Stolzenberg	1975	D-28	R	168
Treiman & Terrell	1975	D-33	R&S	185
Baker & Levenson	1976	D-2	R	102
Featherman & Hauser	1976	D-10	S	121
Snyder & Hudis	1976	D-27	R&S	166
Szymanski	1976	D-30	R	173
Hudis	1977	D-16	R	132

Author(s)	Year	Code	Control	Page
Shapiro	1977	D-26	R	164
Bridges & Berk	1978	D-4	R&S	108
Kluegel	1978	D-18	R	143
McLaughlin	1978	D-21	S	151
Rexroat	1978	D-23	R&S	153
Wright	1978	D-35	R	193
Halaby	1979	D-14	S	126
Hill	1979	D-15	R&S	128
Taylor	1979	D-31	R&S	180
Beck, et al.	1980	D-3	R&S	104
Rosenfeld	1980	D-24	R&S	155
Fox	1981	D-12	S	123
England, et al.	1982	D-9	S	119
Coverman	1983	D-7	S	111
Kaufman	1983	D-17	R	137
Rosenfeld	1983	D-25	S	159
Treiman & Roos	1983	D-32	S	182
Asher & Popkin	1984	D-1	R&S	101
England	1984	D-8	S	116
Major & Konar	1984	D-20	S	147
Fox	1985	D-13	S	125
Martin & Hanson	1985	D-21	S	149
Ward & Mueller	1985	D-34	S	187

Annotated Entries

D-1

Asher, Martin and Joel Popkin
   1984 "The Effect of Gender and Race Differentials
         on Public-Private Wage Comparisons: A Study
         of Postal Workers." INDUSTRIAL AND LABOR
         RELATIONS REVIEW 38:16-35.

     Taylor (D-31) raises the question of whether,
in the presence of a greater proliferation of legal/
regulatory constraints that supposedly protect mer-
itocracy, the federal government does not offer
greater equality of pay, by sex and race, than does
the private sector. Taylor's research reveals that,
in spite of such supposedly greater legal/regulatory
protection, differentials occur by both race and sex
in federal civil service employ. Asher and Popkin
address a similar question, this time analyzing the
Postal Service, as a specific alternative to private sector employ[1]. Analyzed data is from a 1979
Current Population Survey.
     The Asher and Popkin study is highly descrip-
tive--not attempting to analyze the reasons "why"
pay discrepancies arise. However, the study is
brought to the reader's attention, due to its re-
sults--which contrast with those of Taylor (D-31).
Specifically, whereas Taylor finds pay discrepancies by race and sex in the public sector, in general, Asher and Popkin fail to find such to be the
case in their analysis of the Postal Service. In
the general private sector, however, Asher and Popkin do find race and sex-based pay discrepancies.
     Reflecting on the work of such writers as Beck,
et al. (C-1), Hodson (C-8), Coverman (D-6), and
McLaughlin (D-22), any number of social factors may
have been impacting on these findings, exclusive of
differential legal/regulatory constraints--not the
least of which are variant forms of labor-management
relations (in general), the content of specific union contracts (in particular), and issues surrounding variant intra-industry occupational structures
(and/or prestige attached to such structures).

D-1 (continued)

Note

(1) A number of earlier studies, comparing public vs. private sector wage differentials (by race
and/or sex) are summarized by Asher and Popkin--but
are not all included in this book. The reader is
referred to the Asher and Popkin article for a complete listing of these earlier studies.

D-2

Baker, Sally H. and Bernard Levenson(1)
   1976   "Earnings Prospects of Black and White
          Working-Class Women." WORK AND OCCUPA-
          TIONS 3:123-150.

Baker and Levenson argue that, among research
on actual pay discrepancies for women, by race, very
little has been done on that segment of the population that moves directly from high school to employment. Consequently, the authors present results of a 5-year study that compares earnings among
black, Puerto Rican, and white women, all of whom
were trained for blue collar jobs and graduated from
the same high school.
The authors analyze data by means of certain
weighted average indexing procedures. Results are
that, upon entry and thereafter (for the duration
of the study), blacks and Puerto Ricans earned less
than did whites.
So as to address the question of what social
factors might be contributing to such earnings discrepancies, Baker and Levenson test for the effects
of race and industrial location of first job, finding wage discrepancies based on both factors(2).
Baker and Levenson argue that, logically, race and
industry location should not be considered insepar-
able factors, since any discrimination by race can
mean denial of access by racial minorities to more
lucrative employ in certain industrial locations.
Indeed, when controlling for the effects of race,
the authors find blacks and Puerto Ricans to locate
in those type industries that pay consistently lower
wages.

D-2 (continued)

The above finding somewhat parallels that of
Kluegel (D-18) on non-white males. Kluegel (p.
292) finds an overrepresentation of black males in industries "that offer the poorest relative chances for
authority attainment"; and, "authority attainment,"
as Kluegel sees it, is the key to achieving higher
income returns. The Baker and Levenson finding also
infers the very real potential for economic segmen-
tation--a matter more fully developed by such writers as Beck, et al. (C-1), Bibb and Form (C-2), and
Tolbert, et al. (C-18).

Research on differential income returns to education, by race, among male samples, have (in most
circumstances) demonstrated lower returns to equal
education for blacks than for whites (cf., Kluegel,
D-18; Stolzenberg, D-28; Wright, D-35). Since the
Baker and Levenson study is of women with essentially the same level of education, the argument is made
by the authors that (as in the case of most all-male
studies), racially based differences in returns to
education exist for women. Baker and Levenson suggest that this is solely due to racial discrimination. However, Kluegel argues that the degree to
which race is a more important determinant than other variables depends on the nature of "beliefs, values, and attitudes." These are matters which Baker
and Levenson have not tested for.

In any event, Mahoney (A-4) argues that contemporary compensation policy derives, in part, from
perceptions of racial inequities in the "external
market." The findings by such writers as Kluegel
(D-18), Wright (D-35), and Baker and Levenson would
appear, therefore, to lend a degree of "actual" sub-
stance to the "perceived" inequities that Mahoney
finds critically influencing the nature of pay policy.

Notes

(1) This citation is made to the journal, WORK
AND OCCUPATIONS. Actually, in the early part of its
publication history, the journal's main title was
SOCIOLOGY OF WORK AND OCCUPATIONS; and, indeed, the
Becker and Levenson article technically can be found
in the journal, under its earlier title. However,

D-2 (continued)

for the sake of simplicity, all references, taken
from the journal and cited in this book, bear the
later main title.

(2) While both "race" and "industrial location"
are loosely categorized as "social" factors, it is
acknowledged that, in other literature (especially
that on issues of economic segmentation), these two
variables are not considered to be at the same level
of abstraction as each other. Specifically, the
reader will usually find "race" and similar demographic variables to be considered "personal" characteristics (unique to the individual), while a variable, such as "industrial location" is generally
classified as a broader "social structural" characteristic. For an example of the literature that
distinguishes personal from structural characteristics, see Beck, et al. (C-1).

D-3

Beck, E.M., Patrick M. Horan, and Charles M. Tol-
    bert II
    1980 "Industrial Segmentation and Labor Market
          Discrimination." SOCIAL PROBLEMS 28:113-130.

    The more general literature on economic seg-
mentation, such as that reported by these and other
authors (re: Part C annotations) utilizes the nature
of sectoral differences as a social structural explanation for why wage returns to various personal
characteristics (race, sex, age, education, etc.)
vary as they do. In this paper, Beck, et al. concentrate on an examination of differential returns
to race and sex(1).
    Specifically, Beck, et al. suggest that, from
a structural standpoint, variant returns to race
and sex exist because of "differential allocation"
of women and non-whites to sectors and because of
"differential evaluation" of employee credentials
within each sector. Two of the primary purposes of
the Beck, et al. research are to test for the existence of differential allocation and diferential
evaluation as "discriminatory mechanisms."

D-3 (continued)

The issue of differential allocation is discussed, at some length, in the literature on economic segmentation (re: Part C entries), whereby a number of authors argue that non-whites and women are "allocated" in greater proportion to the periphery than to the core sector (in any dual sector model). If it is the case that, as most segmentation theorists argue, lower paying jobs are to be found in the periphery, then, by fiat, women and non-whites can generally be expected to earn less than white males. The argument is often extended that, due to what employers look for in the evaluation of credentials for higher paying jobs, there is no way for minorities[2] to ever achieve compensation equity with most white males. This is because, as Kaufman (D-17) argues, the nature of jobs in the core (which are already disproportionately held by white males) allow for more "stability," over time, than do jobs in the periphery (which are, as the argument goes, disproportinately held by minorities). So, assuming that one "credential," allowing access to better paying jobs, is stability of work history, then it can be expected--based on most segmentation theory--that a predominance of white males (who already occupy core positions) will continue to get the better paying jobs.

With respect to the second issue, of differential evaluation within sectors, the Beck, et al. suggestion is as follows. Even if there were no differential allocation--and, even if there were no "overt" manifestations of prejudice--minorities could still expect lower earnings, compared with white males in the same sector. Based on their reviewed literature, Beck, et al. suggest that, in such a case, differential evaluation could result from: lower levels of minority education; a greater degree of perceived "risk" associated with hiring women and non-whites (perhaps due to the past history of most minorities in lower paying jobs); and, the impact of union policy and/or more general company policies on seniority--favoring the progression of white males[3].

Analyzing Current Population Survey data, Beck, et al. find that, indeed, the more general economic segmentation thinking--to the effect that differential allocation of minority labor results in differ-

<u>D-3 (continued)</u>

ential earnings--is confirmed. The authors become
concerned about whether the differences in earnings,
across sectors, are due to differences in race/sex
or to "human capital" factors (i.e., education and
other credentials). Controlling for the effects of
human capital factors, they find that the effects
of race and sex do not disappear; so, they conclude
that, indeed, differences in earnings reflect variation in race and sex. More specifically, Beck,
et al. proceed to revise earnings figures, under
an assumption that differential allocation does not
exist, while controlling for the effects of human
capital and rates of return to human capital. Upon
doing this, the authors find that, regardless of
race, females experience a percentage gain in earnings, while males experience a percentage decline;
so, the authors conclude that differential allocation makes a difference, especially when such is
done on the basis of sex(4).

On the matter of differential evaluation, Beck,
et al. find the costs to minorities to be greater
within the core sector than in the periphery. The
authors do not find this to be too surprising, given
some of their earlier published findings to the effect that unions have a greater influence on policy
in the core sector(5). In addition, while there is
some controversy on the matter (re: Beck, et al.,
C-1; Stolzenberg, C-16), the finding is not too surprising to the authors, since most segmentation research finds education to be a more important factor
in core than in periphery wage determination (cf.,
Part C entries). Of interest is an additional finding, in this study, to the effect that, within each
sector, "absolute dollar costs are higher for females than for males which suggests that in both
sectors sex discrimination is more severe than race
discrimination" (Beck, et al., p. 124). This finding would appear to correspond with those of a number of earlier writers in this subject area--such
as Treiman and Terrell (D-33)--who also tend to find
sex playing a larger role than race, when defining
the reasons behind wage differentials.

D-3 (continued)

Notes

(1) Beck, et al. do much, in this particular
article, to integrate the literature on economic
segmentation with that on differences by race and
sex. Kaufman (D-17) does much the same, although
he only measures race, as a personal characteristic. The reader will, no doubt, find the literature reviews by Beck, et al. and Kaufman, in this
respect, to be among the more informative--from the
standpoint of summarizing a broad base of other
research and developing linkages among such other
studies.

(2) The concept, "minorities," is used loosely
by Beck, et al. to refer to women and to non-whites;
and, the concept is, therefore, also so used in this
annotation.

(3) Some sample literature, cited by Beck,
et al. on these matters, include: Beck (E-1); L.
Thurow, GENERATING INEQUALITY (New York: Basic
Books, 1975); P. Doeringer and M. Piore, INTERNAL
LABOR MARKETS AND MANPOWER ANALYSIS (Lexington, MA:
D.C. Heath, 1971).

(4) The procedure of revising figures, under
an assumption of no differential allocation, allows
Beck, et al. to assess the degree to which sectoral
variation makes a difference to variation by sex
and/or race. Specifically, what the authors do is
"compute a revised average earnings value for each
race-sex group based on an assumption that human
capital for each group was evaluated at the same
core sector rate" (Beck, et al., p. 124). By doing this, the authors feel that they can determine
whether "minorities would be better off relative to
white males if sectoral differences in rewards to
human capital did not exist" (p. 124). What is
found is that females (both white and non-white)
improve their situations, relative to white males;
but, the positions of non-white males remain un-
altered. From this, Beck, et al. conclude that
sectoral differences, per se, exascerbate unequal
returns to sex more than they exascerbate unequal
returns to race.

D-3 (continued)

(5) The greater influence of unions in core
than in periphery sectors has been well-established
by a number of economic segmentation studies, including the initial one reported by these authors
(Beck, et al., C-1). The argument, being made here,
is that increased unionization influences inequitable sector earnings/income. However, this particular argument (at least with respect to increased inequality by race) is a matter of some debate. The
debate is outlined in the following entries: Hill
(E-6); Beck (E-1); Pfeffer and Ross (E-7).

D-4

Bridges, William P. and Richard A. Berk
    1978   "Sex, Earnings, and the Nature of Work: A
           Job-level Analysis of Male-Female Income
           Differences." SOCIAL SCIENCE QUARTERLY 58:
           553-565.

After reviewing some of the literature on sex-
based wage discrepancies, Bridges and Berk conclude
that, among a variety of reasons given for such discrepancies, two deserve more careful attention: (1)
whether the characteristic of a job, in and of it-
self, has something to do with sex-based differences; and, (2) whether men and women operate under
different structures of remuneration(1).
To investigate these matters, Bridges and Berk
survey white collar employees in 20 Chicago-area
firms. While acknowledging that such a limited sampling frame might "restrict" their ability to gen-
eralize, the authors feel that such a narrowly drawn
sample affords them a better opportunity to focus on
differences within specific rather than broad occupational categories(2).
Writers, such as Fox (D-12) and Snyder and Hudis (D-27) have been concerned with the issue of
whether the presence of women in any occupational
category, historically populated by men, lowers
overall returns in that job category. Other writers have suggested that, perhaps, sharp wage demarcations between male-dominated and female-dominated occupations can be made (cf., Beck, et al.,

D-4 (continued)

C-1; Bibb and Form, C-2). These particular issues
are of salient interest to Bridges and Berk, as they
proceed by: (a) classifying jobs as predominantly
"male" and predominantly "female"; (b) comparing
wages across the job categories; and, (c) suggesting reasons for what wage discrepancies exist.

In general, Bridges and Berk find wage differentials to exist between jobs described as "male"
and those described as "female"; and, they further
find that, in contrast to "male" jobs, monetary returns decrease to increased productivity among "female" jobs(3).

The authors argue that, because of control for
quantity of work done, the wage differentials have
little to do with "differences in job performance"(4). They, therefore, conclude that individuals, working in female-dominated jobs, must operate under different "rules of the game" when it
comes to the structuring of remuneration. Such
different "rules of the game" are not elucidated
upon in this particular article. However, Bridges
and Berk suggest that, until such different "rules"
are understood, researchers will never be able to
fully determine the extent to which sex-based wage
discrimination exists and why it exists.

Notes

(1) Bridges and Berk present some additional
data that substantiates the finding of writers,
such as Beck, et al. (D-3) and Treiman and Terrell
(D-33), to the effect that sex discrimination is
more pronounced than is race discrimination on matters of pay. However, Bridges and Berk do not control for the effects of race, when assessing these
two major areas of analytical interest.

(2) Bridges and Berk, here, seem to be attempting to reconcile some of the criticism leveled at
them by Stolzenberg with certain other statements
made by that author. Specifically, Stolzenberg
(C-16) criticizes Bridges and Berk for using such a
limited sampling frame. However, in an earlier article, Stolzenberg (C-15) seemed to argue for ana-

D-4 (continued)

lytical focusing on wage differences within specific
occupational categories.

(3) The reader will find somewhat similar re-
sults discussed by other researchers in this area.
Examples include: England (D-8); Treiman and Terrell
(D-33).

(4) Although Bridges and Berk control for quantity of hours worked, they do not control for quality of work done. It is because of this lack of
control for work quality, among other things, that
Bridges and Berk are reluctant to identify their
findings, in this study, as definitive evidence
for the existence of dual core and peripheral economic sectors.

D-5

Browning, Harley L., Sally C. Lopreato, and Dudley
    L. Poston, Jr.
   1973 "Income and Veteran Status: Variations Among
         Mexican Americans, Blacks and Anglos." AMER-
         ICAN SOCIOLOGICAL REVIEW 38:74-85.

        Writers, such as Sørensen (C-13) and Spilerman
(C-14) offer general commentary on the importance
of accounting for differences in career-line progression and experiences over the course of careers,
when analyzing perceived and/or actual variation in
pay. Browning, et al. represent writers with a specific interest in the effect of military service experiences on career-line progression. The authors,
therefore, are interested in the differences between
the eventual earnings of those who serve in the military and those who do not. The argument, in brief,
is that professional/managerial type employ is so
tied to seniority and on-the-job experience that,
for employees in these categories, no amount of military experience can act to compensate for time lost
to military service. On the other hand, Browning,
et al. contend that, for employees in occupations
less tied to such items of "career continuity"
(e.g., clerical, sales, and laborer categories),

D-5 (continued)

military service can act as a "bridging environment"
to such employ. The reason provided by the authors
is that military service offers the type training
easily transferrable into these latter types of occupations. Assuming that occupational opportunities (and, therefore, earnings) are generally less
available to non-whites than to whites in the United
States, Browning, et al. hypothesize that the effect of such military "bridging" experiences will
act to increase minority employment opportunities
and, therefore, decrease any racially based pay discrepancies for veterans who pursue non-career continuity jobs.
        Analyzing census data, Browning, et al. find
that, unlike the situation for anglos, black and
Mexican-American incomes are higher for veterans
than for non-veterans. The authors thus conclude
that, among occupations not bound by career-conti-
nuity criteria, military service acts as bridging
environment. Indeed, Browning, et al. argue that
the "bridging" so facilatates the wage enhancement
of minority group members that pay equity results
across race categories. For a contrasting view on
this matter, see Cutwright (D-7).

D-6

Coverman, Shelley
   1983 "Gender, Domestic Labor Time, and Wage In-
          equality." AMERICAN SOCIOLOGICAL REVIEW 48:
          623-637.

        An interest in whether women's wages depreciate
to a greater extent than do men's, due to marital
status (in general) and the assumption of household
duties (in particular), is reflected in the work of
several others, whose work is annotated in this collection (cf., Talbert and Bose, C-17; Ferber and
Loeb, D-11; Rosenfeld, D-24; Rosenfeld, D-25; Suter
and Miller, D-29; Treiman and Roos, D-32; Treiman
and Terrell, D-33).
        Rosenfeld (D-25), in particular, argues that
the assumption of household duties by women sup-
presses their opportunity to move into more finan-

D-6 (continued)

cially lucrative employ (through movement out of
the peripheral economic segment). This specific
issue is the subject of even more succinct study
by Coverman, who analyzes the effect of degree of
involvement in domestic labor activity (DLA) on wage
levels, hypothesizing that such involvement will be
a more important factor in explaining lower wages
for women than for men (due to the fact that women
have a greater propensity to engage in DLA than do
men).
        In brief, the major objective of Coverman's
research is to assess the relative influence of domestic labor time (DLT) on male and female wages.
DLT is operationally defined as the time spent on
housework and child care[1]. In addition to DLT,
Coverman includes a number of other independent variables in the analysis. These are: age, number of
children, spouse's child care time, education, sex-
role attitudes[2], hours spent in market work, establishment size, union membership, sectoral location of employ (core vs. periphery), and social
class[3]. The sample size is over 1500 but is restricted to white, currently married respondents.
The sample is aged 16 and over, and all respondents
were working at least 20 hours per week in 1977.
        Among the study's results, Coverman finds that,
in general, increased DLT contributes to lower earnings for both men and women[4]. However, significant differences, by sex, in the amount of lowered
earnings, due to DLT, are not found. On the other
hand, when controlling for social class, gender differences in earnings begin to emerge. Coverman had,
in fact, not expected to find class-based earnings
differences, hypothesizing that higher class rank
(resulting in greater overall household income)
would "mediate the depressant influence of domestic
activities on labor market outcomes" (p. 634). However, while this expectation is found to hold for
men, it is not found to hold for women; and, as a
consequence, Coverman concludes that "women with
higher earnings potential but few resources for
domestic assistance are most disadvantaged by the
time they spend in domestic work" (p. 634)[5].
        At the same time, Coverman does not find the
allocation of domestic roles, by sex, to vary by
social class; consequently, the author concludes

D-6 (continued)

that the overriding variable conditioning differential earnings is not social class but is the allocation of domestic division of labor, by sex<6>.

Notes

<1> The Coverman "DLT" measure represents an
attempt to introduce more refined analysis, of what
constitutes time spent on familial responsibility,
than simply marital and parental status. An earlier attempt to do this is represented in the writing of Hill (D-15).

<2> It would appear, from the Coverman descrip-
tion of such, that the testing of the "sex role attitudes" variable gets at the question not saliently
addressed by such writers as England (D-8), Rosenfeld (D-25), and Snyder and Hudis (D-27)--as to what
specific social values are being maintained that may
restrict female mobility to a greater extent than
male mobility. While much of the Coverman thinking,
in this regard, surrounds how larger societal values
permeate work place decisions, one must go beyond
the pay equity literature to gain the most broad-
based knowledge of changing societal values on female work roles. An exemplary review of such literature is: V. Oppenheimer, "The Sociology of Women's
Economic Role in the Family." AMERICAN SOCIOLOGICAL
REVIEW 42(1977):387-406.

<3> What Coverman is doing, in this study, is
providing a rather broad-based "map" of macro-level
variables that might be impacting on sex-based pay
differences. In a later published study, Coverman
offers a "merger" of macro and micro-level variables, which might be influencing pay discrepancy,
by saliently focusing on the interplay between selected macro-level variables and perceptions of
stress. The reader with an interest in this study
is referred to B. Reskin and S. Coverman, "Sex and
Race in the Determinants of Psychophysical Distress:
A Reappraisal of the Sex-role Hypothesis." SOCIAL
FORCES 63(1985):1038-1059. This article is not annotated, since its predominant concern is with effects on stress, not on any eventual perceived/ac-

D-6 (continued)

tual pay inequities. Nevertheless, inferences can
be drawn from the Reskin and Coverman research that:
(a) sex-based variance in pay may evolve from the
fact that social factors contribute to sex-based
variation in the effects of "stressors"; and, (b)
differential exposure to paid employment, by sex,
can lead to differences in level of stress. It
might also be added that, unlike the article being
annotated, the Reskin and Coverman piece does control for the effects of race.

        <4> This finding appears to contradict much
other research that uses less refined measures of
familial responsibility that does Coverman. Most
of this other research tends to find that males,
with more responsibility (marriage/children), earn
more than single males--but that there exists a lack
of wage differential among women, regardless of
their level of familial responsibility (cf., Ferber
and Loeb, D-11; Treiman and Roos, D-32; Talbert and
Bose, C-17; Suter and Miller, D-29). On the other
hand, the findings also appear to contradict those
of the earlier-cited study, which also uses a more
refined measure of domestic activity (Hill, D-15).
Since both the Hill and Coverman studies are done
at about the same time (mid to late 1970's), it
might be surmised that the difference in findings
has something to do with different components of the
domestic activity measures used by each researcher
or with a somewhat different demographic composition of the samples. As an example of the latter
possibility, Hill, apparently, includes Hispanics
in her "white" sample. Whether Coverman also includes Hispanics, in the focal sample (which is defined as "all-white"), is not known.

        <5> Szymanski (D-30) emphasizes the importance
of distinguishing earnings/wages from income--where-
by the former is argued to represent an individual
measure, the latter a household measure. If the
Szymanski distinction is accurate, then it might
help explain this particular Coverman finding. Assuming that the greater proportion of any household
income (among those in the Coverman sample) derives
from male than from female earnings, then one might
anticipate that the amount of household income

D-6 (continued)

which is more closely associated with the earnings
of men) would have a greater effect of mediating the
depressant effect of DLT on male earnings than on
female earnings.

(6) Coverman offers two methodological cautions
to the findings--one having to do with the lack of
longitudinal analysis--the other having to do with
lack of control for variations in the use of paid
assistance with domestic work. A considerable degree of detail on these methodological issues is
presented in the focal article.

D-7

Cutright, Phillips
    1974 "The Civilian Earnings of White and Black
           Draftees and Nonveterans." AMERICAN SOCI-
           OLOGICAL REVIEW 39:317-327.

    Browning, et al. (D-5) argue for the reality
of a military service "bridging environment" that
facilitates pay equity among whites and non-whites,
employed in occupations without "career continuity"
criteria (e.g., seniority, on-the-job experience,
etc.). The Cutright article actually represents
more of a rejoinder to the Browning, et al. study,
as the author criticizes Browning, et al. on several grounds and proceeds to re-study the matter--
correcting for the following alleged problems with
the Browning, et al. research:

(1) The Browning, et al. study is limited to five
     southwestern states and, therefore, does not
     sufficiently stratify by region to be consid-
     ered representative of a national population.

(2) Browning, et al. do not control for age. Wri-
     ters, such as Parker (C-12) and Spilerman
     (C-14), point out that differences in both
     perceived and actual inequity may be contin-
     gent on employee age.

D-7 (continued)

(3)   Browning, et al. exclude from analysis vet-
       erans with less than five years of schooling,
       but then to proceed to include individuals of
       that educational level in the non-veteran sam-
       ple--thus potentially inflating earnings ca-
       pability (due to education) among veterans.

       Cutright's re-analysis reveals that, among
those employed without "career continuity," who are
also non-white, veterans do not necessarily earn
more than do non-veterans.   Thus, he concludes that
the Browning, et al. assumption of a military bridging environment cannot be supported(1).

                          Note

       (1) It should be noted that both Cutright and
Browning, et al. rely on data primarily of personnel, who were either serving or not serving in the
military in the 1940's and 1950's. Whether data on
a newer group of veterans, exposed to (perhaps) newer methods of training in the military, would provide alternative findings to these, is not known.

D-8

England, Paula
    1984 "Wage Appreciation and Depreciation: A Test
          of Neoclassical Economic Explanations of
          Occupational Sex Segregation." SOCIAL FORCES
          62:726-749.

       England examines the worthiness of two explana-
tions of occupational sex segregation. Both rest
on an assumption that women make "pecuniary choices"
to become employed in certain jobs that best fit
their circumstances of non-continuity in employ.
       The first, proposed by Polachek(1), argues
the following:

          Segregation results because women, whose
          employment is intermittent, maximize
          lifetime earnings by choosing occupa-

D-8 (continued)

       tions with low depreciation during time
       spent at home (England, p. 726).

       As the theory goes, Polachek (according to
England) views wage depreciation as an "atrophy"
of human capital skills. England adds that firm
and/or union rules, surrounding loss of seniority
upon resignation, could also have something to do
with such wage depreciation. In any event, assuming that some occupations carry a "greater risk" of
depreciation, than do others, the Polachek theory
(as England summarizes it) is that "women who anticipate intermittent employment may maximize lifetime earnings by choosing an occupation with low
depreciation penalties" (p. 728). Sex differences
in earnings occur, because (as the theory goes) men
are more continuously employed than women and, thus,
need not try to minimize the effects of wage depreciation. Since, from the Polachek point of view,
traditionally "male" occupations entail "greater
risk" of depreciation, over time, for intermittently employed persons, then (as England summarizes the
Polachek view), women "choose" to be employed more
in traditionally "female" occupations--so as to compensate for the inability to compete with continuously employed men in any traditionally "male" occupations.
       The second explanation for occupational sex
segregation, examined by England, is proposed by
Zellner(2), to the effect that "many women optimize
lifetime earnings by choosing occupations with high
starting wages but low wage appreciation, while men
optimize in occupations with high appreciation"
(England, p. 726). Assuming that occupations differ, in terms of starting wages and wage appreciation rates, the Zellner theory (according to England) takes on a "human capital" flow, suggesting
that jobs offering more potential for appreciation
have lower starting wages, but, given earlier years
investment in training, there results higher appreciation over the long-run. Since only continuously
employed persons can avail themselves of these type
careers--where long-run training "pays off"--and,
since men are more inclined than women to be continuously employed, then the theory suggests that an
earnings gap will exist, by sex, if both men and

D-8 (continued)

women rather exclusively pursue these type jobs (low
starting wages; high long-run appreciation). The
Zellner argument (as England describes it), therefore, is that women, in reality, tend not to place
themselves at such a competitive disadvantage. Rather, being only intermittently eligible for employ,
most women "choose" to pursue jobs with high starting wages but lower depreciation rates. Given these
differential "choice" patterns, between men and wom-
en, the segmentation supposedly results between traditionally "male" occupations (low starting wage,
high appreciation) and traditionally "female" occupations (high starting wage, low appreciation).

Using data collected in 1973(3), on approximately 3000 individuals, England finds that, contrary to the major assumption made in the Polachek
and Zellnek models, women do not have pecuniary
reasons for pursuing traditionally "female" jobs.
This is because England finds that women earn more
in traditionally "male" than in traditionally "female" occupations(4). What England suggests is that
analysis must be made on the nature of "nonpecuniary
motivations, such as those controlled by sex role
socialization" (p. 742)(5).

Notes

(1) The reader is referred to the England article for a number of references, upon which the
author draws, when discussing the Polachek theory.
The most recent of these citations, as provided by
England, is: S. Polachek, "Occupational Self-selec-
tion: A Human Capital Approach to Sex Differences
in Occupational Structure." REVIEW OF ECONOMICS AND
STATISTICS 58(1981):60-69.

(2) H. Zellner, "The Determinants of Occupa-
tional Segregation." In Cynthia Lloyd, SEX, DIS-
CRIMINATION, AND THE DIVISION OF LABOR (New York:
Columbia University Press, 1975).

(3) The reader will note that this and most
other articles, annotated in this part of the book,
rely on data that is about 10-20 years old. While
this seems to be the case in most journal literature

D-8 (continued)

on individual earnings, there exists, at least, one
case of an article on family income sex differentials (not directly tied to on-the-job earnings)
that uses much more up-to-date information. For
the reader's reference, the article is N. Glenn and
P. Taylor, "Educational and Family Income: A Comparison of White Married Men and Women in the U.S."
SOCIAL FORCES 63(1984):167-183.

(4) For somewhat similar findings, the reader
is directed to the articles by Bridges and Berk
(D-4) and by Rosenfeld (D-25).

(5) The reader will find similar conclusions,
as this, drawn by such other writers as: Coverman
(D-6); Rosenfeld (D-25); Snyder and Hudis (D-27).

D-9

England, Paula, Marilyn Chassie, and Linda McCormick
   1982   "Skill Demands and Earnings in Female and
          Male Occupations." SOCIOLOGY AND SOCIAL
          RESEARCH 66:147-168.

A number of writers, listed elsewhere in this
collection, have commented on how: there exists economic segmentation (whereby less pay is provided
to occupations of lower "skill"); differential allocation by sex occurs among the segments (such
that women end up earning less than men); and, as
a result of the economic segmentation and differential allocation processes, certain occupations become labeled as "traditionally female" and "traditionally male" (cf., Beck, et al., D-3; Bridges and
Berk, D-4; McLaughlin, D-22; Rosenfeld, D-25; Snyder
and Hudis, D-27). England, et al. engage in what
appears to be one of the more salient examinations
of differences in "skill" needed to perform various
occupations, so as to determine: (a) whether there
(indeed) exists variant skill between traditionally
"male" and "female" occupations and (b) whether
there exists differential sex-based wage returns
to occupations of similar skill. Their analysis
is of 1970 census data.

D-9 (continued)

England, et al. define five types of skill
(training requirements, cognitive, perceptual, manual, and social) and match such with occupations
listed in the DICTIONARY OF OCCUPATIONAL TITLES(1).
In general, the authors find the following:

(1)   Cognitive and training requirement skills in-
      fluence earnings the most; yet, "male and fe-
      male occupations average nearly equal demands
      for [such skills]..." (p. 163).

(2)   Sex differences are only found to occur with
      respect to the performance of manual and so-
      cial skills attached to a job(2); however,
      these differences in skills are not found to
      translate into differences in pay.

As a consequence of the above findings, England et al. (p. 164) conclude as follows:

      The skill differences between male and
      female occupations explain virtually
      none of the earning gap between the sex-
      es. Rather, female occupations syste-
      matically pay less than is predicted by
      their skill demands.

Treiman and Roos (D-32) argue that sex-based
wage discrimination persists, in spite of equivalency in occupational "prestige"; and, England,
et al. are, thus, inferring that sex-based discrimination persists, as well, in spite of equivalency
in that occupational "skill" bearing the most on
earnings determination. Much the same as Rosenfeld
(D-25) and Snyder and Hudis (D-27), England, et al.
suggest the need to study sex-based socialization
(and resultant values), so as to discern why such
apparent wage discrimination by sex persists; but,
also like Rosenfeld and Snyder and Hudis, England,
et al. do not engage in any empirical analysis of
such a socialization process and resultant value
formation.

D-9 (continued)

Notes

(1) England, et al. use a coding scheme, developed by S. McLauglin, OCCUPATIONAL CHARACTERISTICS AND THE MALE/FEMALE INCOME DIFFERENTIAL (Ph.D. Dissertation, Washington State University, 1975). Some detail is provided in the England, et al. paper as to how the scheme is applied and on certain methodological issues associated with the use of the scheme.

(2) England, et al. (p. 163) explain the sex-based difference in manual vs. social skill performance as follows: "many male occupations involve manipulation of physical objects or wielding of power over people, while female jobs typically entail clerical skills or nuturant ... skills."

D-10

Featherman, David L. and Robert M. Hauser
    1976   "Sexual Inequalities and Socioeconomic
           Achievement in the U.S., 1962-1973."
           AMERICAN SOCIOLOGICAL REVIEW 41:462-483.

Featherman and Hauser present data which substantiates the thinking of several other writers in the field that, while men and women are approaching equality in terms of occupational and educational status, women continue to receive lower returns to both of these forms of status.

Examples of some others, who essentially report the same finding, are Suter and Miller (D-29) and Treiman and Terrell (D-33). In contrast to these other two analyses, however, Featherman and Hauser restrict their study by only looking at households where a married spouse is present. On the other hand, in contrast to the Suter/Miller and Treiman/Terrell studies, Featherman and Hauser use a broader age-range in their data set, looking at employees aged 20-64.

Featherman and Hauser report trends toward decreasing sex-based wage differentials, over time. However, in contrast with some other studies that

D-10 (continued)

they cite (which demonstrate a corresponding increase in the importance of formal education or
"credentialism" as an evaluative component), the
Featherman and Hauser data does not reveal a trend
toward such an increased importance placed on credentialism.

D-11

Ferber, Marianne A. and Jane W. Loeb
    1973 "Performance, Rewards, and Perceptions of
          Sex Discrimination Among Male and Female
          Faculty." AMERICAN JOURNAL OF SOCIOLOGY
          78:995-1002.

    Reflecting a suggestion of Stolzenberg (C-15)
to compare wages within specific occupational categories, Ferber and Loeb examine why pay differentials by sex exist, among University of Illinois
faculty.
    Ferber and Loeb take note of some data, appar-
ently reported elsewhere[1], that such a salary differential at the university favors males. An assessment is made of the effects of two independent
variables, marital status and parental status, while
holding constant the effects of age, occupational
status (i.e., academic rank), and host of profes-
sionally oriented "status" variables (e.g., number
of articles published, books edited, etc.). The
finding is that, whereas both parental status and
marital status make a difference in male salaries,
only marital status affects female salary levels.
Further, it is found that the marital status effects
are the opposite by sex. Specifically, married
males earn more than do single males; but, single
females earn more than do married females[2].
    From these findings, Ferber and Loeb infer that
the direction of sex discrimination is such that
"reward tends to be scaled to perceived financial
need" (p. 1000). Apparently, the authors are assuming, here (in the absence of reported literature
or empirical support) that university decision-
makers consider married males (especially those with
children) to have greater financial needs than mar-

<u>D-11</u> <u>(continued)</u>

ried females--and, that this, therefore, serves to
explain sex-based discrimination in the academic
setting.
    Ferber and Loeb further find that perceptions
of sex-based wage discrimination are "more accurate"
among women than among men and among married than
among single women. The authors suggest, in this
case, that greater "accuracy" of perception derives
from "having experienced more" discrimination by
sex.

Notes

    <1> The salary differential data is not re-
ported; even in summary form, in this article.
While the authors do not specifically say that they
report the data elsewhere, they do take note of
"a more detailed analysis of the current data"
(p. 1000) that was done in M. Ferber and J. Loeb,
"University Professors: Productivity and Rewards"
(unpublished manuscript, 1972).

    <2> The reader will note how the findings on
female earnings by marital status, in this case,
contrast with those of such writers as: Talbert
and Bose (C-17); Suter and Miller (D-29).

<u>D-12</u>

Fox, Mary Frank
    1981 "Sex Segregation and Salary Structure in
          Academia." WORK AND OCCUPATIONS 8:39-60.

    Writers, such as Snyder and Hudis (D-27), test
for the "competition" hypothesis, whereby the entrance of minorities/women into an occupational category is argued to depress overall income levels in
that category. Fox tests the same hypothesis, in
this study, with respect to specific units of a university (departments, colleges, schools, etc.). In
this case, the author is arguing that such academic
units represent "occupational categories," since all
professional employees within each unit do the same

D-12 (continued)

general form of academic work defined by the specific category.

Other writers, such as Bridges and Berk (D-4), express interest in differences between male and female-dominated occupations. This is an interest shared by Fox, as she tests for the relevance of two other hypotheses: a "concentration" hypothesis, suggesting female salaries to be higher in male-dominated, as opposed to female-dominated units; and, a "compensation" hypothesis, suggesting men to be salary-compensated (i.e., receiving higher salaries) when having to work with women.

In brief, Fox finds none of the hypotheses to be supported by her data. Rather, the nature of sex-based salary allocation in academia can be explained by a "connection between composition of the sexes and the context of achievement" (Fox, p. 55). Specifically, Fox finds the following:

(1)   With respect to the "competition" hypothesis, what effect the entry of women into a male-dominated unit might have on overall salaries in that unit is found to have more to do with the attainments of the men in that unit than with the unit's sex composition.

(2)   With respect to the "concentration" hypothesis, female attainment levels, not the sex composition of units, are found to be determinants of female salary levels.

(3)   With respect to the "compensation" hypothesis, "units with higher proportions of women have more, not less, sex equivalent salaries" (Fox, p. 56). Again, levels of attainment, not sex composition, play a greater role--in this case toward the determination of salary level equivalence.

It would appear, from these findings, that any inferences about sex-based salary discrimination in academia that might be drawn from the work of others (e.g., Ferber and Loeb, D-11; LaSorte, D-19) are not particularly borne out by this, more recent, Fox research.

<u>D-13</u>

Fox, Mary Frank
   1985 "Location, Sex-typing, and Salary Among Ac-
         ademics." WORK AND OCCUPATIONS 12:186-205.

        In an earlier study, Fox (D-12) found that mat-
ters of individual or personal "attainment" play a
large role in defining sex disparity in wages. In
this article, Fox suggests that research on sex-
based wage differentials in academia has tended to
focus rather exclusively on the effects of such at-
tainment--at the expense of assessing the effects
of "employment context" or "location" type charac-
teristics(1). Consequently, in this later effort,
Fox separately analyzes the effects of such "location" characteristics (of both teaching and non-
teaching units of a university) and the effects of
"attainment" characteristics on earnings.
        Fox offers no definitive percentage cutoff, as
to what proportion of a unit must be male or female,
such that the unit becomes labeled as "male" or "female" (in contrast, for example, to the Bridges and
Berk, D-4, breakdowns on what leads to "male" and
"female" occupational categories). Rather, she simply interprets, based on relative percentage breakdowns among units, that the "female" units have
"much higher" concentrations of women employed. In
general, Fox (p. 199) finds

        a particular pattern of salary returns
        to sex-typed locations: Namely, the
        lower-status female-typed professional
        schools are advantageous for women, but
        not for men. The higher status, male-
        typed schools are stongly advantageous
        for men, but not for women.

Thus, in certain circumstances, Fox (p. 200) is able
to conclude that "within each gender group, the separation is rewarding and hence reinforcing...." In
doing this, Fox is, thus, describing, in more specific terms, the type "sex-role socialization" more
generally posited by England (D-8) and others as
perpetuating wage disparity by sex.
        However, in spite of a number of different
findings regarding which units have more advanta-
geous salary returns than others, Fox cannot total-

D-13 (continued)

ly dismiss the importance of individual attainment
characteristics, when controlling for the effects
of such characteristics. Indeed, she finds some of
the location effects to dissipate, when controlling
for the effects of the attainment characteristics.
So, it would appear that any attempt to ascribe preeminent importance to either locational or attainment characteristics, within an academic institution, must be done with some caution.

Note

<1> In her summary of this research, Fox cites
a number of earlier studies, other than her own
(Fox, D-12), that are not annotated in this collection. The reader is referred to the Fox article for
a complete listing of these earlier studies.

D-14

Halaby, Charles N.
    1979 "Job-Specific Sex Differences in Organiza-
          tional Reward Attainment: Wage Discrimina-
          tion vs. Rank Segregation." SOCIAL FORCES
          58:108-127.

        Certain writers, such as Rexroat (D-23) and
Rosenfeld (D-24), distinguish between the dynamics
of wage discrimination and occupational status (or
"rank") discrimination--so as to analyze the potential for differential progression in salary vs. rank
on the basis of race and/or sex. In doing so, for
example, Rexroat finds that, among blacks, women enjoy higher rates of return to a given occupational
status than do men; however, overall, males are
found to earn more than do females--prompting Rexroat to conclude that what wage advantage black
males might have over black females has more to do
with differential access to higher paying ranks not
with differential salaries attached to said ranks,
per se.
        In general, Halaby is interested in further
investigating the same issue of wage vs. rank dis-

D-14 (continued)

crimination effects. Studying managers in a Cali-
fornia-based utility firm, he generally finds what
Rexroat (D-23) found; i.e., what wage advantage that
men have over women has more to do with lack of access to rank than with wage discrimination, per se.
On the other hand, there appear to be some, more
specific, differences between the Halaby and Rexroat findings. To understand what the differences
are, it needs initially be noted that neither Halaby nor Rexroat control for the effects of race.
Rexroat deals solely with black subjects of both
sexes(1), while Halaby provides no information,
whatsoever, on the racial composition of his sample. The matter is brought up because, while Rexroat appears to find women earning higher rates of
return to any given rank than do men, Halaby does
not find significant rates of return differences,
at any rank, by sex(2).
    In any event, dealing with the one issue in
which he is in agreement with Rexroat (that variations in rank occur by sex), Halaby finds that the
individuals in his sample display very few differences in qualifications (based on specifications of
the firm) and that males do not have any rank advantage at the time of entry into the firm(3). Therefore, Halaby concludes that the only plausible reason for rank differentials is sexual discrimination
in the firm's promotion practices.

Notes

    (1) In the content key, at the front of Part D,
Rexroat is identified as "controlling" for the effects of both race and sex. In reality, she does
not fully control for such effects. Rexroat only
controls for race, when comparing data for women;
and, she only controls for sex, when comparing data
for blacks.

    (2) Since Halaby does not report racial com-
position information, it is difficult to determine
whether this apparent difference in the findings,
between the two studies (on variation in rates of
return per rank), has more to do with: any variation in racial composition of the data sets; the

128   PAY INEQUITY

<u>D-14</u> <u>(continued)</u>

fact that Halaby studied one firm, while Rexroat
studied an entire population; or, the fact that Halaby's findings are for one period of time (the year,
1960), while Rexroat's are based on a 10-year period
(1959-1969).

(3) Halaby's finding a lack of rank variance
(by sex) at time of employ, appears to somewhat correspond with a finding of Rosenfeld (D-24) for white
employees throughout the general population.

<u>D-15</u>

Hill, Martha S.
    1979 "The Wage Effects of Marital Status and
          Children." JOURNAL OF HUMAN RESOURCES 14:
          579-593.

    Hill reviews some of the literature, dealing
with the question of what effect familial responsibility has on differential wage allocation. Among
the literature, listed elsewhere in this volume, for
example, it has been found that:

(1) Whether marital status, per se, affects female
     earnings remains open to question. Some stud-
     ies find single women to earn more than mar-
     ried women (cf., Ferber and Loeb, D-11; Trei-
     man and Terrell, D-33). Others are not always
     able to find differences in female earnings,
     due to marital status (cf., Talbert and Bose,
     C-17; Suter and Miller, D-29; Treiman and Roos,
     D-32).

(2) Marital status consistently affects the earn-
     ings of men, whereby married men (regardless
     of parental status) earn more than do single
     men (cf., Ferber and Loeb, D-11; Rosenfeld,
     D-24; Treiman and Roos, D-32).

(3) Sex appears to have a more powerful influence
     on wage differences than does race. Sex dif-
     ferences by marital/parental status tend to
     persist across race categories, although there

D-15 (continued)

is some evidence that the sex differentials
are less pronounced among blacks than among
whites (cf., Rosenfeld, D-24; Treiman and Terrell, D-33).

Hill feels that, even when contradictions in
the literature do not exist, findings, such as the
above, on differential familial responsibility,
might be circumspect. The reason is that Hill argues that marital and parental status represent rather "crude" measures of differential familial re-
sponsibility--not allowing for such other aspects
of differential responsibility as years of training/
work experience, actual "labor force attachment"
(absenteeism, hours worked, etc.), and number/ages
of children. Hill, therefore, proposes a more refined measure of degree of familial responsibility,
that incorporates all of the above matters and applies such to the testing of earnings variance within four race/sex subgroups: white male, black male,
white female, and black female.
    The Hill sample is of over 5000 "household
heads [assumably male] and wives aged 18-64 ...
who worked at least 500 hours in 1975" (p. 581).
Among the findings:

(1) The propensity for married men to earn more
     than single men (as found in several other
     studies) persists; and, the finding appears
     to be a bit more pronounced for whites than
     for blacks. With respect to women, Hill ap-
     pears to support that body of literature find-
     ing no significant differences based on mari-
     tal status(1).

(2) Differences occur on the basis of parental re-
     sponsibility. Whereas white men and black wom-
     en, with greater parental responsibility, earn
     more, such is not found to be as pronounced a
     result among black men and white women.

(3) The findings, with respect to marital and pa-
     rental status persist, when controlling for
     the more refined elements of familial respon-
     sibility (amount of work experience, labor force
     attachment, etc.).

D-15 (continued)

Hill offers no data that potentially explains why the above patterns are found(2). However, she suggests the possibility of value-based "paternalistic attitudes," whereby employers may feel that "workers with greater financial responsibilities to their families deserve higher wages" (Hill, p. 592). The issue of whether "paternalistic attitudes" might be influencing wage differences by sex or by race have been studied in more depth by such writers as Coverman (D-6), Martin and Hanson (D-21), and Shapiro (D-26). However, these writers broaden the scope of their interest beyond the "paternalism" of employers to more general values in the public-at-large; and, none of the writers are saliently interested in whether paternalism exists due to different values toward financial responsibility, per se, independent of sex and/or race. Indeed, the Hill suggestion that such paternalism exists (with respect to the general impact of financial responsibility, per se) does not appear to be very plausible. For example, the suggestion does not explain why differences among black males and white females (based on parental responsibility) are not found to the extent that such differences are found among black females and white males. Also, such a suggestion of rather unilateral impact of degree of financial responsibility does not explain why there is a lack of wage variation among women, on the basis of marital status.

It might be useful to view things more saliently, on the basis of what actually contributes to different "preference mixes" within and among race/sex subgroups. For example, Coverman (D-6) finds social class to be an important variable affecting earnings variance (and, therefore, potential employment choice patterns) among women(3), and Hudis (D-16) argues for racial differences on the basis of types of rewards sought through work.

On another matter (and as a final suggestion for future research), the reader will find Hill arguing that, rather than study how differences in familial responsibility affect wage variation, it might be more fruitful to study how differences in familial responsibility (due to different "family formation decisions") are affected by variation in wage levels(4).

D-15 (continued)

Notes

⟨1⟩ The Hill findings, with respect to marital
status effects on female earnings, appear to contradict those of Coverman (D-6), who also uses more refined measurement of familial responsibility. Of
interest is that Hill apparently finds this lack of
marital status effect, when controlling for degree
of career involvement. Suter and Miller (D-29) also
control for degree of career involvement, but find
the lack of marital status effect only among women,
who are not intermittently employed. Among intermittently employed women, Suter and Miller find that
marital status does make a difference.

⟨2⟩ More generally throughout the literature,
while there is a good deal of data reporting that
marital status is important in differentiating earnings for males, there is, indeed, very little research on "why" such particular patterns exist. For
a review of some of the research on male earnings
patterns, see: R. Bartlett and C. Callahan III,
"Wage Determination and Marital Status: Another
Look." INDUSTRIAL RELATIONS 23(1984):90-96. In
their own research, Bartlett and Callahan appear
to reject the Hill suggestion of male marital status discrepancies due to employer perceptions of
"greater need" or "financial responsibility" of married rather than single men.

⟨3⟩ Coverman's findings of within-sex group
class differences are not expounded upon in the
annotation (D-6). However, as a follow-up to that
annotation, the following exemplifies what is found
in this respect. Coverman reports that the depres-
sing effect of domestic labor time on "non-working
class" female earnings is more pronounced than is
the effect on "working class" female earnings. The
suggestion that this might translate into variant
employment choice patterns is not a matter addressed
by Coverman. Rather, it is simply a possibility
being suggested by the writer of this volume, based
on the discussions of such other writers as Martin
and Hanson (D-21).

D-15 (continued)

(4) Hill suggests that such an analysis would
be best done on a longitudinal, rather than on a
crossectional basis and offers several citations to
longitudinal studies. The role of income/earnings,
as an independent variable (affecting variables other than familial responsibility), has been examined.
For example, the reader with an interest in the effect of compensation/methods of compensation, on
social class formation in the employment setting,
is directed to R. Russell, "Class Formation in the
Workplace: The Role of Sources of Income." WORK
AND OCCUPATIONS 10(1983):349-372.
     In this case, Hill seems to be calling for more
broad-based investigation into the role of pay as
a social force--a matter brought up in this book's
introduction--when quoting from the work of Wallace
and Fay (referenced by note #6 to the introduction).
What Hill is suggesting is that pay can have social
meaning not only to one's on-the-job behavior, but
also to one's off-the-job behavior. However, as
was emphasized in the introduction, any matter of
pay (be it wage variation, compensation administrative practice, or whatever does not occur in a social or cultural vacuum. Thus, the writer of this
volume argues that the true nature of social interaction requires anything but analyses of one-way
flows to influence. Matters of pay may be acting
to influence broader social behavior; but, that
broader social behavior has been acting all along
to influence changes in the matters of pay as well.

D-16

Hudis, Paula M.
   1977 "Commitment to Work and Wages: Earning
         Differences of Black and White Women."
         WORK AND OCCUPATIONS 4:123-146.

     In general, Hudis is primarily interested in
studying the effect of race on earnings. In doing
this, she reflects on the interest of some others
(cited in this book) toward doing certain things
that enhance rigor of independent variable and dependent variable operationalization.

D-16 (continued)

With respect to the independent variable, Kluegel (D-18) and Wright (D-35) represent authors who
question the degree to which race can be considered
an explanatory factor of differential income, independent of other explanatory variables. Hudis
is also interested in this question, as she tests
for the effects of labor force experience and level
of employee commitment to the monetary aspects of
employment--in addition to the effects of race.

With respect to the dependent variable, research on differential income returns, by race,
has led to a debate over whether such differential
returns are to education or to occupational status
(cf., Kluegel, D-18; Stolzenberg, D-28; Wright,
D-35). Hudis examines returns to both education
and occupational status.

It need be noted that, whereas much of the other research, cited above, has been done on all-male
samples, this study is of an all-female sample.

Hudis expresses an initial interest in testing
two broad hypotheses, derivative from the findings
of other research. The first hypothesis is that
any differential returns to education and occupational status can, at least in part, be explained
by differences in race. In general, this hypothesis reflects the type finding reported by Wright
(D-35) as being rather common among sex-exclusive
research on males. However, Hudis also reports on
a body of literature, suggesting that, in terms of
direction of findings among women, blacks achieve
higher returns to education and occupational status
than do whites; and, her second hypothesis is that
this will be found to be the case in her study.

The second Hudis hypothesis would seem to contradict that research on males, which is reviewed by
Wright (D-35)--whereby black men have been found to
earn less than their white counterparts. However,
Wright cautions that it is important to distinguish
the means by which returns are being measured. Specifically, he points out that research on males using a rates of return, rather than an absolute returns measure, finds what Hudis is suggesting for
females--that blacks enjoy an advantage over whites.

Other research by Rexroat (D-23) suggests that
what Wright is discussing as the case among males is
indeed the case among females as well(1); i.e., from

D-16 (continued)

the standpoint of absolute returns, whites have an
advantage over blacks; but, from the standpoint of
rates of return, blacks have an advantage over
whites. So, the Hudis hypothesis that black women
achieve higher returns than do whites would appear
to have empirical grounding, among other writers
cited in this book--if it is the case that she is
using a rates of return measure.

A problem is that it is not overwhelmingly
clear, to the writer of this volume, as to whether
Hudis uses an "absolute" or a "rates" measure; however, the overall context of her discussion creates
the impression that she probably does use a rates
measure(2). In any event, Hudis finds that black
women, as hypothesized, enjoy higher returns to education and occupational status than do white women.
As noted before, Hudis is not convinced that such
differences by race, per se, explain a great deal.
Thus, in order to discern why black women enjoy an
advantage over their white counterparts, the author
develops two additional hypotheses for testing.
These surround her interests in "level of monetary
commitment" and "labor force experience":

(1)   Black women have been found work to supplement
      family incomes to a greater degree than have
      white women--suggesting to Hudis that black
      women have a greater economic need than do
      whites. Hudis, thus, hypothesizes that black
      women demonstrate a greater commitment to the
      monetary aspects of employment than do whites.
      The inference is that greater commitment trans-
      lates into higher returns for black women.

(2)   Because black women have been found to supple-
      ment family incomes to a greater degree than
      have white women, Hudis suggests that black
      women accumulate more job seniority, through
      more continuous labor force experience, than
      do whites. Hudis hypothesizes that this more
      continuous labor force experience will lead to
      higher income returns to education and occupa-
      tional status for blacks than for whites; and,
      Hudis states a belief that such influence of
      labor force experience might be such that it
      offsets (through greater long-run returns) any

<u>D-16</u> <u>(continued)</u>

short-run income advantages that white women
have, due to higher education and/or occupational status.

Hudis finds support for the first of these additional hypotheses, but not for the second one, as
stated. With respect to the second hypothesis, Hudis finds that, rather than having a direct effect
on compensation, labor force experience has an indirect effect. Specifically, it is found that such
work experience enhances the value of schooling for
black females, as well as the occupational statuses
of both blacks and whites. So, Hudis suggests that
what differences in earnings occur reflect the degree of educational and occupational status that a
woman already has--status that can, at best, only be
further enhanced by labor force experience. Therefore, the data do not reveal labor force experience,
<u>per</u> <u>se</u>, to necessarily compensate for any white ed-
ucational advantage (leading to the potential for
blacks to earn more than whites based on experience
alone). If one assumes that black women have greater labor force experience than do white women, then
the inference is drawn that a black woman can only
acquire a <u>greater</u> return than any white counterpart,
if that black woman is, at least, as educated (to
start out with) as any white counterpart.
It might be that, due to lower overall educational levels, those black women, who lack "greater
monetary commitment" cannot expect to achieve higher
returns than white women (based on the Hudis findings). However, if (given their longer histories
of work experience) any black experience enhances
the value of a given educational level more than
does white labor force experience, then the question becomes one of whether black women can, at
least, expect (through the compensatory aspect of
such experience) to achieve <u>equality</u> of pay with
whites. Hudis seems to think that such can possibly happen. However, such an inference might be
questioned based on the work done by Kluegel (D-18)
and Stolzenberg (D-28) on male samples. Kluegel
and Stolzenberg find that education does not, in
reality, have a direct effect on income. Rather,
education, according to these two writers, influences <u>occupational</u> <u>status</u>, which (in turn) influ-

D-16 (continued)

ences level of income. Indeed, Hudis does not find
the effect of occupational status (and, by inference, any returns to occupational status), per se,
to be any greater for blacks than for whites. Rather, variant returns between blacks and whites appear to involve an acknowedged interaction between
educational and occupational status. So, if the
Kluegel and Stolzenberg findings are applicable,
then one surmises that, for any disadvantaged black
woman to achieve equality of pay with whites, increased labor force experience must not only enhance
the value of education, per se, but it must also
lead to that value being translated into enhanced
occupational status--at least to the extent that
the black woman ends up with an occupational status
equal to that of her white counterpart.

                         Notes

        (1) For an example of research on males that
finds blacks achieving higher rates of return than
do whites, see Stolzenberg (D-28). Indeed, Stolzenberg is the individual cited by Wright, when making his disclaimer on the importance of distinguishing "rates" from "absolute" measures of pay. While
it is the case that Rexroat finds this type finding
to be the case among females, it need be noted that
Rexroat actually cites a body of other literature
suggesting the possibility of the opposite being
the case for males--and, thus, potentially contra-
dicting the Wright/Stolzenberg findings for males.
For more information on this issue, the reader is
directed to the Rexroat (D-23) and Stolzenberg
(D-28) annotations.

        (2) The confusion over the Hudis method re-
sults from the following. Stolzenberg (D-28) presents a complex natural logarithmic transformation
of income that contributes to his derived rates.
While Hudis cites Stolzenberg with respect to the
expanded use of certain independent and control
variables in her model, she is vague on the dependent variable measurement. Initially, Hudis operationalizes earnings in an "absolute" sense. The author then mentions the Stolzenberg use of a "rates"

D-16 (continued)

measure, briefly starts to discuss her findings in
terms of rates, and then drops the rates descriptor
from the bulk of the findings presentation. In the
absence of presenting the logarithmic transformation
or of more definitively discussing her findings in
terms of rates, ambiguity results over whether Hudis
is actually discussing most of her findings based on
rates measures, absolute measures, or both. The assumption made by the writer of this volume is that,
since she introduces the Stolzenberg contribution to
her model before entering into the bulk of her findings presentation, Hudis is probably using a rates
measure.

D-17

Kaufman, Robert L.
    1983 "A Structural Decomposition of Black-White
          Earnings Differentials." AMERICAN JOURNAL
          OF SOCIOLOGY 89:585-611.

     Much the same as Beck, et al. (D-3), Kaufman
offers an attempt to integrate the literature on
economic segmentation (re: Part C entries) with that
on specific differences by race. However, unlike
Beck, et al., Kaufman uses an all-male sample; so,
he can offer no new information on the relationship
between economic segmentation and sex differences.
     Kaufman touches upon a number of issues, in
his literature review, that are central to the discussions of writers listed elsewhere in this collection. Some of the issues are these:

(1) The implication that sectoral discrimination--
     where blacks might be overrepresented in the
     periphery (often equated with a secondary la-
     bor market(1))--is transferable into the real-
     ity of pay discrimination (cf., Beck, et al.,
     C-1; Bibb and Form, C-2; Stolzenberg, C-15;
     Tolbert, et al., C-18).

(2) How the periphery is characterized by more un-
     stable work histories--and, since blacks are
     overrepresented in the periphery, how employ-

D-17 (continued)

ers view minorities, in general, not to be
"good, steady employees" (Kaufman, p. 586)(2).

(3) How there not only appears to be black over-
     representation in secondary labor markets, but
     also (reflecting on the conclusions of Stolz-
     enberg, D-28) a circumstance, whereby blacks
     are less successful than whites in converting
     education into better paying jobs. Kaufman
     suggests that this line of thought corresponds
     with that of Wright (D-35)--to the effect that
     social class differences exist in the distri-
     bution of races--and, therefore, in the dis-
     tribution of income by race(3).

    The above-stated line of thinking suggests that
racial differences in pay exist across sectors.
Kaufman notes that only one other study (Beck,
et al., D-3) has also examined the possibility of
racial differences within sectors. However, Kaufman
criticizes Beck, et al. for (among other things)
not empirically comparing their across-sector data
with their within-sector data. Kaufman's main purpose is to present and apply a method that affords
such comparison of across-sector and within-sector
data.
    The importance of looking at within-sector
(not just at across-sector) data is expanded upon
a bit more by Kaufman than by Beck, et al. (D-3).
In the case of race data, Kaufman notes how some
segmentation research, restricted to comparisons
across (i.e., "between") sectors, finds little difference in the distribution of blacks and whites
from one sector to the next(4). If such research
were correct, then one might assume a lack of earnings differential, due to race. By looking within
sectors, however--analyzing racial representation
across occupations within any given sector--one
might detect a pattern of differential returns, due
to (say) overrepresentation of blacks in the lower-
paying jobs of any given sector.
    Beyond the fact that Kaufman seeks to estab-
lish a method for comparing across-sector with
within-sector data, the reader will find him doing a couple of additional things quite different
from other segmentation researchers, in general,

D-17 (continued)

and from the one previous study (Beck, et al., D-3)
that looked at within-sector data, in particular.
First of all, in an earlier written article,
Kaufman, et al. (C-10) criticized segmentation research for shallowly following a "dualistic" pos-
ture. In that article, Kaufman, et al. suggested
that a much broader array of sectors needed to be
looked at (in total, they suggested 16 sectors).
In the article now under consideration, Kaufman puts
into action what he and his colleagues preached in
the earlier piece; i.e., he analyzes a multitude of
different sectoral arrangements. This contrasts
with the work of Beck, et al. (D-3). Whereas, Beck,
et al. acknowledge the shallow quality of research
reliant on only core and peripheral sectors, they
doggedly proceed to only engage in dual sector research, arguing that much can be gained from analysis of the "ideal type" extremes to any continuum.
    Secondly, Beck, et al. (D-3) use the concepts
"differential evaluation" and "differential allocation" to represent, respectively, within-sector and
across-sector mechanisms for pay discrimination.
Kaufman concurs with the broad usage of "evaluation"
and "allocation" in these respects--but, he further
operationalizes these concepts at a more detailed
level. What Kaufman does is divide the evaluation
and allocation components into two parts each, contributing to the following categories:

(1) Evaluation-Composition (EC)--Differences in
     intergroup rewards attributable to intergroup
     differences in personal characteristics. For
     example, this might represent the effect of
     variant education (among core sector blacks
     and whites) on differential earnings, by race,
     within the sector.

(2) Evaluation-Returns (ER)--Differences in inter-
     group rewards attributable to different rates
     of return (or "payoffs") to individual char-
     acteristics. For example, this might repre-
     sent the effect of variant rates of return to
     education (among core sector blacks and whites)
     on differential earnings, by race, within the
     sector(5).

D-17 (continued)

(3) Allocation-Composition (AC)--Differences in
     intergroup rewards attributable to differences
     across sectors in all personal characteristics.
     So, this would represent the differences in
     earnings, by race, attributable to sectoral
     differences in education, age, occupational
     prestige, etc.

(4) Allocation-Returns (AR)--Differences in in-
     tergroup rewards attributable to differences
     across sectors in rates of return to the per-
     sonal characteristics.

     As Kaufman sees it, the addition of this and
some other operational detail (that he goes over in
the article) allows for more salient examination of
the reasons why there may be racial differences in
earnings. Specifically, Kaufman seems to feel that
the further demarcation of evaluation and allocation into the above four subcategories offers a better perspective on the effects of past vs. current
discrimination practices, than can be gathered from
Beck, et al. (D-3). That is, whereas EC might sig-
nify the effects of past educational discrimination,
between blacks and whites, on current earnings, ER
allows for an examination of the effects of current
discrimination (e.g., current rate of return to education differences by race) on current earnings.
An AC vs. AR comparison also provides for a past vs.
current discrimination pattern analysis, in this
case with respect to a comparison of the relative
sizes of discrimination effects across different
sectors.
     Kaufman finds that, although a certain amount
of pay discrepancy can be explained by differences
across sectors (when compared with within sector
patterns), much more pay differential can be explained by the differences within sectors. Apparently controlling for the effects of "human capital"
variables (education and other credentials), Kaufman
finds such within-sector differentials to persist;
and, he thus concludes that the effects of past discrimination (e.g., by education) are not nearly as
relevant as the effects of current discrimination
(by race).

D-17 (continued)

Kaufman finds, as do Beck, et al. (D-3), that, assuming no differential allocation, non-white males experience a percentage decline in earnings as "more blacks ... move into labor market divisions having greater within-division black-white earnings differences" (Kaufman, p. 602)(6). Although he does not measure for male-female differences, Kaufman takes note of the variant findings of Beck, et al.-- to the effect that, if differential allocation did not exist, whereas non-white males may suffer a decline in earnings, females (both white and non-white) would not. Thus, from a policy standpoint, Kaufman argues that, as the matter of differential allocation becomes increasingly resolved, policy-makers will need to become attentive to the different "tradeoffs" confronted by non-white males vs. females; and, whereas current legislation may be focused on "improving the lot" for all minorities, as differential allocation becomes resolved, the effects of differential evaluation on one specific group of minorities (non-white males) may need to be given more salient attention.

Notes

(1) In another article, in which this author is involved (Kaufman, et al., C-10), the issue of conceptually distinguishing segmented "economies" from "labor markets" is brought up. The issue is of no small importance to such writers as Zucker and Rosenstein (C-19) and Ward and Mueller (D-34). At first glance, the reader of this article might feel that the issue is not one that Kaufman wants to deal with, since he appears (from the standpoint of labels) to be using economies and labor markets interchangeably. However, the most important distinction, made later in this article, between the nature of across-sector and within-sector comparisons, signals that Kaufman is very much interested in the difference between economy and labor market comparisons (per the Ward and Mueller definition of such, in particular).

(2) This type "vicious cycle effect" (which is also commented upon by Beck, et al., D-3), derives

D-17 (continued)

from general commentary on sectoral differences in
work histories (cf., Beck, et al., C-1; Bibb and
Form, C-2; Tolbert, et al., C-18), as well as from
certain general statements made about the very real
potential for race discrimination (cf., Kluegel,
D-18; Stolzenberg, D-28; Wright, D-35). For more
specific information on the nature of the "vicious
cycle" effect, under discussion, Kaufman recommends
that the reader consult: B. Bluestone, "The Tripartite Economy: Labor Markets and the Working Poor."
POVERTY AND HUMAN RESOURCES 5(1970):15-35; P. Doeringer and M. Piore, INTERNAL LABOR MARKETS AND MAN-
POWER ANALYSIS (Lexington, MA: D.C. Heath, 1971);
D. Gordon, THEORIES OF POVERTY AND UNEMPLOYMENT
(Lexington, MA: D.C. Heath, 1972).

(3) Kaufman does not pick up on it; but, the
Wright (D-35) and Stolzenberg (D-28) conclusions
are not exactly the same. Wright talks specifically about direct income returns to education; Stolzenberg does not. For more information on the matter, the reader is directed to the Wright and Stolzenberg annotations.

(4) The emphasis, here, is on what "some"--
but not necessarily "most"--studies have found.
While some controversy does exist (among segmentation researchers) over the racial distributions between different sectors, a review of the articles
annotated in Part C of this volume suggests that it
would be overstating the case to say that many, let
alone most, of these studies find relatively equal
distribution across sectors. Indeed, most of the
segmentation studies seem to suggest that whites
are overrepresented in the core, while blacks are
overrepresented in the periphery.

(5) Wright (D-35) points out that changes in
"rates" of return to such items as education do not
necessarily reflect changes in the magnitude of
"actual" returns. For example, Wright argues that
blacks might be much more equal to whites in terms
of rates of return than in terms of actual returns.
However, Wright does not measure for the effects of
variant rates of return on actual returns.

D-17 (continued)

(6) Using their two-sector model, Beck, et al.
(D-3) find that greater wage discrimination by race
occurs in the core than in the peripheral sector.

D-18

Kluegel, James R.
    1978 "The Causes and Cost of Racial Exclusion
          From Job Authority." AMERICAN SOCIOLOGICAL
          REVIEW 43:285-301.

        In another article, published shortly before
this one, Wright (D-35) suggests that, while the
discrepancy in returns to education varies by social class standing, in an absolute sense whites
enjoy a greater income return than do blacks--re-
gardless of class standing. Wright equates social
class standing with the formal authority to make
certain decisions; so, in other words, he is stating that whites enjoy a greater income return to
such decision-making authority than do blacks.
        Kluegel engages in a similar analysis of the
question of racial discrepancies in income returns
to social class standing; however, unlike Wright
(D-35), he does not primarily measure for formal
class standing by means of "fixed" Marxist categories. Rather, Kluegel relies on a "continuously" measured index of formal job authority. In any
event, because the Kluegel interest is in constructing a measure that is reliant on degree of "decision-making authority," his theoretical basis for
the development of a method is much the same as is
that for Wright(1). Like Wright, Kluegel also ex-
cludes his analysis to males--thus preventing any
examination of differences by sex; and, the Kluegel
findings end up reflecting those of Wright, to the
effect that blacks receive a lower income return to
class standing (i.e., to job authority) than do
whites(2).
        The question arises as to why the above is
found to be the case. Both Wright (D-35) and Kluegel address the question. In the former case,
Wright analyzes racial discrepancies in returns
to formal education, finding such to vary by class

D-18 (continued)

level. However, since absolute income discrepancies, by race, remain within all classes, Wright
concludes that a man's race, rather than his class
standing, contributes more to the income discrepancies. Although other factors (age, seniority, father's occupation, etc.) contribute to such discrepancies, Wright does not separate out the effects of such other factors and continues to argue
that race, more than any other factor, contributes
to such discrepancies in income returns.
     Kluegel also accounts for variables other than
race and class, in his analysis; but, unlike Wright
(D-35), he separates out the effects of these other
variables. For example, while Kluegel is not interested in variant returns to similar levels of
formal education, he (nevertheless) tests for the
influence of education on the relationship between
race and job authority. It appears that his purpose, in this respect, is to see whether (at any
given class position) a lower level of black education might be contributing to lower black than
white returns to such a position of decision-making
authority. Kluegel finds that education, per se,
has no direct effect on the relationship. However,
he does find that education influences "occupational status" or the type of job performed, independent
of authority level; and, to the extent that black
men are found to "experience poorer access to authority positions than white men" (Kluegel, p. 295),
the inference is drawn that blacks are not able to
convert equal education into occupations of equal
status (to those of whites); or, if they do acquire
occupations of equal status, then the inference
drawn from the Kluegel results is that blacks are
being deliberately kept out of more critical decision-making processes. Thus, Kluegel comes to the
same conclusion as does Wright; i.e., "race" is the
primary factor contributing to lower income returns
for blacks than for whites. On the other hand, the
actual degree to which race is more important than
other variables (in determining such income discrepancy) is something that Kluegel cannot discern,
inasmuch as he acknowledges not having tested for
actual "beliefs, values, and attitudes"(3).
     The reader will also find Kluegel (p.292) pre-
senting some data on an overrepresentation of blacks

D-18 (continued)

In "industries that offer the poorest relative chances for authority attainment (principally in manufacturing industries)." This line of argument infers the possibility of economic segmentation effects on a relationship between race and earnings variation. However, the Kluegel development of such argumentation is not nearly as comprehensive as is that of writers with a more specialized interest in such segmentation effects (e.g., Beck, et al., C-1; Bibb and Form, C-2).

Notes

(1) Wright's fixed categories are "proper managerial," "nominal supervisor," and "worker." While Kluegel relies primarily on his continuous job authority index, he also offers some fixed categories for consideration, labeled: "manager," "foreman," "non-managerial," and "self-employed." Wright has nothing comparable to Kluegel's self-employed class, and his nominal supervisor is not exactly the same as Kluegel's foreman. Nevertheless, both writers report the same type of racial discrepancies in absolute income within whatever discrete classes that they measure.

(2) The inference is drawn, from the Kluegel discussion, that the use of his continuous measure should allow for as definitive an analysis of race-based pay variation within classes as there is between classes. While Kluegel reports both "within" and "between" occupational data, he seems to concentrate most of his emphasis (when interpreting his results) on the advances in job authority that result from mobility between classes--not so much on differences in authority within the classes. In any event, while reporting that Kluegel's findings appear to (in the end) reflect those of Wright, the writer of this volume does not want to leave the impression that the Kluegel demarcation of "within" vs. "between" class effects comes across as saliently as does that presented by Wright.

(3) In a later work, Kluegel offers an analysis of such racially based "beliefs, values, and

D-18 (continued)

attitudes"--at least from the standpoint of white
beliefs about blacks. Readers with an interest in
such are directed to: J. Kluegel and E. Smith,
"Whites' Beliefs About Blacks' Opportunity." AMER-
ICAN SOCIOLOGICAL REVIEW 47(1982):518-532. The
Kluegel and Smith study does not deal with earnings
patterns, per se; but, rather, it deals with a notion of differences in "opportunity"--where opportunity appears to broadly refer to advancement in
"any areas of life" (Kluegel and Smith, p. 520).
Because the article does not separate out earnings
from other forms of opportunity, it is difficult to
discern what specific worth the Kluegel and Smith
findings have to the study of pay variation, per se.
Nevertheless, the nature of held beliefs, in general (as Kluegel points out), is fundamental to discerning whether any type variation in opportunity
(be it earnings opportunity, occupational opportunity, educational opportunity, or whatever) results
primarily from racial prejudice.

D-19

LaSorte, Michael A.
    1971 "Sex Differences in Salary Among Academic
          Sociology Teachers." AMERICAN SOCIOLOGIST
          6:304-307.

     Following the thought of Stolzenberg (C-15;
D-28) toward analyzing wage differences within specific occupational categories, LaSorte, like Ferber
and Loeb (D-11) and Fox (D-12; D-13), expresses an
interest in sex-based differences in academia. In
this case, the specific interest is in what differences of this type exist among college faculty.
     LaSorte reports on data collected by the Na-
tional Register of Scientific and Technical Personnel. The Register compares salary information
across different academic disciplines. LaSorte's
sample constitutes a 54 percent response rate from
faculty in sociology, chemistry, mathematics, psychology, and the biological sciences.
     Among the five selected disciplines, LaSorte
finds the greatest male-female salary differential

D-19 (continued)

(representing lower female salaries) to be in sociology. However, he reports that the sociology differential can be largely explained by "merit"-
related criteria (academic rank, academic degree,
and type of work engaged in), while a much smaller
proportion of the differentials in the other fields
can be explained by the same criteria. LaSorte,
therefore, concludes that sex discrimination might
be playing a larger role in the determination of
salaries in fields other than sociology.
      On the other hand, LaSorte does not address
the possibility of sex-based occupational status
(i.e., academic rank) discrimination--and, the degree to which such may be variant among disciplines.
Indeed, other writers have opened the question of
how important it might be to analyze such variation
in access to rank--since it serves as a potential
key to explaining earnings differences by sex (For
example, see Halaby, D-14.).

D-20

Major, Brenda and Ellen Konar
    1984 "An Investigation of Sex Differences in Pay
          Expectations and Their Possible Causes."
          ACADEMY OF MANAGEMENT JOURNAL 27:777-792.

      A number of entries, annotated in Part D of
this volume, comment on the potential of broad social values, surrounding "sex role socialization,"
to be influencing pay differentials by sex (cf.,
Coverman, D-6; England, D-8; Rosenfeld, D-25; Snyder and Hudis, D-27). Major and Konar add information on the potential quality of such sex role
socialization.
      The authors find variant perceptions of ineq-
uity, given different pay expectations among a se-
lective group of subjects (83 upper-division/gradu-
ate business students). The question of how representative their findings are of any larger population is not as important to the issue-at-hand, however, as is the authors' discourse on the potential
reasons for the discrepancies in pay expectations.
Based on reviewed literature, Major and Konar pro-

D-20 (continued)

vide an outline of social variables, the analysis
of which appears largely absent from the other literature annotated in this part of the book. These
variables, as outlined by Major and Konar, would
appear quite relevant to any intensive social analysis of what values lie behind inequity and how such
values are formed. Some of the variables are as
follows:

(1) Variant methods (between men and women) of es-
     timating pay. Such could, for example, have
     something to do with the differential quality
     of information provided to employees in tra-
     ditionally "male" vs. traditionally "female"
     occupations.

(2) The different quality of interaction/social
     comparisons made by men and women, with re-
     spect to "same-specialty others."

(3) The different quality of interaction/social
     comparisons made by men and women, with re-
     spect to "same sex others."

     The importance of considering the quality of
internal social comparisons, for example, has been
long established in the literature on perceived inequity (cf., Adams, A-1; Livernash, A-3; Mahoney,
A-4). What appears suggested by the Major and Konar
discussion is that, by analytically focusing more
saliently on the processes of such comparisons
(i.e., on variations in how such comparisons are
made and on what might be contributing to such variant comparisons), a firmer perspective can be gained
on what specific mix of values are contributing to
what specific forms of sex-based pay variation(1).
Indeed, writers, such as Spilerman (C-14), have
commented on how employees will form variant "preference mixes," when engaging in social comparison;
and, researchers, such as England (D-8), have expressed more specific interest in whether any existent sex-based differences in preference mix can
be attributed to pecuniary or non-pecuniary sets of
values. Consequently, it would appear useful to
engage in more salient analysis of the dynamics of
the social comparison process--such as that being

D-20 (continued)

called for by Major and Konar. In a sense, this
might require merging some of the more general literature on sources of variant job satisfaction with
the literature on sources of pay equity. For more
information on this particular suggestion, see Martin and Hanson (D-21).

Note

(1) By focusing on social comparison interactive processes, Major and Konar engage in more micro-level analysis than do the majority of other
writers in this part of the annotated collection.
Indeed, the Major and Konar emphasis is quite similar to that of J. Martin, "Relative Deprivation:
A Theory of Distributive Justice for an Era of
Shrinking Resources" and F. Crosby, "Relative Deprivation in Organizational Settings." The Martin
and Crosby articles are respectively found in Volumes 3(1981) and 6(1984) of RESEARCH IN ORGANIZA-
TIONAL BEHAVIOR (Greenwich, CT: JAI Press--L. Cummings and B. Shaw, co-editors). However, by further reflecting on the potential for variant value
formation, Major and Konar introduce an element of
potential social analysis to their discussion that
is not as saliently found in the Martin and Crosby
reviews.

D-21

Martin, Jack K. and Sandra L. Hanson
    1985   "Sex, Family Wage-Earning Status, and Sat-
           isfaction with Work." WORK AND OCCUPATIONS
           12:91-109.

    Much the same as Coverman (D-6), Martin and
Hanson are interested in evaluating the effects of
"combined family and occupational roles." However,
whereas Coverman focuses attention on what effect
such combined role performance has on earnings, Martin and Hanson are more interested in assessing the
dynamics of "worker satisfaction," under the assumptions that: (a) men and women might respond differ-

D-21 (continued)

ently to their employment conditions; and, (b) given
different combinations of "family time" and "work
time," people might manifest different "values"
about employment. Thus, Martin and Hanson are interested in assessing, from the standpoint of differences between and within sex groups, the more
general thesis of variant "preference mixes" discussed by such writers as Spilerman (C-14).
       Analyzing data from a 1972-73 University of
Michigan Quality of Employment Survey, Martin and
Hanson (p. 98) are able to estimate "whether the
pressures of family roles are mediated, intensi-
fied, or suppressed as a function of wage-earning
status." This assessment is important toward determining the degree to which persons, performing
what Coverman (D-6) calls "domestic labor activity,"
will seek more non-pecuniary than pecuniary features
attached to any job outside the home.
       In general, Martin and Hanson find that both
working men and women seek "rewarding and challenging" features to their jobs. However, upon closer
examination of non-pecuniary emphasis, the authors
find marked differences among women with different
degrees of household responsiblity. Specifically,
it is found that the more that women must combine
familial responsibilities with work responsibilities, the more that "comfort and/or convenience,"
attached to a job, defines their satisfaction with
that job. Therefore, reflecting on the thinking of
such writers as Spilerman (C-14) and Major and Konar
(D-20), it would appear that the nature of different
"preference mixes" for job rewards (inferring variant interpretations of "equity" through social comparison) are operable in this circumstance--such
that variant "values" on the relevance of specific
rewards help define the type jobs sought by different people. As England (D-8) suggests, non-pecuniary motivation is very much involved in the process. Martin and Hanson have simply provided some
empirical information on what the specific quality
of that non-pecuniary motivation is.

D-22

McLaughlin, Steven D.
  1978 "Occupational Sex Identification and the
        Assessment of Male and Female Earnings In-
        equality." AMERICAN SOCIOLOGICAL REVIEW 43:
        909-921.

        The major interest for McLauglin, in this pa-
per, is on "occupational structure"--which focuses
on the "occupation," as a unit of analysis, when
assessing earnings variation. The author argues
that such an analytical focus is important in research on earnings variation by sex, given that most
research of this type, to date, has relied on "human
capital" theory; i.e., most sex-based earnings variation research has centered on the individual, not
on the focal occupational structure, as a principal
unit of analysis.
        This interest in assessing returns to variant
occupational structures, argues McLaughlin, is what
separates his work from that of such writers as Featherman and Hauser (D-10), Suter and Miller (D-29),
and Treiman and Terrell (D-33). What these other
authors might call "returns to occupation," argues
McLaughlin, are not really returns to "structure"
but, rather, are returns to "prestige" or "status"(1). Prestige, according to the author, is a
human capital characteristic--i.e., something pos-
sessed by the "individual"--much the same as education and experience.
        McLaughlin's point is this. If men and women
possess equal credentials, occupational prestige,
etc.--but receive unequal returns to such human capital characteristics--then it might be concluded
that overt sex discrimination is transpiring. If,
however, there does not exist differential returns
to human capital--but, rather, differential returns
to occupational structure--then the explanation for
such discrepancies might be regarded as less overt
and more tied to the quality of the type "sex role
socialization" discussed by England (D-8). Such
socialization, as England discusses it, results in
women performing tasks that yield less income than
the tasks performed by most men.
        Based on secondary research into the 1965 DIC-
TIONARY OF OCCUPATIONAL TITLES and 1970 census reports, McLaughlin finds "labor force participation"

D-22 (continued)

data providing evidence of a sex-segregated occupational structure (82 percent of all women are in
traditional "female" occupations; 74 percent of all
men are in traditional "male" occupations). Utilizing certain "prestige scores"(2), McLaughlin finds
that some "female" tasks are of equal prestige to
some "male" tasks; and, since (due to their "structures") such "female" tasks often yield less earnings than the "male" tasks, the author feels that
potentially variant returns to prestige cannot necessarily be neglected and should be given a "second look." McLaughlin's findings are that, indeed,
differential returns to prestige exist, due to less
than equal returns to occupations of different
structure. Consequently, when making judgments
about "equal pay for equal work," McLaughlin recommends that such assessments not be made on prestige alone, but on some combination of prestige and
structural factors.

Notes

(1) Some controversy in the literature, over
the synonomous usage of "status" and "prestige,"
is discussed by McLaughlin. However, in his general discussion, McLaughlin uses the terms rather
synonomously.

(2) The scores represent a derivation of the
"Hodge-Siegel-Rossi Index." An apparent source for
such scores, as reported by McLaughlin, is R. Van
Dusen and N. Zill, BASIC BACKGROUND ITEMS FOR U.S.
HOUSEHOLD SURVEYS (Washington, DC: Social Science
Research Council, 1975).

D-23

Rexroat, Cynthia
   1978 "The Changing Cost of Being a Black Woman."
   WORK AND OCCUPATIONS 5:341-359.

     In the content key, this article was listed
among those controlling for the effects of both
race and sex. However, a caveat on that description needs to be noted. Rexroat does not allow for
full statistical control of this type. Rather, she
only controls for race with her female sample; and,
she only controls for sex among blacks. Rexroat
reviews a body of literature that determines the
economic "cost" of being a black male and of being
a woman (irrespective of race). Her objective is
to expand this discussion with an analysis of the
cost of being a black woman; and, given the nature
of her statistical controls, Rexroat compares black
female costs with white female costs, as well as
black female costs with black male costs.
     The general procedure involves, first, measur-
ing the contributions of the following independent
variables to mean earnings[1]: age, marital status,
number of children, region of residence, and occupational distribution. Next, the total contributions of the independent variables to income are
subtracted across categories, yielding differences
in earnings between women, by race. A substitution
of means procedure is then applied to calculate the
actual cost of being a black woman. These findings
are then compared with the findings of Johnson and
Sell[2] on the cost of being a black man.
     Comparing 1959 and 1969 census data, Rexroat
reports that, relative to the earnings of white wom-
en, the black female earnings gap, as well as the
cost of being black, decreased over the 10-year period in question. Increased educational status of
black women was found to be predominantly responsible for the closing of the absolute earnings gap,
although when strictly analyzing rates of return,
black females (over the period) experienced greater
returns to occupational than to educational status.
     Whereas the cost of being a black female de-
clined, over the 10-year period in question, Rexroat reports on the Johnson and Sell finding that
the cost of being a black male increased over the
same decade. This particular phenomenon for black

D-23 (continued)

males occurred, even though the percent of absolute
earnings differences (due to educational and occupational status), by race, declined for males over
the same decade.
     The contradictory findings on the cost of being
black for males and females are explained by Rexroat
as follows. Since black male absolute earnings differences declined, due to increased educational and
occupational status, such males experienced greater
upward mobility over the period in question. However, black males still received lower rates of return on their investments; i.e., they were paid less
than average wages for higher status occupations.
In contrast, while black females experienced higher
rates of return on their investments, absolute earnings differences between black and white females,
due to differences in educational and occupational
status, actually increased over the same period(3).
Thus, Rexroat finds that, unlike black males, black
females did not experience increased upward mobility
over the period in question. Therefore, the author
concludes that, while the social force determining
change in the economic status of black males and
females might have been hypothesized to be the same
(degree of racial discrimination being that social
force), the social consequence ends up taking a different form, based on sex variation; i.e., the consequence for males is lack of wage progression,
while the consequence for females is lack of occupational status progression.

                          Notes

     (1) Szymanski (D-30) argues for the importance
of conceptually separating "income" from "earnings,"
since the former represents a household figure that
that can misrepresent individual earnings. Rexroat
does not appear to make such a conceptual separation; and, as best this writer can tell, she uses
income and earnings interchangeably. Consequently,
this writer cannot determine, with any degree of
certainty, whether Rexroat is using the same data
to report income and earnings or different data--
but he is operating on the assumption that it is the
same data. In any event, when reporting procedures,

D-23 (continued)

findings, etc. from this article, the language used
by Rexroat will be followed as closely as possible;
and, the reader, who is concerned about the matter,
is advised to consult the article being annotated,
so as to formulate her/his own conclusions on the
matter.

    <2> M. Johnson and R. Sell, "The Cost of Being
Black: A 1970 Update." AMERICAN JOURNAL OF SOCIOLOGY
82(1976):183-190.

    <3> In this case, Rexroat is speaking of the
absolute income blacks lose, because of their not
having occupational and educational characteristics
equal to those of whites; she is apparently not con-
tradicting her earlier stated finding that the absolute income gap, by race, actually declined.

D-24

Rosenfeld, Rachel A.
    1980 "Race and Sex Differences in Career Dy-
          namics." AMERICAN SOCIOLOGICAL REVIEW
          45:583-609.

    Some articles, listed elsewhere in this col-
lection, touch upon the importance of analyzing career patterns in pay equity/inequity, often tying
this analysis in with an evaluation of membership
in different economic segments, over time (cf., Parker, C-12; Spilerman, C-14)<1>. Economic segmentation theorists consider race and sex differences to
be two of several variables that define differential membership in sectors. However, as Rosenfeld
points out, "sorting" by race and sex occurs not
only among sectors but also within sectors<2>. It
is Rosenfeld's objectives to (a) focus succinctly
on the nature of this "sorting" by race and sex
identity and (b) discuss what potential there is
for career inequality based on this sorting process.
    The data evaluated by Rosenfeld is from the
National Longitudinal Surveys of Labor Market Experience. The portion, which Rosenfeld uses, is
restricted to career measurements for young people,

D-24 (continued)

aged 14-24 and tracked for 10 years. The following
represents a brief overview of what Rosenfeld hypothesizes and finds(3):

(1) "All women and non-white men will have lower
     average initial and potential wages." This
     hypothesis is based on literature, cited by
     Rosenfeld, that demonstrates wage differen-
     tials, due to within and among sector "sorting"
     by race and sex. More specifically, Rosenfeld
     hypothesizes that the ordering of wages, from
     highest to lowest, will be as follows: white
     male, non-white male, white female, non-white
     female. The author's data, indeed, reveal this
     to be the case.

(2) "The gap in average wages between white males
     and other groups will increase over the work
     life." The hypothesis is based on reviewed
     literature demonstrating that initial denial
     of access to better-paying jobs leads to less
     access to training that can contribute to even
     greater returns, over time. Again, the Rosen-
     feld data confirm this to be the case.

(3) "The average [occupational] status of non-white
     men will be lower initially and at their po-
     tential than status of white men, although the
     average status of white women will be about
     the same as that of white men at their poten-
     tial and perhaps run slightly higher at career
     entry." This hypothesis is based on literature
     reviewed by Rosenfeld and is confirmed by her
     data(4).

     Rosenfeld calls the reader's attention to the
different "sorting patterns" of wages vs. status.
The findings, with respect to Hypothesis #1, suggest that "the ordering of wages is first by sex
and then, within sex, by race.... [whereas] status
is determined first by race and then, within race,
by sex" (Rosenfeld, p. 596). The variant form of
social consequence (lowered wages vs. lowered status) is an issue of importance to Rexroat (D-23).
For example, based on her findings, Rexroat suggests that race may, indeed, be a most important

D-24 (continued)

element, here, with respect to females. Specifically, while Rosenfeld finds that occupational status
does not vary, by sex, for whites, Rexroat suggests
that status does vary, by sex, for blacks (re: note
#4).
    Rosenfeld offers a discourse on potential reas-
ons for different forms of "sorting" of wages vs.
status, although she does not reach firm conclusions
on the subject. In terms of absolute wage and status differentials (based on race/sex), the author,
nevertheless, does examine variant returns to education and other resources. The findings are that:
(1) women and non-white men earn lower returns to
such resources than do white men; (2) the differences between white male and white female returns
are less, when career position is measured in terms
of status than in terms of wages; and, (3) marital/
parental circumstance affects the wage and status
returns for males but not for females. In this last
case, Rosenfeld finds that, being married and having children has a positive effect on male returns.
The findings, with respect to women (of marital status not affecting wage returns), appears to somewhat
correspond with the findings of such writers as Talbert and Bose (C-17) and Suter and Miller (D-29)--
but, at the same time, contradicts the findings of
such writers as Ferber and Loeb (D-11) and Treiman
and Terrell (D-33).
    Of interest is further measurement, done by
Rosenfeld, with respect to the "speed" of wage and
status achievement. Comparisons are made among all
four race/sex groups. Rosenfeld finds, for example,
that non-white females reach their wage potential
before black males (a finding that concurs with that
of Rexroat, D-23). However, Rosenfeld also finds
the following: Non-white females reach their status
potentials faster than they reach their wage potentials, while the circumstances for non-white males
are, apparently, less clear. By contrast, Rexroat
finds that, among non-whites, females do not reach
status potentials faster than wage potentials, while
males do clearly do so. The differences between
the Rosenfeld and Rexroat findings, on this matter,
could have something to do with different methods
of collecting/analyzing data, somewhat different
time periods analyzed, and/or different age ranges

D-24 (continued)

being analyzed(5). The reader is directed to the
two articles, in question, for detail on methodological differences.

Notes

(1) Among the articles, listed in this collection, that deal with career patterns, the reader
will find what is, perhaps, the clearest explanation of what is meant by a "career pattern" in this
Rosenfeld discourse.

(2) A comparable line of argumentation is
developed by other writers, such as Beck, et al.
(D-3).

(3) The statements of hypotheses represent
direct quotations, taken from pp. 585-588 of the
Rosenfeld article.

(4) The third hypothesis, and findings com-
mensurate with it, appear to negate the logic of
the second hypothesis, when comparing white males
and females. Specifically, the second hypothesis
is stating that white male wages will continue,
over the course of careers, to be above those of
white females--even though, as the third hypothesis states, white females suffer no occupational
status disadvantage, when compared with white males.
The issue is, however, potentially resolved, if one
assumes that (as Rexroat, D-23, finds among blacks)
there exists a difference between absolute earnings
variation and variation in rates of return to occupational status. Looking at such "absolute" vs.
"rate" differences, Rexroat, concludes that black
females are at a disadvantage, in terms of achieving occupational status, that does not affect black
males. Rosenfeld seems to be suggesting that, unlike black females, white females are at a wage disadvantage, not necessarily at an occupational status
disadvantage, relative to white males. While Rosenfeld does not really develop the matter for whites
to the extent that Rexroat does for blacks, nevertheless, the general context of her discussion on
rates of return leads to the impression that this

D-24 (continued)

might have been every bit as critical a variable in
explaining the Rosenfeld results (on white sex differences) as it is for Rexroat, when discussing
black sex differences.

(5) Rexroat does not specify the age range of
her sample; however, the general use of census data
infers that she might have used a broader range of
ages than does Rosenfeld.

D-25

Rosenfeld, Rachel A.
   1983   "Sex Segregation and Sectors: An Analysis
          of Gender Differences in Returns From Em-
          ployer Changes." AMERICAN SOCIOLOGICAL
          REVIEW 48:637-655.

     Rosenfeld has three baseline empirical objec-
tives in this paper:

(1)   to examine mobility between and within economic
      sectors, with a focus on movement between tra-
      ditionally-defined "male" and "female" occupa-
      tions;

(2)   to examine what factors might promote movement
      into a sex-atypical occupation, as well as
      movement between periphery and core sectors of
      the economy;

(3)   to examine what effects such mobility patterns
      have on chances for wage gain.

     The author's literature review, establishing
the basis for her research, comes across as being
quite rich, both in terms of writing quality and
depth of discussion. In that literature review,
Rosenfeld does much to tie together a number of
points of confusion and debate, derivative from
the works of others whose work is annotated in
this collection.
     As an example of the quality of Rosenfeld's
review, she expands a bit upon Spilerman's (C-14)

D-25 (continued)

discussion on intersector mobility (over the course
of careers), discussing such items as:

(1)   difficulties associated with movement out of
        the periphery into the core;

(2)   the fact that, since not all core sector jobs
        are "primary" and not all periphery sector jobs
        are "secondary," there can actually exist, over
        the course of a career, voluntary movement from
        the core to the periphery(1);

(3)   the fact that, as a consequence of the place-
        ment of "primary" and "secondary" jobs in both
        sectors, wage advance can occur (in some cir-
        cumstances) through movement from the core to
        the periphery.

     As another example of what the literature re-
view, by Rosenfeld, has to offer, the author expands
upon the theme (so important to such other writers
as Fox, D-12) of potential movement between traditionally male and female dominated occupations. In
this respect, Rosenfeld provides illustrations and
a good amount of documentation that supports the
reality of some mobility (of this type) by both men
and women.
     The flow of the Rosenfeld empirical analysis
is to, more specifically, analyze the probability
of three types of mobility: out of sex-typed occupations; out of the periphery; and, up in wages.
She assesses these probabilities, based on the effects of two independent variables: the quality of
one's commitment to the labor force and the quality
of one's skills/credentials. These rather "sex-
neutral" independent variables appear, on the surface, to reflect the Fox (D-12) finding that such
variables have more to do with mobility and wage
attainment than does sex identification. However,
Fox's research was done in a more restrictive occupational environment (academia); Rosenfeld's data
set reflects a broad range of occupational categor-
ies(2). As a consequence, it does appear relevant
that Rosenfeld also compares her findings by sex.
     In terms of results, Rosenfeld acknowledges
that, in general, the explanatory power of her da-

D-25 (continued)

ta is low. However, she does report the following
trends.

On the matter of movement between traditional
"male" and "female" occupational categories (apparently within sectors), Rosenfeld finds that an often
used explanation for female concentration in traditionally female jobs--that women are bound by family
status to work, at most, intermittently outside the
home--does not tend to hold. Indeed, Rosenfeld cannot find any consistent pattern between female familial status and propensity to work in traditionally
female jobs. Rosenfeld finds that familial status
can only be said to affect the placement of males,
as married men are more inclined than single men to
work in traditionally male occupations.

On the matter of movement from the periphery
to the core sector, the effects of labor force commitment and skills/credentials have a greater impact
on the chances of women than men moving out of the
periphery. Specifically, being married, only having
a part-time work history, and having less education
were all found to have a rather pronounced effect
on "blocking" female mobility out of the periphery,
during the middle range of one's life cycle.

As a consequence of the findings, summarized
in the above two paragraphs, Rosenfeld concludes
that what blockage exists, preventing female mobility into better-paying jobs, occurs primarily between, rather than within sectors. The conclusion
is drawn, given the fact that most "core" jobs are
described as "male." However, one can possibly sur-
mise that, since chances of such mobility are related to rather "sex-neutral" factors (marital status, level of education, work history, etc.), the
blockage occurs not necessarily because of employer
negative reactions to hiring women, per se<3>, but
because of a broader range of societal values. The
specific values, being referred to, sanction married
women assuming such a level of household maintenance
duties that they cannot acquire the necessary credentials (education, work history, etc.) to adequately compete for core sector employ<4>.

As for the effects of such mobility patterns
on wage changes, Rosenfeld generally finds movement
out of the periphery to result in wage gains for
both sexes. However, although (as the data shows)

D-25 (continued)

males are more mobile than females in this respect,
there is very limited support for the notion that
males gain more than females, once members of both
sex groups have moved out of the periphery. Also,
controlling for type of sector mobility (between or
within), Rosenfeld apparently finds what Fox (D-12)
suggests--that there are no significant wage gains
to women, simply due to movement into "male" occupations.

In earlier research, Rosenfeld (D-24) could
not conclude that marital/parental status affected
the wage returns for women. What the above-noted
findings, of the more current study, seem to suggest is this: By more saliently focusing on what
is involved in "labor force commitment" and by separating forms of mobility into two types (male/fe-
male job movement; movement among sectors), Rosenfeld has been able to draw more definitive conclusions about possible female wage disadvantages to
the assumption of household duties(5).

Notes

(1) Rosenfeld is concluding, here, that any
economic segmentation assumptions of a clear correspondence between primary vs. secondary labor
markets and core vs. periphery segments is much
too shallow. However, while (in the literature
review) the author offers a number of rather novel
alternatives to traditional "periphery to core"
mobility, she ends up only testing for the traditional periphery to core movement in the empirical part of this paper.

In addition to the suggestion of both primary
and secondary labor markets existing in any economic sector, Rosenfeld argues that the characteristics, defining membership in a sector, are more complex than some segmentation theorists will acknowledge, because the quality of personal characteristic
demarcations are not as "clear-cut" as some theorists argue them to be. Such a line of argumentation is offered by others, listed in this collection, as well. Along these lines, for more information on the complexities associated with defining
sharp demarcations between sectors, the reader is

D-25 (continued)

referred to: Kaufman, et al. (C-10), Zucker and Rosenstein (C-19), Kaufman (D-17), and Ward and Mueller (D-34).

(2) Rosenfeld uses Current Population Survey data that tracks career information over a 5-year period between 1968-1973. A broad range of ages are represented by the data (16-50), but there is no control for the effects of race. Only data on whites are included in the study.

(3) The circumstance, whereby an employer might discriminate against a woman, under the assumption that her household duties will negatively impinge upon her occupational duties, has been referred to as "statistical discrimination" by E. Phelps, "The Statistical Theory of Racism and Sexism." AMERICAN ECONOMIC REVIEW 62(1972):659-661. As does the data of Fox (D-12; D-13), the Rosenfeld data infers the possibility that matters of attainment, rather than such statistical discrimination, may be more involved in the selection of males over females. This inference appears to counter the thinking of several other writers, who (at least) assume the preeminent effects of statistical discrimination on matters of selection, pay, etc. For a review of this other thinking, beyond that provided by Rosenfeld, see Coverman (D-6).

(4) Rosenfeld "hints" at the possible effect of such societal values and discusses the political/legal remedy of Affirmative Action programs. However, like most writers on the matter of race/sex-based wage differentials, whose works are annotated in this collection, Rosenfeld offers no definitive analysis of the nature of such values. For an exception to this rule, offering somewhat more developed analysis and thinking on the matter, see Coverman (D-6).

(5) There appears to exist no small amount of debate, in the literature, over whether the degree of labor force attachment (as a part of one's work history) conditions levels of wage gain, over time. In effect, Rosenfeld seems to be stating that her research demonstrates such to be the case. For a

D-25 (continued)

review of contrasting perspectives on the matter,
the reader is referred to Coverman (D-6).

D-26

Shapiro, E. Gary
    1977   "Racial Differences in the Value of Job
            Rewards." SOCIAL FORCES 56:21-30

        Martin and Hanson (D-21) saliently test for the
nature of differential values that might influence
variation in "preference mixes" for rewards, as discussed by Spilerman (C-14). However, whereas Martin and Hanson are interested in analyzing sex categories, Shapiro is interested in studying race categories. Further, the Shapiro analytical focus is
a bit more narrow than is that of Martin and Hanson.
The latter authors analyze differences both between
and within sex categories; Shapiro only studies differences between race categories.
        Nevertheless, using national survey data from
approximately the same era as the data used by Martin and Hanson (1973-1974), Shapiro has a somewhat
similar interest in whether employees will place
greater values on pecuniary or non-pecuniary rewards. In this respect, Shapiro discusses not only
pecuniary, but also other forms of "extrinsic" rewards, as alternatives to "intrinsic" non-pecuniary
rewards[1].
        Shapiro infers, from the work of Maslow[2],
that variant preference mixes for extrinsic vs. intrinsic rewards exist not so much because of race,
per se, but because of the variant social classes
that are predominantly occupied by one racial group
or another--contributing to different levels of
needs. Using education, occupation, and income (as
indicators of social class), Shapiro tests the "Maslow assumption" that whites value more intrinsic
rewards, due to higher levels of education, occupation, and income--thus prompting higher-order
needs. Blacks, by inference, are thought to value
more extrinsic rewards, due to lower levels of education, occupation, and income--thus prompting
lower-order needs.

D-26 (continued)

The Maslow theory, therefore (as Shapiro reports it), rests on class more than race being a crucial determinant of the nature of reward preference mixes. Shapiro finds this not to be the case. Blacks are found to value extrinsic rewards more than do whites, irrespective of social class; and, by comparing the effects of race on preference mix before and after the control for class variables, the author determines that roughly half of the effect of race on reward preference can be explained by class and half cannot(3).

If roughly half of the race effects cannot be explained by variation in class, Shapiro addresses the question of what might be explaining the differential race effects. Some economic segmentation theorists have argued for the importance of parental occupation/education and family size (cf., Beck, et al., C-1). However, Shapiro controls for these effects and does not find either explanation to reduce the race effects beyond that explained by class alone. As a consequence, Shapiro argues that the variant racial effects are probably due to broader differences in race-based cultural values and/or to the effects of racial discrimination (perhaps, for example, resulting in any suppression of the ability of blacks to secure the level of extrinsic rewards that whites can secure). However, neither of these potential explanations are empirically tested for by Shapiro.

Notes

(1) The point being made is that the rewards, studied by Shapiro, differ somewhat from those studied by Martin and Hanson (D-21). Shapiro actually does not use such labels as pecuniary and non-pecuniary—preferring, instead, to use the labels extrinsic and intrinsic. The resultant more specific differences between the authors' reward categories are these: (a) Shapiro's "extrinsic" category broadens its focus beyond just the pecuniary or monetary quality of a reward to also encompass "job security"; (b) whereas Martin and Hanson consider a rather broad range of non-pecuniary alternatives to money as a reward (e.g., intrinsic challenge, more

D-26 (continued)

convenience, etc.), Shapiro restricts his analysis
mainly to intrinsic challenge and associated rewards
that correspond with Maslow's higher-order needs.

<2> The reference, provided by Shapiro, is to
A. Maslow, MOTIVATION AND PERSONALITY (New York,
Harper and Row, 1964).

<3> The independent effects, here, appear to
somewhat correspond with those of Wright (D-35)--
even though Wright uses different measures of class.
Specifically, when studying differences in actual
earnings, Wright cannot report on either race or
social class being a consistently dominant explanatory variable.

D-27

Snyder, David and Paula M. Hudis
     1976   "Occupational Income and the Effects of Mi-
            nority Competition and Segmentation: A Re-
            analysis and Some New Evidence." AMERICAN
            SOCIOLOGICAL REVIEW 41:209-234.

     In an attempt to discern the reasons why some
groups earn less for comparable work than do other
groups, Snyder and Hudis demonstrate an interest in
analyzing the nature of what they call "competition"
and "segregation" processes.
     The competition process relates to the circum-
stance whereby the entrance of minorities<1> into
an occupational category depresses overall income
levels in that category. Albeit not under the "competition" label, the reader will find this type effect also being discussed by such writers as Beck,
et al. (D-3), Kaufman (D-17), and Szymanski (D-30).
     Beck, et al. (D-3) also discuss, at much great-
er length, the issues of "differential allocation"
and "differential evaluation" which, respectively,
deal with the exclusion across and within economic
sectors--of minorities--from higher paying occupations. Snyder and Hudis appear to more generally
be using "segregation" to refer to the differential
allocation and evaluation processes.

D-27 (continued)

Writers, such as Beck, et al. (D-3) and Kaufman (D-17), assume segregation processes to incorporate both the effects of occupational segmentation and (as a consequence) wage segmentation. Snyder and Hudis do not disagree; however, they feel that it is important to empirically separate the circumstances, where wage differentials describe occupational segmentation, from those circumstances, where "factors other than wages have determined ... occupational distribution..." (Snyder and Hudis, p. 232). From a conceptual standpoint, Snyder and Hudis prefer to use the term, "segregation," to describe the circumstance where occupational segmentation is being defined in terms of wage discrepancies; and, the authors prefer to use the term, "historical factors," when referring to non-wage oriented variables that influence occupational segmentation. As Snyder and Hudis argue the point, historical factors may, in the end, actually be responsible for the different wage distributions accompanying occupational segmentation; so, historical factors might be responsible for the segregation processes. It is a consideration of such historical factor influence that Snyder and Hudis feel separates their research from much of that published during the 1960's<2>.

In general, the authors find (re-analyzing the data of several 1960's writers) that competition and segregation are either race or sex-specific processes. Specifically, what wage differential can be attributed to competitive effects seems to define the circumstances for women, regardless of race, while what wage differentials can be attributed to segregative effects seems to define the circumstances fairly exclusively for black men. By further analyzing trends of occupational distribution by race and sex, over time, Snyder and Hudis conclude that overriding any effects of competition and segregation, however, are the effects of those historical factors that "stabilize" the concentration of white males in higher paying occupations and that "stabilize" the concentration of women and black males in lower paying occupations. However, the reader looking for salient identification of (let alone empirical testing for) the effects of

D-27 (continued)

specific historical factors will not find it in
this particular article.

Notes

(1) Like many writers, Snyder and Hudis include women in their "minorities" category; and,
such is, therefore, assumed in this annotation.

(2) Among the several studies cited, those
which particularly appear to have provided the im-
petus for the conclusion about the importance of
historical factor influence are: R. Hodge and P.
Hodge, "Occupational Assimilation as a Competitive
Process." AMERICAN JOURNAL OF SOCIOLOGY 71(1965):
249-264; A. Tauber, et al., "Occupational Assimilation and the Competitive Process: A Reanalysis."
AMERICAN JOURNAL OF SOCIOLOGY 72(1966):273-285.
     Snyder and Hudis cite several sources of po-
tential "historical" factors, including one (Hill,
E-6), which leads the authors to feel that minority
underrepresentation has, historically, been particularly pronounced in higher paying craft occupations. The matter is concurred upon by the research
of others, such as M. Johnson and R. Sell, "The Cost
of Being Black: A 1970 Update." AMERICAN JOURNAL OF
SOCIOLOGY 82(1976):183-190. The reader will find
Johnson and Sell expanding the argument to underrepresentation in higher paying managerial occupations, as well.

D-28

Stolzenberg, Ross M.
   1975 "Education, Occupation, and Wage Differences
         Between White and Black Men." AMERICAN JOUR-
         NAL OF SOCIOLOGY 81:299-323.

     Stolzenberg reviews a body of literature on
variant wage returns to schooling by race--and proceeds to re-examine the question. The reader will
find a certain correspondence, in this respect,
between Stolzenberg's intent and that of Wright

D-28 (continued)

(D-35). Also, like Kluegel (D-18), Stolzenberg has
an additional interest in the role of education,
per se, as a determinant of wages. Like both Wright
and Kluegel, Stolzenberg restricts his analysis to
males only.

Analyzing census data on earnings of employees
in 62 detailed occupational categories, Stolzenberg's findings appear to contradict not only the
later work of Wright (D-35), but also to the body
of previous research done on the subject[1]. Specifically, the author finds the following:

> Within-occupation race differences in
> wage returns to schooling are not large
> enough to cause substantial race differ-
> ences in pay for incumbents of those oc-
> cupations employing the vast majority of
> black men in the labor force (Stolzen-
> berg, p. 299).

Stolzenberg does not interpret this finding to
mean that race differences in returns to education
are "inconsequential." Rather, he seems to be arguing that: (1) the matter of differential returns
to education needs to be re-interpreted; and, (2)
the manner in which occupational variation has been
measured by others needs to be re-evaluated.

Specifically, with respect to the first argument, Stolzenberg seems to agree with Kluegel (D-18)
that level of education does not directly affect
wage differentiation--but, rather, influences one's
occupational status or type of job performed. Thus,
from Stolzenberg's point of view, it is more logical
to think about returns to a level of occupation rather than returns to education. The author is,
therefore, arguing that what race differences in
wage returns occur, do so because of differences
(by race) in an ability to convert what may be equal
education into employment of equal quality[2].

With respect to the second argument, Stolzenberg states that it is more realistic to do what he
has done--examine detailed occupational categories
(teacher, accountant, sales clerk, etc.) rather than
the normally used broad census-based categories
(professional, technical, kindred worker)--as any
individual might apply to be a "sales clerk," but

D-28 (continued)

will not apply to be a "kindred worker." By focusing more on detailed occupational categories, argues the author, one can get a better picture of
how employees may be paid differently when actually
occupying what appears to be the same broad occupational category (or occupational "status"). The
reason is that, within any broad occupational category, a number of more detailed jobs are performed;
and, the argument, advanced by Stolzenberg, Kluegel
(D-18), and others is that blacks may be overrepresented in the lower paying jobs within any given
occupational category(3).

An alternative explanation for the Stolzenberg
findings, however, is offered by Wright (D-35)--who
basically discounts the validity of the Stolzenberg
arguments. Wright, like most other writers on the
subject, does find differential returns to education by race; and, he seems to feel that the deviant
findings of Stolzenberg have more to do with a methodological decision by that author to use a natural
logarithmic transformation of income, rather than to
use "raw dollars." As Wright (p. 1369) puts it:
"This means that Stolzenberg is estimating rates of
returns to education rather than absolute returns."
Wright feels that such "rates" of return may be
greater for blacks than are "absolute" returns to
education(4).

                       Notes

    (1) Stolzenberg cites a large body of litera-
ture, from the 1960's, that the reader with a specialized interest in this issue, will want to investigate. As examples, two of the more important
sources of earlier information (based not only on
the Stolzenberg review, but also on that of Wright)
would appear to be: P. Siegel, "On the Cost of Being a Negro." SOCIOLOGICAL INQUIRY 35(1965):41-57;
O. Duncan, "Inheritance of Poverty or Inheritance
of Race?" In D. Moynihan, UNDERSTANDING POVERTY
(New York: Basic Books, 1969).

    (2) Kluegel takes the matter a bit further.
He argues that an inability by blacks to convert
educational level into equality of occupational

D-28 (continued)

status--if such occurs--means that blacks are not
allowed to occupy positions with critical decision-
making authority attached to them; and, it is this,
therefore, that Kluegel feels contributes to wage
variation within certain occupationally based "social classes" (managers, foremen, etc.).

(3) Of course, as Kluegel sees it (re: note
#2), the overrepresentation of blacks into lower
paying jobs (within an occupational category) derives from the fact that they are not allowed to advance to positions, with the degree of decision-
making authority, that whites are allowed to advance to.
The perspective being taken, here, by Stolzenberg and Kluegel, would appear to be in concert
with that of M. Johnson and R. Sell, "The Cost of
Being Black: A 1970 Update." AMERICAN JOURNAL OF
SOCIOLOGY 82(1976):183-190. Johnson and Sell find
black-white absolute income differentials to decline, due to increased black occupational status;
but (as Rexroat, D-23, interprets the Johnson and
Sell data), white males still enjoy an advantage in
returns to occupational status. On the other hand,
unlike Kluegel, Rexroat does not interpret this phenomenon to be due to a lack of advancement to positions (within an occupational category) with greater decision-making authority; Rexroat interprets it
simply to be an artifact of race-based pay discrimination, whereby blacks and whites of similar position are not paid the same.
It should be noted that Rexroat finds the opposite to be the case for black females, who enjoy
higher rates of return to occupational status than
do whites. However, noting that black females are
at an absolute income disadvantage, Rexroat suggests
that this is due to lack of general black upward
mobility to higher paying statuses. Since Rexroat
does not account for the same "fine" differences
in decision-making authority, however, that Kluegel
does, one does not know whether the situation for
females has more to do with lack of progression between or within occupational ranks.

(4) Rexroat (D-23) interprets the findings of
Johnson and Sell (re: note #3) to be in concert with

D-28 (continued)

those of Wright; i.e., that black males enjoy lower
returns to education than do white males. However,
after reviewing the content of the Johnson and Sell,
Rexroat, and Wright articles, it is still unclear,
to the writer of this volume, whether Johnson and
Sell's measurement of "returns" is more similar to
that of Wright or to that of Stolzenberg. Obviously, if the latter, then Johnson and Sell (who are
not cited by Wright) would be calling this Wright
conclusion (about the difference in findings, due
to different measures of return) into question.

D-29

Suter, Larry E. and Herman P. Miller
    1973 "Income Differences Between Men and Career
          Women." AMERICAN JOURNAL OF SOCIOLOGY 78:
          962-974.

        Writers in the area of economic segmentation
have often commented on sectoral differences by sex
(cf., Beck, et al., C-1; Bibb and Form, C-2). At
the same time, several of these writers (whose findings are briefly reviewed by Suter and Miller) have
attempted to explain why women earn less than men,
often testing for the effect of "less overall job
experience" or "more intermittent" patterns to career paths.
        The primary objective of the Suter and Miller
study is to analyze census earnings data that compares men and career women--thus controlling for
any intermittency of female labor force behavior
that might lead to differences from the wage patterns of more continuously employed males. The Suter and Miller comparison, however, does not offer
the optimum in control over age, as it is made within a restrictive age cohort (30-44).
        Controlling not only for the effect of "life-
time career experience," but also for the effects
of education and occupational status, Suter and Miller find that women earn less than men are able to
earn.
        Of interest is an additional finding by Suter
and Miller that, among career women, marital status

D-29 (continued)

does not significantly affect earnings. Although
not all other researchers in the area exclusively
study "career" women, the measurement of marital
status effects on female earnings has led to a number of conflicting results in the literature--with
not everyone being able to conclude, as do Suter
and Miller, that there is a lack of significant effect (cf., Coverman, D-6; Ferber and Loeb, D-11;
Hill, D-15; Treiman and Roos, D-32; Treiman and
Terrell, D-33).

D-30

Szymanski, Albert
  1976 "Racial Discrimination and White Gain."
        AMERICAN SOCIOLOGICAL REVIEW 41:403-414.

        Several writers, listed elsewhere in this col-
lection, concern themselves with the effect of race
on wage variation, in general, and whether whites
in the United States accrue greater returns, due
to discrimination against non-whites (For example,
see: Hudis, D-16; Kluegel, D-18; Stolzenberg, D-28;
Wright, D-35). As the title of this article infers,
the issue is of central importance, as well, to Szymanski[1].
        Szymanski reviews a body of literature, some
of which argues that whites benefit from economic
segregation against blacks, but some other of which
argues that whites do not so benefit. In the latter category, Szymanski, for example, cites some
studies that reveal attempts at racial discrimination to suppress incomes and earnings of whites as
well as of blacks. At a more specific level of discussion, there are four basic themes that Szymanski
finds to be posited throughout the research literature. The themes are hereby outlined.

(1) The level of racist belief is such that white
     employers resist hiring blacks--only doing so
     at lower paying jobs--even when it means loss
     of profit. Consequently, through loss of over-
     all profit, such white employers are the "net
     losers" from their economic discrimination

D-30 (continued)

practice. The "net winners" of such policy are
white employees, who get better paying jobs at
the expense of blacks. The argument, therefore, is that to change such discriminatory
practice, employer attitude must change before
employer behavior can be expected to change(2).

(2)   White employers, recognizing larger returns to
the hiring of blacks (not just whites), will
do so. In such a case, white employees will
not necessarily benefit at the expense of
blacks. However, under these circumstances,
employers will have not necessarily changed
their racist attitudes. They are simply "ex-
ploiting" blacks to make more profit. Thus,
this line of thinking suggests that employer
behavior can change without necessarily being
accompanied by change in employer attitude(3).

(3)   Depending on more detailed dynamics of the hiring process, white employees might either gain
or lose from an employer's practice of economic discrimination. The matter is outlined by
Glenn(4) as follows:

(a)   If blacks, are hired at lower paying jobs,
then white employees could be the net beneficiaries of such practice by having exclusive access to the better paying jobs
(re: #1 above).

(b)   If, however, the effect of such deliberate
occupational segmentation by race so sup-
presses the efficient utilization of labor
that it retards overall economic productivity and growth, then white employees
will "lose" from the policy, as well.

(c)   Further, if the result of deliberate occupational segmentation by race only allows
black entry into lower paying jobs, then
this restriction on the number of employment opportunities for blacks could actually contribute to some white employee
"losses," since whites would confront the
probability of increased taxes to pay for

<u>D-30</u> <u>(continued)</u>

increased welfare and law enforcement
costs.

(d)   If increased automation is used to sup-
plant lower paying employ, then, it will
mean that not only blacks, but also whites
(currently working in lower paying capacities) will be denied employ. Increased
costs associated with welfare and law enforcement (re: item "c" above) will be ac-
centuated.

(4)   Reich(5) also feels that the more detailed dynamics of the hiring process might negatively
impact on whites, not just blacks; but, he adds
a couple of reasons not noted by Glenn in #3
above:

(a)   Any growth in income returns to white employees that could accrue through "union
growth and labor militancy" will be in-
hibited through the "racial antagonism"
that results from deliberate discrimination against blacks.

(b)   Racial antagonism in the broader environment (outside the firm), generated by employer practices of discrimination, prevents the "interracial unity" necessary to
bring about a high quality of public education and services for all members of a
community--not just blacks.

An empirical examination of the above four
themes lies at the heart of the Szymanski paper.
Theoretically, Szymanski argues that what benefits
whites, at the expense of blacks in the United
States, also benefits whites, at the expense of
"other national minorities." Therefore, the author
seeks to separate all "third world" people, living
in the United States, from the "white" population.
Since some "third world" people are anything but
"non-white," Szymanski (p. 405) operationalizes
"third world" people to include: "blacks, persons
of Spanish origin, Asians, and American Indians."

D-30 (continued)

"Whites," then, refer to "everyone else." The following hypotheses are tested:

(1)   Other things being equal, whites will enjoy
      higher income returns than third world people
      in areas where economic discrimination against
      such third world people are more pronounced.

(2)   Earnings inequality among whites will be great-
      er in areas where economic discrimination
      against third world people is less pronounced.

      The Szymanski logic behind the second hypothe-
sis is this. The more that third world people are
dispersed, vertically, throughout occupational categories, the more that whites will have to share in
occupations at all levels of an organization. On
the other hand, Szymanski acknowledges that the
thinking of Reich(6) would suggest the opposite;
i.e., white earnings inequality would be greater
in areas where economic discrimination is more pronounced. The reason is that, the greater the degree of discrimination, the greater the degree of
"racial antagonism" and "weakened unions." As a
consequence, if Reich is correct, then when economic
discrimination is practiced to a greater extent, employers can exploit the weakness of unions to, in
general, keep all wages relatively low and promote
greater inequality in white earnings that might otherwise be more equal, were unions strong.
      In general, Szymanski finds neither of his hy-
potheses to be supported. Whites do not gain from
economic discrimination, and white earnings inequality is greater in areas where economic discrimination is more pronounced. So, the direction of the
relationship suggested by Reich is supported. At
the same time, Szymanski finds that the reason given
by Reich (that "weakened unions" depress circumstances for both whites and blacks) is only par-
tially supported. This leads Szymanski to suggest
that, perhaps, greater equality of pay among whites,
as well as between whites and third world people,
arises from a greater recognition by employers of
the applicability of certain points made by Glenn(7)
to their own circumstances; i.e., that certain
"costs" of pay discrimination, resulting in lower

D-30 (continued)

productivity/growth and a lower quality of public
services, are a disadvantage to everyone--employers
and employees alike(8).

On some technical matters, Kluegel (D-18) notes
that to attempt to measure for any pattern of race
discrimination is one thing; to attempt measurement
of the degree to which race dominates as a variable,
in pay decisions, is another. Szymanski actually
attempts to assess such degree of importance to race
by means of an "intensity" of racism measure. This
involves a "ratio of third world to white median
earnings" (Szymanski, p. 406)(9).

In all of the Szymanski measurement, the reader
will find that, like such writers as Kluegel (D-18)
and Wright (D-35), the author relies on an all-male
sample. Szymanski argues that this allows him to
separate out the effects of racism from the effects
of sexism. Szymanski also argues that, since his
data involves the "entire" United States population
(i.e., census data), and he is, thus, not generalizing to a larger population of males, there is no
need to establish statistical significance(10).

The reader will find Szymanski making a case
for measurement by states than by SMSA's, since (as
he sees it) the former provides a better picture of
proportionate representation of certain racial minority groups; and, the reader will also find Szymanski making a conceptual distinction between
"earnings" and "income." Empirically, Szymanski's
interest, in this study, is in earnings, since it
more closely approximates pay for the individual
employee. Income is viewed by Szymanski as a more
global measure of pay for a household (which could,
therefore, include spouse earnings). Of course, the
author cannot use income data, as defined, since he
is only interested in male wages; i.e., he would not
be able to separate out female wages, if using in-
come(11).

Notes

(1) It need be noted that, based on the literature reviewed in this and other annotated articles,
it can be said that the issue of white gain through
racial discrimination has been addressed through a
rather large body of pre-1971 journal literature,

D-30 (continued)

as well as through a good number of non-journal
sources. For the reader's information, Szymanski
appears to offer one of the more thorough reviews
of such literature, among the many provided by authors of the articles (considering the race variable) in this annotated collection.

(2) The major reference, provided by Szymanski,
for this line of argument, is: G. Becker, THE ECO-
NOMICS OF DISCRIMINATION (Chicago: University of
Chicago Press, 1971).

(3) The major reference, provided by Szymanski,
for this line of argument, is: L. Thurow, POVERTY
AND DISCRIMINATION (Washington, DC: The Brookings
Institution, 1969).

(4) N. Glenn, "Occupational Benefits to Whites
from Subordination of Negroes." AMERICAN SOCIOLOGI-
CAL REVIEW 28(1963):443-448; and, N. Glenn, "White
Gains from Negro Subordination." SOCIAL PROBLEMS
14(1966):159-178.

(5) M. Reich, "The Economics of Racism." In
D. Gordon, PROBLEMS IN POLITICAL ECONOMY (Lexington, MA: D.C. Heath, 1971).

(6) See note #5 for the reference to Reich.
Reich's line of argumentation appears to serve as
the basis for that literature examining the more
salient effects of unionization on pay equity. For
examples, see: Hill (E-6); Beck (E-1); Pfeffer and
Ross (E-7).

(7) See note #4 for the references to Glenn.

(8) These particular findings would not appear
to be too surprising, given certain other research
that has found sufficient black gains in both personal earnings and family income during the 1960's.
Further, this other research demonstrates that, in
spite of the recessionary trends of the 1970's, such
a movement toward greater income equality, by race,
continued. As an example of research, demonstrating the general trend, the reader is directed to:
R. Farley, "Trends in Racial Inequalities: Have the

D-30 (continued)

Gains of the 1960's Disappeared in the 1970's?"
AMERICAN SOCIOLOGICAL REVIEW 42(1977):189-208. The
reader is reminded that, in spite of the general
trends, certain caveats are issued by Rexroat (D-23)
surrounding fine distinctions made on the basis of
absolute income/earnings and rates of return. In
his descriptive essay, Farley addresses some, but
not all, of the issues introduced by Rexroat.

(9) Actually, for this particular ratio, Szymanski does not have available data on "third world"
earnings; so, he uses a ratio of "black" to white
earnings as a proxy. In doing this, the author argues that blacks constitute a reasonable facsimile
for any broader third world data, since blacks "are
the biggest third world group in the U.S." (Szymanski, p. 406). Although such is not stated by the
author, one assumes that whites in the more general
third world group are not part of the "whites" in
this ratio. It need also be noted that Szymanski's
intensity measure does not control for the effects
of other variables (education, age, job experience,
etc.). Kluegel infers that it is not really possible to assess the degree of race variable dominance, in the absence of control for such other variables.

(10) Of course, by not controlling for sex,
there is no way to know how generalizable the Szymanski data is to the female population. Further,
the author only includes "full-time, year-around
workers"; so, there is no way of knowing whether
his findings are generalizable to individuals in
other categories of employ.

(11) The distinction between earnings and income, as Szymanski makes it, is assumed to be im-
plicit to many, if not most, other authors of the
annotated articles. However, many of the other writers do not as carefully provide a definitive distinction between the two concepts as does Szymanski.
While Szymanski states that he is only interested
in measuring earnings (and, indeed, appears to only
measure such), he offers no apparent explanation
for why the first hypothesis is stated in terms of
potential "income" differences.

<u>D-31</u>

Taylor, Patricia A.
   1979 "Income Inequality in the Federal Civilian
        Government." AMERICAN SOCIOLOGICAL REVIEW
        44:468-479.

This part of the book is devoted to commentaries on the potential for wage differentials by race
and/or sex. Taylor notes that, given the weight of
federal laws and regulations governing its hiring/
promotion actions, if there is one employer that
should consistently demonstrate the use of merit-
related criteria (unrelated to race and sex) toward
determing levels of pay, it is the federal government. Taylor's research objective is to examine
the degree to which any wage inequality, by race
and/or sex, actually remains in federal service.
   The author establishes a conceptual distinction between "institutional" discrimination and
"employer" discrimination(1). The former results
from "the equal application of universalistic criteria to groups that meet these criteria unequally"
(Taylor, p. 469). An example would be the case of
black students scoring lower than whites on standardized college admission tests. The latter form
of discrimination often results from "the placement
of individuals into particular job streams" (Taylor,
p. 470). "Tracked" through a particular stream, for
the duration of one's career, an individual could
end up earning much less than an alternative employee "tracked" through some other job stream. The end
result could, for example, be certain traditional
"female" jobs (i.e., streams into which most women
are tracked) that pay less than certain traditional
"male" jobs (cf., Bridges and Berk, D-4).
   Taylor argues that the distinction between institutional and employer discrimination is rarely
made in the literature; and, yet, it would appear
to be of critical importance when trying to discern
the effects of discrimination that relies less on
merit (employer-based) from the effects of that
which (at least) demonstrates a certain intent to
consider merit (institutional). It is Taylor's intention to separate the effects of the two forms of
discrimination, so as to determine what amount of
wage discrimination is derivative from each. The
study is done by means of analysis of secondary data

D-31 (continued)

on a systematic random sample of approximately
17,500 white collar federal employees.
    First of all, in contrast with the "theory"
that might suggest otherwise for the federal government, but in concert with the more universal findings in other parts of the economy, Taylor finds
wage discrepancies by race and sex, with white males
consistently earning more than women and non-white
males(2). Taylor also finds that differences exist
among non-white males, non-white females, and white
females, leading the author to conclude that: "each
minority/sex group has a substantially distinct pay
structure which, in part, contributes to different
average salary for the four groups [white males con-
stituting the fourth group]" (Taylor, p. 474).
    Utilizing a "substitution of means" procedure,
similar to that of Rexroat (D-23), Taylor is able to
establish the importance of the variant pay structures. The author then compares wage discrepancy
data in two models. One of the models includes a
number of employment attributes over which an employer can exercise control (e.g., assignment to
a particular occupational group, dispensing of supervisory status, etc.); the other model does not
include such attributes. Taylor concludes that
"pay disparity differences in pay structure probably falls somewhere between the estimates from Model I and Model II" (p. 477). Thus, the author is
arguing that each type of discrimination (employer
and institutional) accounts for about half of all
wage variation by race and sex in the federal government. From this finding, Taylor further concludes that the assumed protection against non-merit
oriented pay discrepancy in the federal government
is far from being reality.

Notes

    (1) "Employer" discrimination, as Taylor de-
scribes it, bears some resemblence to the type "differential allocation" discussed by such writers as
Beck, et al. (D-3) and Kaufman (D-17). From the
standpoint of sex-based occupational segregation
(irrespective of any pay inequity consequences),
as well as from the standpoint of female "adapta-

D-31 (continued)

tion" to such differential allocative processes in
the public sector, the reader with an interest in
these matters is directed to the following study,
which provides information beyond that found in the
Taylor article: W. Markham, et al., "Gender and
Opportunity in the Federal Bureaucracy." AMERICAN
JOURNAL OF SOCIOLOGY 91(1985):129-150.

      (2) The reader is advised that Asher and Popkin
(D-1) offer a contrasting finding, to this, through
their study of the Postal Service.

D-32

Treiman, Donald J. and Patricia A. Roos
   1983   "Sex and Earnings in Industrial Society:
          A Nine Nation Comparison." AMERICAN JOUR-
          NAL OF SOCIOLOGY 89:612-650.

      The objective of this study is to test for the
viability of three alternative explanations, to sex
discrimination, that might be contributing to what
Treiman and Roos report as lower female wages(1)
across all industrialized countries. Analyzing
data from nine such countries(2), the three competing explanations are as follows:

   (1)   "Human Capital"--Where returns to education
         and experience are roughly equal, this expla-
         nation, according to Treiman and Roos, claims
         that any wage discrepancies are influenced by
         lower female than male educational and exper-
         ience levels.

   (2)   "Occupational Segregation"--Where returns to
         occupation are roughly equal, this explana-
         tion, according to Treiman and Roos, claims
         that women will still earn less than men, due
         to their concentration in lower level jobs.

   (3)   "Dual Career"--According to Treiman and Roos,
         this explanation claims that women, who must
         manage both labor market and household respon-

D-32 (continued)

   sibilities, earn less than women who only have
   to manage labor market responsibilities.

   The reader will find a rather well-presented
literature review, by Treiman and Roos, on each of
the above three alternative perspectives and the
fourth alternative (sex-based pay discrimination).
The authors then outline their empirical procedure.
In brief, Treiman and Roos rely on "national probability samples" in each of the nine countries. The
age range for each sample is rather broad (20-64);
however, the samples are excluded to full-time employed.
   One of the advantages to rather broad-based
economic segmentation models (such as those discussed in Part C of this collection) is that they,
often, rely on a multitude of occupational meas-
ures--rather than simply on something so narrow as
"occupational prestige." Treiman and Roos point
out that some of these writers have doubts about
the validity of the "occupational segregation" explanation, since, at times, studies have found that:
"men and women tend to work in substantially different kinds of jobs, even though on average they
work in jobs of equivalent prestige" (p. 623)(3).
This matter would appear to be of no small interest to those who evaluate, formulate, and/or im-
plement comparable worth policy; and, the reader
will find Treiman and Roos utilizing a number of
measures of differences in occupation (beyond just
"prestige"), most of which derive from the economic
segmentation research tradition.
   In terms of results, the data reveals that,
across all nine countries studied, men and women
are found to work in very different kinds of jobs,
whereby women tend to be

      substantially overrepresented in high-
      prestige clerical occupations and in
      low-prestige sales and service employ-
      ment; they are substantially underrep-
      resented in administrative occupations
      and in high- and medium-prestige pro-
      duction occupations (Treiman and Roos,
      p. 641).

D-32 (continued)

Translating this into wage differentials (adjusting for what women would earn, if they had the same average education and experience characteristics as men), in no country could women be found to earn wages equal to what men could earn.

Although they acknowledge some potential methodological difficulties, Treiman and Roos, nevertheless, reject all three alternative explanations to sex discrimination. The following summarizes their arguments.

(1)   "Human Capital"--Gender differences in human capital (education and experience) are found to be small, although differential returns to such human capital are found to be large.

(2)   "Occupational Segregation"--There are no gender differences, with respect to prestige and other elements attached to particular positions; but, the differential returns to such occupational attributes, by sex, are found to be large.

(3)   "Dual Career"--Marital status is not found to affect the earnings of women; rather, it is found to only affect the earnings of men<4>.

Based on the above results, Treiman and Roos conclude that the only explanation for differential returns to human capital and occupation must be sex discrimination.

Notes

<1> In this paper, Treiman and Roos acknowledge not making the distinction between "income" and "earnings" suggested by such writers as Szymanski (D-30). However, the authors do not find the distinction too overly important to make, thus offering a contrasting point of view to that of Szymanski.

<2> The nine countries are: Austria, Denmark, Finland, Germany (Federal Republic), Israel, the Netherlands, Norway, Swedan, and the United States.

D-32 (continued)

(3) For more information on the derivation
of this particular statement, Treiman and Roos refer readers to P. England, "Women and Occupational
Prestige: A Case of Vacuous Sex Equality." SIGNS
5(1979):252-265.

(4) The reader will find these results on "dual
career" impact to correspond with those of such writers as Suter and Miller (D-29) but to, apparently,
be at variance with earlier published findings by
the senior author (Treiman and Terrell, D-33). The
findings also appear to be at variance with those of
Coverman (D-6), although Coverman: (a) uses a different measure of degree to which household duties
are performed ("domestic labor time" rather than
simply marital status); and, (b) apparently includes
intermittently, not just full-time, employed persons
in the data set.

D-33

Treiman, Donald J. and Kermit Terrell
   1975   "Sex and the Process of Status Attainment:
          A Comparison of Working Women and Men."
          AMERICAN SOCIOLOGICAL REVIEW 40:174-200.

A number of themes of interest to writers,
listed elsewhere in this volume, are addressed by
Treiman and Terrell in this analysis of census data
within a specific age cohort (30-44). The themes
and some selected references are:

(1)   The importance of assessing differential re-
      turns to education and/or occupational status
      (Hudis, D-16; Kluegel, D-18; Rexroat, D-23).

(2)   The degree to which wage differentials exist,
      by sex, exclusive of any impact of race (Fer-
      ber and Loeb, D-11; Suter and Miller, D-29).

(3)   The effect of marital status and/or career-
      orientation on sex-based wage differentials
      (Ferber and Loeb, D-11; Suter and Miller,
      D-29).

D-33 (continued)

(4)   The influence of racial differences on sex-
        based wage differentials (Beck, et al., D-3;
        Rosenfeld, D-24).

        Treiman and Terrell find, as do most other wri-
ters in the field, that (in general) women earn less
than do men for work of comparable occupational status and for which they are equally qualified on the
basis of formal education. The reader will, for example, find these results corresponding with those
of Suter and Miller (D-29)--although the latter authors compare all men and women, while Treiman and
Terrell only compare husbands and wives. Treiman
and Terrell also report that there exist lower earnings for women, per increases in productivity.
        The authors introduce the reader to the poten-
tial problem of lower female earnings being due to
more intermittent employment patterns than those
existent for most males. However, unlike Suter and
Miller (D-29), they do not control for the problem;
so, there is no way to determine, from the reported
data, whether the earnings of career-oriented women
more closely correspond with those of men than do
the earnings of more intermittently employed women.
However, Treiman and Terrell do report on the effects of marital status, arguing that single women
earn more than do married women. The reader will
find that this particular result corresponds with
that of Ferber and Loeb (D-11); but, it apparently
contradicts the findings of Suter and Miller, as
well as some later reported findings by the senior
author (Treiman and Roos, D-32).
        The Treiman and Terrell results tend to per-
sist, when comparisons are made by race, thus apparently corresponding with general conclusions
drawn by such later writers as Beck, et al. (D-3)--
to the effect that sex discrimination is more applicable than race discrimination toward explaining
wage differentials. However, this does not mean
that race makes no difference, whatsoever. Indeed,
the sex-based differentials, reported by Treiman
and Terrell, are less pronounced for blacks than
for whites. In a later published article, which
compares race-based pay differentials for females
only, Hudis (D-16) hypothesizes that black women
have a greater amount of labor force experience,

<u>D-33</u> <u>(continued)</u>

and place a greater emphasis on the attachment of
monetary rewards to work, than do white women.
Treiman and Terrell appear to concur with this type
of judgment and feel that such might lie behind more
narrow male-female pay differentials among blacks
than among whites.

<u>D-34</u>

Ward, Kathryn B. and Charles W. Mueller
    1985   "Sex Differences in Earnings: The Influence
           of Industrial Sector, Authority Hierarchy,
           and Human Capital Variables." WORK AND OC-
           CUPATIONS 12:437-463.

        A number of writers, such as Lord and Falk
(C-11) and Fligstein, et al. (C-5), argue for the
relevance of not only looking at pay differences by
economic segment, but of also examining the impact
of social class differences on such pay variation.
However, whereas some writers will combine "economic segments" and "social class" into the same broad
conceptual category (e.g., the "social position"
category for Fligstein, et al.), Ward and Mueller
point out that such writers, inevitably, measure
segmentation and class effects separately. The
authors state an opinion that such separate measurement is appropriate, because (in doing so), a
researcher correctly assumes that segmentation effects, <u>per</u> <u>se</u>, do not necessarily reflect class effects. This is argued to be the case, because measures of social class emphasize the degree of control
over means of production--a matter not necessarily
accounted for by studies of segmentation differences
alone.
        In building their case for separating segmenta-
tion from class effects, Ward and Mueller cite the
work of Robinson and Kelley(1). The latter authors
question the practice of some of the writers, listed
in Part C of this collection, who suggest theoretical (and, in some cases, empirical) relationships
between segmentation and social class. For example,
such writers as Beck, et al. (C-1) and Hodson (C-7)
consider class to be an essential component of eco-

D-34 (continued)

nomic segmentation; and, they tend also to infer
that differing measures of socioeconomic status
(e.g., occupational status, employment status, etc.)
are proxies for social class. However, it is the
Robinson and Kelley (and, by fiat, the Ward and
Mueller) position that such measures of socioeconomic status (SES) do not conceptually correspond
with what Wright and Perrone (B-7), for example,
call social class. The reason is that what Wright
and Perrone refer to as "class" infers variation,
in control, over modes of production; SES does not.
The issue is an important one for Ward and Mueller,
as they wish to emphasize that a social class emphasis on mode of production control goes further in
explaining sex-based pay inequity than does any segmentation theory (with its inclusion of SES concepts).

A number of writers, listed in this volume,
argue that, in order to understand pay differentials by race and sex, one must analyze "sorting"
or "allocation" patterns; however, in doing this,
they often speak of race or sex-based allocation,
but not both. Examples are Kaufman (D-17) and
Wright (D-35), who exclusively discuss race-based
allocation patterns. Ward and Mueller also restrict
the nature of their allocation discussion, in this
case to sex-based patterns.

In addition to rather exclusive emphasis on
allocation by race or by sex, writers will often
argue, rather exclusively, about allocation into
social "classes" or into economic "segments"--not
into both. Wright and Perrone (B-7) and Wright
(D-35), for example, emphasize analysis of allocation patterns into different classes, while Beck,
et al. (D-3) and Kaufman (D-17) emphasize allocation patterns into different economic segments. In
this respect, however, Ward and Mueller offer a
broadened discussion. In general, the authors attempt to analyze variant allocation into social
"classes," but, in doing so, they also have something to say about variant allocation into economic
"segments." More specifically, after arguing for
the preeminent importance of class over segmentation effects (due to the former's emphasis on an accounting for degree of mode of production control),
Ward and Mueller then attempt to build a case for

D-34 (continued)

"synthesizing" the class and segmentation research
traditions.
    The attempted "synthesis" begins with a dis-
course that, essentially, differentiates "dual labor
markets" from "dual sectors" and, thus, "re-defines"
the roles of labor markets and segments. For example, Hodson (C-7) and Spilerman (C-14) have discussed a definitional distinction between the two--
arguing that "labor market" differences emphasize
qualitative differences in occupational skill ("primary" vs. "secondary" occupations), whereas "sectors" are more broadly defined--with occupational
differences being one defining element essential to
sectoral differentiation (i.e., primary labor markets are often argued as helping to define a core
sector; secondary labor markets are often argued as
helping to define a peripheral sector). However,
Zucker and Rosenstein (C-19) criticize such thinking, arguing that sectoral (what they call "economic") demarcations are at the level of "industry"--labor market demarcations are at the level of
"firm"--and, variant reliance on industry vs. firm
analysis, among studies, have lead to variant findings from one study to the next. In a sense, Ward
and Mueller agree with the Zucker and Rosenstein
assessment, stating that the problem is that (counter to what Hodson, Spilerman, and other early segmentation writers suggest), labor market differences
(which infer "firm-specific" analysis) can be found
within each sector (core, periphery, etc.). Thus,
Ward and Mueller argue that labor market variation,
per se, is not useful toward defining differences
between sectors(2).
    The Ward and Mueller "synthesis" between seg-
mentation and class perspectives moves into full
gear, as the authors proceed next to discuss sectoral differences in control over mode of production (the essential determinant of social class,
as such is defined in their paper)--utilizing knowledge about variant labor markets to illustrate their
points. The literature reviewed by Ward and Mueller
suggests that firms operating within the core sector
(of any two-sector model) have more formally developed internal labor markets (ILMs) than do firms operating within the periphery. What this means is
that, when evaluating individual credentials, and

D-34 (continued)

then allocating persons to primary and secondary occupations, firms located in the core do things differently than do firms located in the periphery.
Specifically, Ward and Mueller argue that core sector firms exercise "bureaucratic" control, putting
a much greater degree of emphasis on well-defined
"job ladders," "positions of formal authority," and
the "credentials" needed to achieve placement into
positions of "higher authority" than do firms in the
periphery<3>.
     The Ward and Mueller argument for what "bureau-
cratically" controlled firms do differently than
those which are not so bureaucratically controlled
is developed as follows. Whereas women are more
likely than men to be allocated to secondary jobs
in the periphery, this is not necessarily the case
in the core. Indeed, following a line of more general thought by Wright and Perrone (B-7), on equality of income returns to men and women of similar
occupational category, Ward and Mueller argue that
women are no less likely than men to be allocated to
primary jobs in the core and can expect similar in-
come<4> returns, to the broad primary occupations
(to which they are allocated), as can men. The
problem, argue Ward and Mueller, is that the "top
authority positions" (within any one core "primary"
occupational category) are dominated by males. Assuming no variant returns to such human capital
characteristics as education and job experience,
then what pay inequity occurs, in the core sector,
must be due to differential evaluation by sex or to
differential allocation (to top positions) by sex<5>.
     The above-stated argument is tested by Ward and
Mueller through an analysis of NORC data. They find
that, indeed, "men receive greater benefits from
high authority position than do women" (Ward and
Mueller, p. 456). However, the authors cannot establish that this is strictly a core sector phenomenon. Returns to differential authority, leading to
sex differences in pay, can also be found in the periphery. On the other hand, differential returns to
human capital variables (education, experience,
etc.) are still found to be much more pronounced in
the periphery, than in the core. This leads Ward
and Mueller to infer that differential allocation,
strictly by sex, is still more of a core than a pe-

D-34 (continued)

ripheral sector phenomenon<6>. On the other hand,
the authors offer no data on the "distributional
mechanisms" that allocate women to one sector or
the other, to primary vs. secondary jobs within a
sector, or to different authority levels within an
occupational category. Such, acknowledge Ward and
Mueller, remains as "needed future research."

Notes

<1> R. Robinson and J. Kelley, "Class as Con-
ceived by Marx and Dahrendorf: Effects on Income
Inequality, Class Consciousness, and Class Conflict
in the United States and Great Britain." AMERICAN
SOCIOLOGICAL REVIEW 44(1979):38-58.

<2> While the Ward and Mueller statement, on
the demarcation between sectors and labor markets,
contrasts with that of some early or more traditional segmentation writing, it would appear that,
in later writing, Hodson (C-8), for one, has somewhat come around to the Ward and Mueller point of
view. It also needs be noted that the message on
variant labor markets being found within sectors is
something that others have, at least, inferred as
a possibility. For example, see: D'amico (C-4) and
Kaufman (D-17).

<3> Firms in the periphery, argue Ward and
Mueller, exercise "hierarchical" control, where
"there are fewer differentiated levels of control
and supervisory relations are less formal" (p. 441).
The literature on ILMs, as well as on the distinction between bureaucratic and hierarchical control,
is not particularly novel; and, Ward and Mueller do
review a good deal of the literature on this subject. For the person, with an interest in reading
about the nature of ILMs, per se, one of the earli-
est definitive discussions, on the formal quality of
"well-developed" ILMs, appears to be: P. Doeringer
and M. Piore, INTERNAL LABOR MARKETS AND MANPOWER
ANALYSIS (Lexington, MA: D.C. Heath, 1971). Recent
empirical evidence of the more formal quality of
ILMs in the core sector can be found in J. Pfeffer
and Y. Cohen, "Determinants of Internal Labor Mar-

D-34 (continued)

kets in Organizations." ADMINISTRATIVE SCIENCE QUAR-
TERLY 29(1984):550-572.
    The manner in which Ward and Mueller are us-
ing control over modes of production reflects what
might be referred to as "control over personnel resources." The reader is directed to another article, published at about the same time as that by
Ward and Mueller: J. Spaeth, "Job Power and Earnings." AMERICAN SOCIOLOGICAL REVIEW 50(1985):603-
617. Spaeth broadens the examination of "control"
to not only account for personnel, but also for
"monetary" resources. Although the Spaeth data does
not directly assist in understanding the forces underlying differential allocation by sex, some information is provided of potential relevance to the
Ward and Mueller study. Specifically, Spaeth finds
that: "Among men, control over monetary resources is
a stronger determinant of earnings than other work-
related variables" (p. 603). However, Spaeth finds
that, among women, both monetary and personnel resource control are important. Consequently, if
Spaeth is correct, then Ward and Mueller might have
been able to more definitively assess sex differences in class allocation by looking at differences
in the degree of monetary control, not just personnel control.

    (4) Like some of the other writers, listed
elsewhere in this collection, Ward and Mueller do
not differentiate "pay" or "earnings" from "income"
and are, thus, subject to criticism for not doing
so, given the arguments put forth by Szymanski
(D-30).

    (5) For detail on the nature of differential
evaluation and allocation processes, see Beck,
et al. (D-3); Kaufman (D-17). The Ward and Mueller perspective, here, is somewhat akin to that addressed by Rexroat (D-23) on women not being able
to vertically advance within an organization. It
would appear to bear even closer resemblance to the
arguments advanced by Kluegel (D-18) and Wright
(D-35), who (albeit offering race-exclusive discussions) are assessing how advancement within occupational categories constitutes advancement in decision-making authority.

D-34 (continued)

    (6) The importance of "human capital" vs.
"structural" (i.e., "sectoral") variables, toward
explaining earnings variation, has been recently
discussed by D. Jacobs, "Unequal Organizations or
Unequal Attainments? An Empirical Comparison of Sectoral and Individualistic Explanations for Aggregate
Inequality." AMERICAN SOCIOLOGICAL REVIEW 50(1985):
166-180. Perhaps because of the wealth of literature (annotated throughout this collection) on the
impact of sectoral variables, Jacobs spends most of
his time analyzing the potential impact of human
capital variables; and, unlike most other writers,
cited in this volume (especially in Part C), Jacobs
is not as inclined to dismiss the independent explanatory power of certain human capital variables
(particularly, education). Indeed Jacobs views education, in particular, as being every bit as important as more "structural" variables in an analysis.
Consequently, if Jacobs is correct, then the potential for certain human capital explanations (such as
educational effects) playing a larger role than sex
differences and/or class differences--in explaining
the type "within periphery" wage discrepancies described by Ward and Mueller--would appear to be a
worthwhile empirical consideration. Further, if a
case can be made for education playing a larger role
toward wage determination in the periphery than in
the core, this would seem to contradict most economic segmentation research to date (See Beck, et al.,
D-3, and most Part C entries.).

D-35

Wright, Erik O.
    1978 "Race, Class, and Income Inequality." AMER-
          ICAN JOURNAL OF SOCIOLOGY 83:1368-1397.

    As is evident, throughout Part C of this vol-
ume, many writers on the issue of economic segmentation argue for the impact of aspects of social
structure on any relationship between personal characteristics and income variation (cf., Beck, et al.,
C-1; Hodson, C-7; Stolzenberg, C-15). Utilizing
"social class" as an aspect of social structure(1),

D-35 (continued)

Wright seeks to test for the impact of class differences on a relationship between personal characteristics and wage variation. Along these lines,
he becomes interested in the combined effects of
social class, race, and education[2] on income.
Specifically, the author intends to ultimately demonstrate that any "observed racial difference in
returns to education is a consequence of the distribution of racial groups into class categories"
(Wright, p. 1368).

In this particular article, Wright uses (as do
Wright and Perrone, B-7, and Fligstein, et al., C-5)
Marxist definitions of social class[3], whereby individuals are grouped into employer, petit bourgeois, manager, and workers categories. The reader
is directed to the Fligstein, et al. and the Wright
and Perrone annotations for definitions of these
categories. From the standpoint of measurement,
a degree of ambiguity was noted in the Fligstein,
et al. annotation, concerning the extent to which
those authors actually include the "workers" class
in their data set; and, it was noted how Wright and
Perrone combine their "employers" and "petit bourgeois" into a single "owners" class.

In the study, now under consideration, Wright
clearly retains both workers and manager classes;
however, it is unclear, to the writer of this volume, what Wright has done with the other two categories. The author demonstrates how he distinctly
collected employer and petit bourgeois data; but,
he appears to drop all discussion of the petit bourgeois, utilizing an "employer" label as if he has,
like Wright and Perrone (B-7), combined employers
and petit bourgeois into a single "owners" type category. In any event, Wright appears only to include
whatever passes for owners data when engaging in
some broad "all black" vs. "all white" type comparisons; he does not appear to include owners data for
the purpose of more specific across-class hypothesis testing. For example, when testing hypotheses,
Wright becomes very concerned about what is going
on within and between the managerial and workers
classes; but, he apparently has little (if any) interest in what is going on among the "owners" or
between them and the other classes.

D-35 (continued)

Wright offers no explanation for the relative
non-inclusion of owners class data in most of his
analysis<4>. Nevertheless, he does proceed to examine six specific relationships. The tested relationships and the reported results are as follows.

(1) "Managers as a whole ... receive much higher
returns to education than workers" (Wright,
p. 1371).
      The data reveals that, as is the case
in the research by Wright and Perrone (B-7),
Wright has now found that managers do receive
higher returns to education than do workers.
      Fligstein, et al. (C-5) suggest that it
might be useful to examine the relationship
between personal characteristics and pay variation among different managerial categories.
To an extent, Wright does this by separating
"proper managers" from "nominal supervisors."
The former are distinguished from the latter,
insofar as they are found to have input into
subordinate pay and promotion decisions. Thus,
proper managers are considered by Wright to be
at a higher level of managerial class than are
the nominal supervisors. The finding that managers have higher returns to education than do
workers suggests, in a broader sense, that social class makes a difference, with respect to
pay variation. This same broad inference (that
class standing makes a difference) is applicable to the within-class analysis; i.e., Wright
finds that proper managers have greater returns
to education than do nominal supervisors<5>.

(2) "Black males ... [are] more concentrated in
the working class than white males" (Wright,
p. 1372).
      It is not known why Wright chooses not to
control for differences by sex, particularly
when his earlier research (Wright and Perrone,
B-7) emphasized a need to look at both race and
sex differences. In any event, restricting his
analysis to racial differences, Wright (indeed)
finds a greater percentage of black than white
males concentrated in the "workers" class<6>.

D-35 (continued)

(3)   In general (not controlling for the effects of
       class), "black males ... receive lower re-
       turns to education than white males" (Wright,
       p. 1372).
            The author finds this to be the case[7].
       The next three hypotheses control for the ef-
       fects of class on this particular relationship
       between race and income returns to education.

(4)   Within the workers class, "the returns to ed-
       ucation for black and white males ... [are]
       much more similar than for all blacks and all
       whites" (Wright, p. 1372).
            Wright appears to essentially find this
       to be the case; and, he justifies the finding
       on the basis of literature revealing that re-
       turns to education legitimate class distinc-
       tions (re: note #5)--especially when such class
       distinctions can be made on salient differences
       in formal authority. So, since both managers
       and workers are included in "all black vs. all
       white" comparison and since the finding (re:
       hypothesized statement #2) is that blacks are
       more concentrated than whites in the class with
       less formal authority (i.e., the workers class),
       then it would be expected that differential re-
       turns to education would be more pronounced in
       any all black vs. all white comparison than in
       any comparison, exclusive to a given class.
       Simply put, formal authority differences are
       more pronounced between than within classes.

(5)   Within the nominal supervisor subcategory, "the
       returns to education for black and white males
       ... [are] more similar than for all blacks and
       all whites" (Wright, p. 1372).
            Wright finds this to be the case; and,
       he explains it on the basis of the same reas-
       oning as hypothesized statement #4--that more
       pronounced differences will be found between
       occupational categories than within categories.

(6)   Within the proper managerial subcategory,
       "black males ... have lower returns to edu-
       cation than white males" (Wright, pp. 1372-
       1373).

D-35 (continued)

The differential effect of class is demonstrated by the existence of this finding by
Wright, in that it appears to deviate from the
quality of the relationships found through
testing hypothesized statements #4 and #5. In
other words, Wright is arguing (in this case)
that differential returns to education are not
significantly reduced by measurement within a
particular class. Wright assumes that this
finding might be due to an overrepresentation of blacks at lower proper managerial levels; however, he presents no literature to defend this particular point of view.

In his discussion of the above findings, Wright
does not claim an overall superiority of class over
race effects, even though the testing of statements
#4 and #5 indicate that race differences (in returns
to education) diminish among nominal supervisors and
among workers. The reason is that, even though returns gaps "diminish" within these two categories,
significant gaps in mean income, between the races,
still remain in the classes. Thus, it would appear
to be an open question as to whether what occurs
within the nominal supervisor and workers classes
is, in reality, all that different from what is oc-
curing within the proper managerial class.
In any event, the reader will find Wright presenting the implications of his findings through rather extensive theoretical discussion on the interplay between race-based compensation policy and
class relations; however, it need be emphasized that
Wright does not necessarily claim class and race to
be the only variables influencing discrepant returns
to education. Through the introduction of a number
of other variables into his analysis (age, seniority, father's education, father's occupational status, employee occupational status, etc.), Wright
finds several of his conclusions to be enhanced;
however, he does not measure for the separate contributions of these other variables.

D-35 (continued)

Notes

(1) The use of social class as a "structural"
characteristic is controversial. The reader is
directed to the following entries for an outline
of the debate: Fligstein, et al. (C-5); Kalleberg,
et al. (C-9); Wright and Perrone (B-7). Also, the
citation to Beck, et al., Hodson, and Stolzenberg,
is not meant to infer that they define social class
in a manner that would allow empirical comparabil-
ity to what Wright is defining as class. This is
because Beck, et al., Hodson, and Stolzenberg actually discuss the importance of measuring socioeconomic status (SES); and, some question exists
as to whether SES is an appropriate proxy for social
class (cf., Ward and Mueller, D-34).

(2) In this study, Wright measures income in
terms of "returns to education." Education, per se,
is measured by means of "years of schooling." The
matter is important, given some controversy over
how best to measure the educational variable (cf.,
Beck, et al., C-1; Stolzenberg, C-16).

(3) In this article, Wright spends some time
outlining the conceptual difference between Marxist
and certain non-Marxist treatments of the class variable. For example, some non-Marxists operationalize class as any common position in a status hierarchy; the Marxist operationalization, however, em-
phasizes a class as being any common position in
the social organization of production. Whether the
"production" emphasis of the Marxist definition
makes a difference is not known, given the dearth
of literature (to date) that works with the class
variable in pay equity analysis, let alone compares
results across different operational uses of class.

(4) In his later discussion of the findings'
implications, Wright tries to accentuate the nature of class differences by demonstrating differences between white employer and white workers incomes; but, it remains the case that no exhaustive
owners vs. non-owners testing is fundamental to this
analysis. It could be that owners responses are not
actively measured against non-owners responses, due

D-35 (continued)

to a low number of blacks in such owners categories;
however, such is not stated by Wright, in this article. So, there is no way of knowing why the own-
ership classes are not included in the across-class
comparisons.

(5) The stated conclusions, in this annotation,
(such as this particular conclusion), simply represent an "overview" of the Wright discussion. In a
more detailed sense, Wright discusses the degree to
which returns to education should be considered conceptually separate from returns to class, as well
as how returns to class come to somewhat dominate
returns to education, per se--due to an administrative reliance on educational differences (in part)
to legitimate class distinctions. In a general
sense, Stolzenberg (C-16) makes a similar point, by
noting how "level of education" represents a con-
venient, low cost, body of data that can apply to
achievement evaluation. The reader is directed to
the Wright article for more detailed argumentation
on this point, as it relates to the interactive effects of education and class differentiation on pay
variation.

(6) Unlike other comparisons, Wright appears
to rely only on descriptive statistics to reach this
conclusion. However, the percentage differences
are quite noticeable. Approximately 61 percent of
blacks and approximately 40 percent of whites are
in the workers class.

(7) This particular finding is divergent from
the finding of Stolzenberg (D-28); but, the literature reviewed by both Wright and Stolzenberg suggests that the Wright finding more closely corresponds with that of other researchers in this subject
area. Wright feels that this difference in findings
has to do with a decision by Stolzenberg to rely on
"rates" of return, not absolute returns. For more
detail on the matter, see the Stolzenberg entry.

PART E: PAY INEQUITY POTPOURRI

PART E: PAY INEQUITY POTPOURRI

Content Key

Entries are listed by subject area. Years of publication are listed by the "unionization" entries, should the reader prefer to review them chronologically.

Annotated Entries

E-1

Beck, E.M.
   1980   "Labor Unionization and Racial Income In-
          equality: A Time-Series Analysis of the
          Post-World War II Period." AMERICAN JOUR-
          NAL OF SOCIOLOGY 85:791-814.

     In an earlier published study, Hill (E-6) es-
tablishes a difference between two competing hypotheses regarding the effect of unionization on
race-based wage differentials: (1) the "competition"
hypothesis, inferring that greater unionization will
enhance such inequality to the detriment of blacks;
(2) the "exploitation" hypothesis, inferring that
greater unionization will enhance equality of pay
by race--that, indeed, less unionization will depress wages for all employees, regardless of race.
Beck re-labels the Hill "competition" and "exploitation" explanations as "white protectionist" and
"class-consciousness," proceeding to then re-eval-
uate what Hill and others have found in research on
the worthiness of the alternative hypotheses(1).
     Hill (E-6) argues for the demarcation of "in-
dustrial" vs. "craft" unions, in any empirical work,
given a differential history of racial discrimination within the unions. However, Beck does not so
demarcate the data. Rather, Beck argues that: (a)
substantial enough changes in the structure of unions has occurred over time (beginning with the
merging of the AFL-CIO), such that the contemporary
distinction between craft and industrial unions has
become "increasingly blurred"; (b) inasmuch as such
leading "class consciousness" advocates as Szymanski
(D-30) do not make the distinction, it is not clear
that such a craft vs. industrial demarcation is all
that important to the class consciousness perspective. Consequently, Beck relies on aggregated census data, not demarcating the unions into different
types.
     Hill (E-6) acknowledges that his data must be
interpreted with "caution;" given its cross-section-
al quality and the fact that comparisons were not
made, within racial categories, of unionization effects. It is for this reason that Beck engages in
longitudinal analysis (examining data over the per-

E-1 (continued)

iod, 1947-1974), as well as in intraracial comparison.
     In addition, Beck criticizes the Hill (E-6)
usage of median income, whereby (for example) the
latter author concludes that the "class consciousness" perspective is potentially valid because unionization is found to increase median black incomes. The problem, argues Beck, is that reliance
on median income, alone, provides assessment of
"racial differences at only one point on the income
distribution, the fiftieth percentile" (p. 797).
Therefore, Beck uses "total" income figures to allow for "racial discrepancies throughout the income
distribution" (p. 797). Also, whereas Hill only
assesses discrepancies in familial income, Beck compares such familial income discrepancies with discrepancies in male income only.
     Beck's findings (in comparison with those of
Hill, E-6) are as follows:

(1) Using the median familial income measure, Hill
     did not find that, overall, unionization sig-
     nificantly affected the level of inequality
     between black and white workers. Beck sub-
     stantiates this conclusion, utilizing the total
     familial income measure. What differences do
     occur for Beck are at the lower-income levels,
     where unionization leads to lower racial in-
     equality; but, even at these income levels,
     the differences are of "small magnitude"(2).

(2) On the other hand, when looking solely at male
     workers, Beck finds that, over time, there is
     actually more support for the "white protec-
     tionist" than for the "class consciousness"
     position--inasmuch as increased unionization
     contributes to increased racial inequality(3).
     Beck feels that the discrepancy between this
     finding and that noted above might be explained
     by "the likelihood of secondary [assumably fe-
     male] wage earners securing employment in un-
     ionized labor markets" (p. 809). However, for
     this explanation to hold, the assumption must
     be made that any "white protectionist" practice
     of general discrimination against non-whites,
     within unions, does not necessarily apply to

E-1 (continued)

        such "secondary" workers. This matter does
        not appear to be saliently addressed by Beck.

(3)   Hill (E-6) finds that both hypotheses (white
        protectionist and class consciousness) predict
        reduced inequalty among whites. Beck also
        finds this to be the case, although the ef-
        fects are quite small.

(4)   Within the non-white racial group, Beck's find-
        ings reflect those of the overall population;
        i.e., "gains in unionism are associated with
        increasing inequality among males, but have no
        discernable influence on the inequality among
        families" (Beck, p. 809). Beck argues that the
        finding, in this respect, of inequality among
        non-white males, might be due to unions only
        benefitting "skilled" occupations, in which
        non-whites are underrepresented. As for the
        lack of unionization influence on overall fam-
        ilial income, however, Beck argues that this
        might arise due to male earnings making up a
        relatively "small" proportion of overall non-
        white familial wage contributions.

        In the case of the findings within the non-
white racial group, Beck appears to be saying the
following: (a) within black families, the pay contributions of supposedly "secondary" wage earners
(females) are not all that secondary; and, (b) non-
white female employees are more skilled than non-
white males. Neither assumption is tested for in
this study. Also, to assume that, because non-white
females (being more "skilled") can avail themselves
of "union protection" against race-based pay discrimination (a "class-consciousness" conclusion),
Beck would have to explain away the potential for
any "white protectionist" discrimination within the
unions, themselves. As noted earlier, this is a
matter that the author does not appear to saliently
address, even though the argument is posited that,
in general, the white protectionist position might
help explain the effect of inequality among males
(re: finding #2 above). In other words, the question is begged: Is Beck claiming that racial discrimination within unions only exists among males--

E-1 (continued)

not between whites (male and/or female) and non-
white females(4)?

Notes

(1) Beck is not only re-analyzing the work of
Hill but also that of other authors. The works of
these other authors are not annotated in this collection; however, they do appear to generally report
results that are in concert with those of Hill. In
addition to attempting to reconcile certain methodological problems associated with such cross-sec-
tional studies as these, Beck is also attempting to
reconcile certain methodological questions brought
up in earlier longitudinal studies. The reader will
find the Beck review of all of this additional literature to be quite thorough and well-written.

(2) It need be noted that Hill (E-6) and Beck
apparently operationalize "unionization" differently. Beck defines unionization as the percent be-
longing to unions, thus putting an emphasis on "union membership." Hill defines unionization as the
percent employed by organizations with union agree-
ments. So, Hill appears to emphasize success in
"union organizing," while leaving the door open as
to whether one actually belongs to a union. From
a methodological standpoint, the question has been
raised as to whether an even more broad-based definition of unionization might produce different results, by entertaining the "threat effect" of non-
union employees who have provided an inclination,
to management, of organizing potential. For a review of the literature on the "threat effect" and
its potential for providing different findings than
either "union membership" or "organizing success"
operationalizations, see: S. Welch, "Union-nonunion
Construction Wage Differentials." INDUSTRIAL RELA-
TIONS 19(1980):152-162.

(3) The inference made--that unionization contributes to wage discrepancies among males--does
not correspond with the findings of J. Pfeffer and
J. Ross, "Union and Non-union Effects in Wages and
Status Attainment." INDUSTRIAL RELATIONS 19(1980):

E-1 (continued)

140-151. In that article, Pfeffer and Ross infer
lowered male race-based pay inequality, due to unionization. However, Pfeffer and Ross apparently
measure unionization differently than does Beck.
Whereas Beck relies on "union membership," Pfeffer
and Ross only ask whether a respondent's wages result from collective bargaining. Thus, Pfeffer and
Ross (like Hill--re: note #2) seemingly leave open
the question of whether the respondent actually belongs to a union.

(4) To assume equality of returns to skill,
due to unionization, one not only must assume a lack
of differential returns to race, but also a lack of
differential returns to sex. In a pair of articles,
Pfeffer and Ross infer that unionization dimin-
inishes differential returns to race, regardless of
sex. The study measuring unionization effects for
males was cited in note #3; the study measuring unionization effects for females is: J. Pfeffer and
J. Ross, "Unionization and Female Wage and Status
Attainment." INDUSTRIAL RELATIONS 20(1981):179-185.
This finding might appear to somewhat contradict the
Beck implication that unions do not protect non-
white males as much as they do non-white "secondary
wage earners" (assumably female). However, as inferred in note #3, any divergence between the Beck
and the Pfeffer and Ross findings might have something to do with the studies employing different
measurements of unionization.
In any event, Pfeffer and Ross note that, while
unionization enhances female returns to certain general skills, it depresses female returns to certain
"specific" job skills. While Pfeffer and Ross do
not come out and say it, one wonders whether this
infers some "within union" discrimination against
women (whereby, for example, a union might press
for certain benefits for more senior employees and,
by fiat, the more senior employees tend to be male).
The degree to which these Pfeffer and Ross findings
might "spill over" into the Beck findings is not
known, since Beck did not really look, specifically,
at male-female differences.

E-2

Bornschier, Volker and Thanh-Huyen Ballmer-Cao
   1979 "Income Inequality: A Cross-National Study
         of the Relationships Between MNC-Penetra-
         tion, Dimensions of the Power Structure and
         Income Distribution." AMERICAN SOCIOLOGICAL
         REVIEW 44:487-506.

     In discussing (as the annotated articles in
this collection have) aspects of social structure
that contribute to the existence and/or perceptions
of pay inequity, the concern has been, in most
cases, with the potential for external social comparison among occupations in different United States
economic sectors, labor markets, or whatever.
     Perhaps, the relative lack of interest in ex-
ternal comparisons made beyond the boundaries of
the U.S.(1), stems from the relative superiority
of U.S. wage levels to most others throughout the
world--thereby providing little basis for cross-
national comparative influence on any American ac-
tual/perceived inequity, in the form of "underpayment." Bornschier and Ballmer-Cao are not really
specifically interested in what economic sectoral/
labor market differences, across societies, might
contribute to actual/perceived pay inequity. However, their interest is in reminding readers that
the total social structural context that defines
any compensation analysis cannot be viewed within
a given societal vacuum--simply as a matter of variation brought about by internal economic/labor market forces. Rather, what affects the distribution
of pay in any society has something to do, as well,
with social forces generated by governments and the
influences of multinational corporations (MNC's).
     Specifically, Bornschier and Ballmer-Cao study
50 countries, finding that the penetration of any
MNC into a society brings about such change in the
distribution of that country's political power--that
actual income inequality is enhanced. Through both
qualitative and quantitative presentation, the authors defend this particular finding; and, the reader will find an among-country comparison presented,
as well, on the matter of measured inequality.

E-2 (continued)

Note

(1) Although not actually involved in external
comparison, from the standpoint of perceived inequity, the article by Treiman and Roos (D-32) can be
viewed as one exception to the rule, as it attempts
to discern the potential for some actual differences
across societies. Another exception to the rule is
the relatively early theoretical discourse by E.
Bonacich, "A Theory of Ethnic Antagonism: The Split
Labor Market." AMERICAN SOCIOLOGICAL REVIEW 37
(1972):547-559. The limited quantity of comparative work has been discussed elsewhere. For example, the reader might refer to K. Gaskin, OCCU-
PATIONAL DIFFERENTIATION BY SEX: AN INTERNATIONAL
COMPARISON (Ph.D. Dissertation, Univ. of Washington,
1979).

E-3

Burstein, Paul
    1979   "Equal Employment Opportunity Legislation
            and the Income of Women and Nonwhites."
            AMERICAN SOCIOLOGICAL REVIEW 44:367-391.

    The vast majority of the articles, annotated
in this collection, deal with methodological and
theoretical issues that surround the analysis of
social influences on pay inequity, without necessarily addressing "policy application" issues surrounding such an analysis. The Burstein article
represents an exception to the rule, as it is the
author's intention to examine the impact of equal
employment opportunity (EEO) law/policy "on the economic situation of women and minority group members" (Burstein, p. 368).
    Burstein reviews a predominance of economic
pieces, finding them to be wanting on three scores:

(1) The literature ignores certain "complexities"
     surrounding the treatment of EEO law impacts.
     For example, it tends to assume that EEO law
     impacts equally on all protected groups.

E-3 (continued)

(2)   The literature has not, more specifically, an-
      alyzed the potential variant impact of the law
      on white women vs. non-whites (both male and
      female).

(3)   A consideration, in the literature, of white
      male "taste for discrimination" does not ade-
      quately measure "change" in attitudes, over
      time; and, that particular consideration rests
      on a somewhat controversial assumption that
      any change in "behavior" (such as the appli-
      cation of EEO law) will automatically result
      in a change in "attitude" (in this case, a
      "lessened" taste for discrimination)(1).

      With respect to the third matter, Burstein ar-
gues that economic empirical analysis is in error
by, for all intent and purposes, using changes in
EEO enforcement (a "behavioral" matter) as a proxy
for changes in taste for discrimination (an "attitudinal" matter). Further, with respect to the
"complexities" of EEO law impact (re: the first
and second matters), Burstein argues that economic
studies have failed to do two things: (a) they have
failed to separate out the effects on white women
vs. other protected groups (thus not measuring for
the degree to which sex discrimination may be more
or less pronounced than is race discrimination);
and, (b) such studies have failed to accurately
assess the "costs" of discrimination to employers.
      On the matter of costs, Burstein notes that
studies have tended to use EEO enforcement activity
expenditures as a proxy for employer costs--which
may or may not be accurate. Burstein can offer no
alternative measure of employer costs, per se. However, even if one assumes (as do the reviewed econ-
omists) that EEO activity is an appropriate proxy
for employer costs, then Burstein still takes issue
with the use of cumulative Equal Employment Opportunity Commission (EEOC) expenditures as a sole
measure of such EEO activity. He, thus, broadens
the EEO activity measure to encompass not only cumulative EEOC expenditures, but also "expenditures
per black and female member of the labor force, ...
expenditures per charge processed, and equal pay
act underpayments disclosed" (Burstein, p. 373).

E-3 (continued)

Beyond this more detailed operationalization of expenditures, Burstein further measures EEO enforcement activity by: (a) the quality of "judicial enforcement" or "annual and cumulative number and proportion of race and sex discrimination [court] cases
decided in favor of women and minorities" (Burstein,
p. 373); and, (b) the "demand for EEO enforcement
complaints of discrimination--race, sex, and total--
processed by the EEOC each year" (Burstein, p. 373).
      All other things being equal, Burstein hypothe-
sizes that greater EEO enforcement activity based on
the above-noted items (i.e., "behavioral" change),
decreased discriminatory attitudes (i.e., "attitudinal" change), increases in protected group productivity, and decreases in unemployment "should
have independent positive effects on the income of
nonwhite men, nonwhite women, and white women relative to those of white men" (p. 373).
      Analyzing census data, however, Burstein finds
a difference between the nature of the effects of
EEO activity on the income(2) of non-whites (both
male and female) and the income of white women.
      With respect to non-whites, Burstein finds (as
hypothesized) that lowered unemployment rate and
increased EEO enforcement activities contribute to
higher incomes. The matter of productivity effects
is a bit vague, since Burstein seems only to speak
of it in terms of "labor force participation." In
this respect, the finding would seem to counter that
which was hypothesized, since the author finds decreased labor force participation to influence increased incomes. As for attitudinal change, Burstein is unable to separate the effects of changed
attitudes from the effects of education (which was
introduced as an additional variable) on non-white
income changes.
      For white females, Burstein is (apparently)
able to separate attitudinal effects from education
effects, noting that there have been more favorable
attitudes toward white female labor force participation. In addition, the unemployment rate has declined, white female labor force participation has
increased, and EEO enforcement activities have increased. However, counter to what was hypothesized,
Burstein finds all of these matters resulting in
decreased white female incomes.

E-3 (continued)

Burstein offers the following possible explanations for his results:

(1)   The study did not account for the "strength"
       of certain "preexisting factors" that are as-
       sociated with the fact that "labor market dis-
       crimination against women is [actually] 'worse'
       than discrimination against nonwhites...."
       (p. 386). Among these "preexisting factors,"
       Burstein discusses the possibility of more "un-
       ified" interests among blacks than among women
       and women being a "more educated" group than
       blacks (thus, historically, restricting their
       labor force activity to a more narrow range of
       jobs than do blacks).

(2)   A greater number of white women than non-whites
       are available for employ. This makes it more
       difficult for white women (as a group) to
       achieve gains, relative to white men, than it
       is for non-whites to achieve such gains.

(3)   There exists different statutory application to
       women than to non-whites. For example, Bur-
       stein notes the following:

       (a)   Whereas the "supreme court has interpreted
              the constitution so as to make race a
              'suspect classification'.... [d]istinc-
              tions between the sexes have not attained
              this status" (p. 387).

       (b)   An initial "lack of clarity" over the re-
              lationship between federal and state law,
              on female labor force participation, may
              have slowed "female progress."

       (c)   "Women can still be treated unequally in
              those cases where sex is a bona fide oc-
              cupational qualification for a job; race
              is never considered a bona fide occupa-
              tional qualification" (p. 387).

(4)   The more recent differences in labor force
       participation (female increase; non-white de-
       crease) might be explained as follows. The

E-3 (continued)

"entry of white women into the labor force
could bring down the median range of those
who are working..." (p. 387)<3>. On the other
hand, the decline in non-white participation
makes it "easier to detect" income changes
not "confounded by trends in labor force participation" (p. 387).

Notes

<1> The controversy over whether attitudinal
change "automatically" results from behavioral
change, as well as the often suggested alterna-
tive--that behavioral change can only result from
a prior attitudinal change--is discussed in a number of social psychology and organizational behavior textbooks. As an example, the reader will find
an overview of such literature in D. Organ and W.
Hamner, ORGANIZATIONAL BEHAVIOR: AN APPLIED PSYCH-
OLOGICAL APPROACH (Plano, TX: Business Publications,
1982).

<2> In line with the suggestion by Szymanski
(D-30), Burstein does conceptually distinguish between "earnings" and "income"; however, he chooses
only to analyze income patterns in this study. The
reason given by Burstein is that he considers income
to be a better predictor of "overall economic well
being" (p. 372). For a contrasting point of view
on the relative merits of utilizing earnings vs.
income data in compensation research, see the Szymanski entry.

<3> Reference is being made, here, to what Sny-
der and Hudis (D-27) call the "competition" hypothesis. For at least one finding that it does not apply (at least in academic organizations), see Fox
(D-12).

E-4

Freedman, Sara M.
1978 "Some Determinants of Compensation Deci-
      sions." ACADEMY OF MANAGEMENT JOURNAL 21:
      397-409.

Due to the potential for variation in management practice across firms or even industries, writers, such as Livernash (A-3) and Grandjean (B-3),
comment on the need to be skeptical about the nature of external social comparisons. Other writers,
such as Spilerman (C-14), Stolzenberg (C-15), and,
Talbert and Bose (C-17), comment on the types of
social structural forces that might create wage level variance on occupation by occupation, organization by organization, or even industry by industry
bases.
    Variation in management practice, as a partic-
ular "social force" potentially contributing to per-
ceived/actual inequity, has not been subjected to
empirical examination in any of the above-noted articles. The Freedman research, in some respects,
acts to fill this apparent gap in the literature.
    Freedman's concern is with managerial decision-
making on compensation matters. Her specific research question is this: Given differential subordinate perceptions of pay inequity and differential
expressed desires, by subordinates, for a raise in
pay, to what extent will managers act to reduce
any actual pay inequity, through increases in pay?
Therefore, Freedman is testing for the quality of
fundamental manager-subordinate interaction over
wage matters.
    The Freedman study takes the form of a lab ex-
periment, using 275 undergraduate students as subjects. In general, the author finds that managers
will act to somewhat restore equity (though pay
raises), when they perceive subordinate employees
to be actually underpaid. Further, managers will
be more inclined to so restore equity, when they
perceive that underpaid employees have engaged in
some inequitable exchanges off the job and/or when
they are the recipients of employee demands for pay
raises. However, Freedman reports that managers
will not raise pay enough to totally restore actual
equity. She suggests that this might be due to certain "cultural norms," shared by managers, toward

E-4 (continued)

"cost minimization" and/or managerial judgments that
subordinate employees will perceive the magnitude
of a pay raise as being "large enough," even though
it does not perfectly restore pay equity. If the
writing of some others has any merit, however, then
the latter argument would only seem to hold under
conditions where subordinates lack knowledge of comparison others' earnings (cf., Cook, B-2) and/or
where subordinates have a different "preference mix"
with respect to organizational rewards (cf., Spilerman, C-14).

Freedman raises questions about the complete-
ness of her explanations--given the limited amount
of information provided to subjects in her experi-
ment. For example, the subjects were not provided
information regarding the manager's own pay equity/
inequity circumstance--which, apparently, has been
shown in other research to influence managerial decisions toward restoring subordinate of pay equity.
Another methodological matter, which Freedman does
not acknowledge (but which is a constant, whenever
generalizations are made from an experimental to an
actual business setting) is the degree to which the
judgments, in this case, of undergraduate students
can be considered representative of those of practicing managers(1).

From the standpoint of social forces that contribute to perceived/actual wage variation, a larger
question is still left unanswered by this particular
research; i.e., whether variation in the quality of
the social interaction (tested for by Freedman) acts
to heighten or reduce perceptions of pay inequity
among different subordinate groups(2).

Notes

(1) For a reference on the debate over this
particular methodological matter, see: E. Locke,
GENERALIZING FROM LABORATORY TO FIELD SETTINGS
(Lexington, MA: Lexington Books, 1986).

(2) It would appear that this type of question is being addressed throughout much of the more
micro-behavioral literature. A few of the better
reviews, in this respect, include those cited under

E-4 (continued)

note #1 in the Adams (A-1) annotation, as well as:
B. Staw, "Organizational Behavior: A Review and Re-
formulation of the Field's Outcome Variables." In
M. Rosenzweig and L. Porter, ANNUAL REVIEW OF PSY-
CHOLOGY, Vol. 35 (Palo Alto, CA: Annual Reviews,
Inc., 1984).

E-5

Freedman, Sara M.
    1979 "The Effects of Subordinate Sex, Pay Equity,
          and Strength of Demand on Compensation Deci-
          sions." SEX ROLES 5:649-658.

    In another article, Freedman (E-4) comments on
how variation in managerial strategy can be considered a social force influencing pay equity. In this
paper, Freedman is concerned with how variation in
subordinate strategy can also affect pay equity<1>.
    Acknowledging the findings of so many others
that sex discrimination influences equity of pay
(cf., Suter and Miller, D-29; Treiman and Terrell,
D-33), Freedman suggests that different strategies
employed by women than by men, when demanding equity, might hold the key for the eventual realization
of such equity<2>. Specifically, Freedman hypothesizes that, in the case of underpayment, if a woman
uses a more aggressive or "threatening" appeal, then
this will be better received by management than a
non-aggressive appeal, since "a female, who behaves
contrary to sex-role expectations ... conveys more
information to the manager about the seriousness of
[her] complaint" (Freedman, p. 651). However, previous research has suggested that either mode of appeal will yield roughly similar favorable results
for an underpaid male. So, Freedman further hypothesizes that, strategically, males can use the
more aggressive "threatening" or the less aggressive "pleading" appeals/demands with equal success.
    Freedman studies 88 undergraduate business stu-
dents<3>, and, her findings support the hypotheses.
Under conditions of underpayment, men can achieve
equity, regardless of strength of demand, whereas

E-5 (continued)

women can only achieve such equity through use of
a threatening demand.
     Freedman introduces a control for whether fe-
male subordinates can secure a raise in pay, using
a threatening appeal, under conditions of pay equity. She finds that they cannot. This leads Freedman to believe that the actual existing inequity,
not just the strength of appeal, might contribute
to the achievement of a pay increase. The inference, therefore, is that future research might measure for separate effects of strength of appeal and
presence/absence of inequity.
     In addition, Freedman finds **both** female and
male managers to respond equally well to threatening
subordinate female appeals, under conditions of inequity. However, the author thinks that the issue
of managers responding positively (under conditions
of inequity) to women, who do not behave according
to an "expected sex role," applies only to the reasoning of male managers. Freedman argues that, when
female managers respond positively to a threatening
appeal (under conditions of inequity), it has more
to do with the actual existence of inequity--less
to do with the female subordinate behaving contrary
to an expected sex role. Again, however, Freedman
cautions that more research is needed on the subject.

Notes

     (1) What is being inferred, through the two
Freedman articles, is how the nature of manager-
subordinate "exchange" becomes reflected in variant perceptions of pay equity. The reader with a
salient interest in this area is directed to the
references cited in note #2 of Freedman (E-4), as
well as to: S. Gould, "An Equity Exchange Model of
Organizational Involvement." ACADEMY OF MANAGEMENT
REVIEW 4(1979):53-62. Gould discusses (with mathe-
matical presentation) how an accounting for variation in the quantity and quality of subordinate involvement in organizational activities so instigates
"inducement contribution" exchange that it conditions both the perceptions of inequity and decisions
made on means to resolve perceived inequity.

E-5 (continued)

(2) The suggestion is based on a body of research, reviewed by Freedman, that (indeed) finds
this to be the case. Freedman's primary reference,
in this respect, appears to be: B. Rosen and T. Jer-
dee, "Effects of Sex and Threatening Versus Pleading
Appeals on Managerial Evaluations of Grievances."
JOURNAL OF APPLIED PSYCHOLOGY 60:442-445.

(3) As was the case with Freedman (E-4), questions can be raised about the potential generali-
zation to an actual business setting. Again, for
reference on the debate over this matter, see: E.
Locke, GENERALIZING FROM LABORATORY TO FIELD SET-
TINGS (Lexington, MA: Lexington Books, 1986).

E-6

Hill, Richard Child
   1974 "Unionization and Racial Income in the Me-
         tropolis." AMERICAN SOCIOLOGICAL REVIEW
         39:507-522.

   As noted among the entries in Part C of this
collection, economic segmentation theory challenges
more traditional human capital theoretical assumptions of homogeneous labor markets and solely ex-
planable pay variation within the context of job
qualifications. The economic segmentation view is
that investment in the development of employee skill
does not occur uniformly across sectors; and, two
of the factors contributing to such sectoral differences in human capital development are degree of
unionization and racial composition. The specific
argument is, thus, proposed by economic segmentation theory that employees, in some occupations,
do not benefit as much as do those in other occu-
pations--due to the fact that their occupational
categories are not represented by unions and are
largely populated by non-whites (cf., Beck, et al.,
C-1; Bibb and Form, C-2; Kalleberg, et al., C-9;
Parker, C-12).
   While Hill does not develop a formal theory of
economic segmentation, he does investigate the question of income differential on the basis of union

status and race. Indeed, Hill is actually interested in the preeminent role, played by unionization, toward defining any income differential by
race. In this respect, the reader will find a rather extensive and well-written literature review,
whereby Hill initially establishes how theorists
might approach his central research interest differently. Specifically, Hill argues that the literature proposes two fundamental hypotheses about
the effect of unionization on race-based income inequality: The "competition" hypothesis and the "exploitation" hypothesis.

The competition hypothesis, argues Hill, is
derivative from an assumption that the inequity effects of racial discrimination are more predominant,
under conditions of less economic competition; and,
since unionization is viewed as antithetical to
"competitive labor markets," such union activity
acts to reinforce race-based pay discrimination.
Hill states the competition hypothesis, as follows:

> The higher the level of unionization in
> a metropolitan area, the lower the level
> of black income and the higher the racial
> inequality (p. 510).

The competition hypothesis, therefore, assumes
the beneficiaries of race-based pay discrimination
to be white labor. From the standpoint of those
segmentation theories cited earlier, it could be
argued that this is, indeed, the case, since differential allocation of whites into core sector jobs
ensures that whites (a) can better avail themselves
of career-ladder training and (b) are offered the
greater protection of unions representing jobs in
that sector.

The exploitation hypothesis, however, does not
assume either white or black labor to benefit from
race-based pay discrimination. The only beneficiaries are assumed to be white employers. Unionization is viewed, not only as a protective mecha-
nism for white labor but for black labor as well.
The exploitation hypothesis is stated by Hill in
the following manner:

E-6 (continued)

> The higher the level of unionization in
> a metropolitan area, the higher the level
> of black income and the lower the racial
> income inequality (p. 512).

Like Wright (D-35), Hill establishes a case for
differential income returns by social class. However, unlike Wright, Hill only roughly demarcates
two classes: "employer" and "worker." Hill presents
the exploitation hypothesis on the basis of members
of the employer class (largely white) suppressing
the income of both white and black members of the
"worker" class, through racial discrimination practice. It happens, according to this hypothesis, due
to weakened unions(1):

> Racial divisions weaken the ability of
> workers to organize effectively when
> bargaining with employers. As a result,
> economic discrimination fosters lower
> incomes for black workers and their fam-
> ilies, but also lowers the income of
> white workers while elevating the income
> of white employers (Hill, p. 510).

The exploitation argument, therefore, is that
only strong unions can correct for the class differentiation effects that foster such racial divisions, lowered bargaining power, and overall lowered
incomes.

With its emphasis on equal harm to all workers,
regardless of race, the exploitation hypothesis does
not assume any potential discrimination, by race,
within unions proper. Consequently, Hill feels that
the exploitation hypothesis might only be applicable
to metropolitan areas where there is an predominance
of "industrial" unions (with a history of racial integration within unions). In non-metropolitan areas, Hill argues that "craft" unions predominate;
and, since craft unions have, historically, acted
to discriminate against non-whites, Hill feels that
the competition hypothesis might be more applicable
to such non-metropolitan areas. In any event, since
Hill selects a metropolitan sample, in this study,
he expects the exploitation hypothesis to be more
applicable.

E-6 (continued)

Utilizing 1960 census data, Hill measures for the effect of unionization, both on median non-white family income and on non-white income as a percent of white family income. While doing such, he controls for the effects of: regional difference (assuming greater racial discrimination in the South in the 1950's), percent of labor force in manufacturing industries, median non-white education, and non-white education as a percent of white education. Controlling for all of the moderating variables, Hill finds that, counter to either hypothesis, there exist no significant effects of unionization on racial income inequality. Nevertheless, Hill seems to still feel that the exploitation hypothesis offers the greater potential for explaining the effects of unionization, since: (a) counter to the competition hypothesis, there is no evidence that unionization raises the level of income inequality by race; and, (b) the level of unionization does affect the median level of non-white income, per se, in the manner hypothesized by the exploitation thesis. In other words, the higher the level of unionization, the higher the level of non-white income.

Note

(1) Hill's exploitation hypothesis is derivative from the thought of M. Reich. A more complete outline of the Reich thinking can be found in the Szymanski (D-30) annotation.

E-7

Pfeffer, Jeffrey and Jerry Ross
    1981   "Unionization and Income Inequality."
           INDUSTRIAL RELATIONS 20:271-285.

Hill (E-6) and Beck (E-1) analyze alternative hypotheses, surrounding the effects of unionization on differential income returns to race. The first hypothesis has been labeled as "competition" or "white protectionist"; the second hypothesis as "exploitation," "class consciousness," or "neo-

Marxist." Both Hill and Beck provide rather thorough literature reviews on the competing hypotheses.
The reader will now find Pfeffer and Ross not only
reviewing the work of Hill and Beck, but also adding
even more information on what previous research has
been done on the two competing hypotheses--than had
been presented in the earlier articles by Hill and
Beck(1).

While his findings are not the most conclusive
on the matter, Hill (E-6) infers that, at least in
metropolitan areas, the "neo-Marxist" explanation
might have more merit; i.e., that since employer
action to block unionization depresses income for
all, unionization acts to the benefit of all work-
ers--thereby, if anything, lowering (rather than
raising) racial income inequality. On the other
hand, Beck (E-1) argues that the "white protectionist" hypothesis is more applicable; i.e., that increased unionization contributes to enhanced race-
based income inequality. As stated in the Beck annotation (re: notes #3 and #4 to that entry), Pfeffer and Ross have called the Beck conclusions into
question through some of their work published before
the one hereby being annotated(2); and, the reader
will find the Pfeffer and Ross point of view being
somewhat expanded upon, both theoretically and meth-
odologically, in this particular article. Specifically, the authors provide a more definitive analysis of data on the matters of whether unionization
enhances or lowers equality of returns to race. Un-
fortunately, however, the data reported in this paper is on males only; and, thus, some of the questions "begged" by the Beck research (regarding differences by sex) are not addressed in this particular article(3).

In any event, based on their review of the literature, Pfeffer and Ross note that most research,
to date, tends to contradict white protectionist
activity. Specifically, the empirical work reviewed by Pfeffer and Ross seems to (by and large)
not be arguing the question of whether unionization
lowers race-based income inequality--only the degree
to which inequity reductions are strictly interracial or both inter and intraracial. Although not
accounting for sex and (apparently not) age differences (re: note #3), Pfeffer and Ross do con-

E-7 (continued)

trol for the effects of education and skill levels,
socioeconomic/occupational status (measured in several different ways), and size of city (thereby
somewhat addressing the metropolitan/non-metropol-
itan issue of concern to Hill, E-6). Pfeffer and
Ross also control for the degree to which differences in occupational distributions, between union
and non-union sectors, might affect the degree to
which inequality is reduced.

The authors generally find, as they had anticipated, that interracial differences are reduced, in
the presence of unionization. The effects of unionization on reducing intraracial inequality, however, is much more pronounced for whites than for
blacks. Pfeffer and Ross suggest that this might
result from a more general trend of blacks (regardless of union status) enjoying lower returns to education than do whites.

Notes

(1) Pfeffer and Ross, like Hill and Beck, review a good body of sociological literature; however, exemplifying what Pfeffer and Ross add, from
a substantive standpoint, these authors appear to
review a larger body of economic theory than do Hill
or Beck. By doing so, Pfeffer and Ross are able to
point out some rather "fine" distinctions between
more economic and more sociological approaches to
the subject matter--such as the following point:
"Economic theories [unlike more sociological theories] presuppose no overall
strategic action on the part of either
labor or capital; rather, the effects
... are seen as resulting from the un-
anticipated consequences of both sets of
actors pursuing their own self-interests"
(p. 273).

(2) Reference is to the following two articles
by Pfeffer and Ross: "Union-nonunion Effects on Wage
and Status Attainment." INDUSTRIAL RELATIONS 19
(1980):140-151; "Unionization and Female Wage and
Status Attainment." INDUSTRIAL RELATIONS 20(1981):
179-185. As best this writer can determine, Pfeffer

E-7 (continued)

and Ross use "income" and "wages" interchangeably,
not making the operational distinction argued for
by Szymanski (D-30).

(3) This matter is particularly troublesome,
given an implied criticism by Pfeffer and Ross (in
this article) of Beck for not adequately accounting
for sex differences in the the latter's research.
Also, Pfeffer and Ross seem to complain that Beck
does not adequately control for the effects of
"age"; but, this writer is not convinced that Pfeffer and Ross have done so either.
First of all, Pfeffer and Ross use a "mature
male" bracket of National Longitudinal Surveys data
(aged 45-59). Data on this group was apparently
examined at two points in time: 1966 and 1975. Assuming that data on the same individuals was looked
at longitudinally (not simply cohorts of the same
age bracket at two different points in time), then
there is still a rather pronounced age group (under
45 years) that has not been tested.
More importantly, however, this writer cannot
detect, either from the Pfeffer and Ross discussion
or from the tabular presentation, where age is ex-
plicitly introduced as a control. It might be that
Pfeffer and Ross have somehow "built in" age, as
part of their socioeconomic/occupational status
measurement at different points in time; but, based
on the information, as presented, this writer could
not draw such a conclusion.

E-8

Remick, Helen
   1981 "The Comparable Worth Controversy." PUBLIC
        PERSONNEL MANAGEMENT 10:371-383.

As noted in the Burstein (E-3) entry, most of
the annotated articles in this collection deal with
methodological and theoretical issues--but not policy application issues--surrounding the analysis of
social influences on pay inequity. At the level of
that policy application, which aims to resolve sex
discrimination, in particular, the issue (as noted

E-8 (continued)

in this book's introduction) is sometimes referred
to as the achievement of "comparable worth." There
exists no shortage of journal articles that reflect
the legal and methodological problems of trying to
operationalize comparable worth (when attempting to
develop "fair" and "effective" policy at the same
time). However, most of this literature, at best,
appears only to offer cursory discussion of the social environment in which comparable worth policy
is debated and developed(1). Nevertheless, in an
excellent review of the legal literature on comparable worth, Milkovich and Broderick(2) note the
impossibility of assessing the "fairness" of any
comparable worth policy, devoid of in-depth analysis of that social environment.

The Remick article is included in this book,
as it serves as something of an exception to the
rule among writing on comparable worth. While Remick does not provide extensive empirical analysis
on the matter of social environmental dynamics, she
does (nevertheless) provide a theoretical commentary
on the detailed quality of those social forces that
might be impinging on policy formation.

For example, a number of writers listed elsewhere in this volume, such as Beck, et al. (C-1),
Hodson (C-7), and Spilerman (C-14), comment on how--
from the standpoint of dual sector analysis--there
exists an overrepresentation of women and less educated individuals among lower paying jobs in the
periphery. From the standpoint of compensation policy, therefore, one could argue that, if employees
in the periphery deserve to be paid less, then it
should be due to lower educational levels--but, not
due to the fact that they are women. Remick argues
that a more detailed analysis of the situation reveals these more general sectoral findings to be
somewhat deceiving. Presenting some census data on
the matter, Remick notes that: (a) women are actually more likely than men to graduate high school,
and the "gap" between the number of male and female
employees of higher education is closing--yet, within all educational categories, males (on average)
earn substantially more than do females; (b) the
wage differentials continue, even within similar
occupational categories(3).

E-8 (continued)

Such writers as Parker (C-12), Sørensen (C-13),
Spilerman (C-14), Coverman (D-6), and Rosenfeld
(D-24), comment on how the social force of differential "career progression" can serve as a basis
for variant compensation; and, Remick notes how,
indeed, the argument is often made by policy-makers
that--since women have more "interrupted" career
patterns than do men--women cannot expect to accrue
salaries that men can accrue. It is Remick's point
of view that, while a recent "influx" of female participation in the workforce might result in less pay
for the less experienced female employee (in the
short run), over the long-run, what "interruptions"
occur over the course of a woman's career (e.g.,
child birth) should be no greater than "interruptions" in the work histories of men (e.g., armed
forces participation)(4).

Issues surrounding disputes over "distributive
justice," derivative from perceived discrimination
by sex--as well as the "norms" that derive from ad-
ministratively-held "beliefs" about differential
career patterns--represent the type aspects of the
social environment that Mahoney (A-4) argues as mit-
igating against any classical/neoclassical economic
assumption of how "equity" derives solely from market exchange. In addition to Mahoney, many of the
writers, cited throughout Part C of this collection
(on economic segmentation), have commented on how
other structural factors--such as economic concentration and variant quality of unionization--serve
as social forces that belie the reality of market-
based equity. All of these matters are discussed
by Remick as impacting on the quality by which compensation policy is developed.

What is missing from the discussions of many
other writers, listed throughout this book, however,
is definitive thinking on the nature of those cultural "values" that determine "perceptions of status
and fair compensation" (Remick, p. 375). Remick offers, for consideration, one "value"-based policy--
that of "job evaluation," whereby jobs are ranked
by weighted "factors" involving "some variation of
effort, skill, responsibility, and working conditions" (Remick, p. 374)(5). The fact that such an
"evaluation" system is used represents a "value"
that its utility is "good"; but, it is Remick's con-

E-8 (continued)

tention that the subjectivity of the job evaluation
process represents the thinking of those who are
"wedded" to what makes male-dominated occupations
valuable--not necessarily what makes female-dominated occupations valuable. Consequently, argues
Remick, one is confronted with such evaluation factors as: the degree to which one supervises others,
the amount of money and/or equipment that the employee is responsible for, the more decisions one
makes, etc.
     Remick presents no empirical evidence to sub-
stantiate the dominance of these type factors in
job evaluations or the fact that they derive from
the quality of "male" dominated (vs. "female" dominated) occupations. However, the point is that
the author has (at least) presented some thinking
on the more detailed quality of how social values
influence policy. She, thus, provides a quality
of thought that is absent from many other policy-
oriented articles. Remick acknowledges that such
values (and evaluation factors based on such values)
are subject to change. Her section on "the future
of comparable worth," albeit brief, does offer some
suggestions on how changing values are becoming reflected in changed personnel policies (compensation
and otherwise), as well as in legal changes(6).

                         Notes

     (1) While the literature, in question, appears
limited on the matter of social environmental discussion and/or analysis, much of it does offer substantial detail on legal matters, as well as on
problems of operational definition. Per the reader's potential interest in such matters, the following are a few examples: D. Thomsen, "Compensation
and Benefits." PERSONNEL JOURNAL 60(1981):348-354;
M. Carter, "Comparable Worth: An Idea Whose Time Has
Come?" PERSONNEL JOURNAL 60 (1981):792-794; R. Schon-
berger and H. Hennessey, Jr., "Is Equal Pay for Comparable Worth Fair?" PERSONNEL JOURNAL 60(1981):964-
968; E. Brennan, "Sex Discrimination and Comparable
Worth." PERSONNEL JOURNAL 63(1984):56-59; M. Wallace, Jr. "Methodology, Research Practice, and Pro-
gressing Personnel and Industrial Relations." ACAD-

E-8 (continued)

EMY OF MANAGEMENT REVIEW 8(1983):6-13; T. Mahoney,
"Approaches to the Definition of Comparable Worth."
ACADEMY OF MANAGEMENT REVIEW 8(1983):14-22; E. Coop-
er and G. Barrett, "Equality and Gender: Implica-
tions of Court Cases for Personnel Practices." ACAD-
EMY OF MANAGEMENT REVIEW 9(1984):84-94; Thirteen
articles contained in a Special Issue on Comparable
Worth (N. Reichenberg, editor), PUBLIC PERSONNEL
MANAGEMENT 12(1983):323-466.

(2) G. Milkovich and R. Broderick, "Pay Discrimination: Legal Issues and Implications for Research." INDUSTRIAL RELATIONS 21(1982):309-317.

(3) The reader will note similarity, here, with
the findings of others listed elsewhere in this collection. For example, both Halaby (D-14) and Rexroat (D-23) comment on the potential for variant
pay within occupational categories. Halaby finds
such pay variation (as Remick seems to suggest),
to be the result of variant rates of return to education within ranks; Rexroat sees it more as a
matter of inability to be promoted to appropriate
ranks. The reader is reminded that Ward and Mueller (D-34) extend much of the discussion, arguing
for: the existence of primary and secondary labor
markets within all sectors; differential allocation
to positions of formal authority; and, as a consequence, variation (by sex) in rates of pay.

(4) For information on how salary differentials, by sex, continue to persist, even when such
"interruptions" are controlled for, see Suter and
Miller (D-29).

(5) "Job Evaluation" involves analysis, at the
level of "job content," on issues of no small interest to less policy-oriented writers, listed elsewhere in this collection--such as Bridges and Berk
(C-3) and Talbert and Bose (C-17). While it can be
said that, at the level of policy-oriented discussion, all of the articles, cited in note #1, offer
some useful information on "job evaluation" legal
and methodological issues, perhaps the most comprehensive information of this type can be found in the
Cooper and Barrett article (ACADEMY OF MANAGEMENT

E-8 (continued)

REVIEW, Vol. 9), as well as in three of the articles that are part of the PUBLIC PERSONNEL MANAGE-
MENT Special Issue (Vol. 12). These three articles
are: L. Eyde, "Evaluating Job Evaluation: Emerging
Research Issues for Comparable Worth Analysis" (pp.
425-444); D. Pierson, et al., "Equal Pay for Jobs
of Comparable Worth: A Quantified Job Content Approach" (pp. 445-460); R. Fredlund, "Valuing Work:
Complications-Contradictions-Compensation" (pp. 461-
466).

    (6) For a general discussion and references,
relevant to the issue of values, resulting in sex-
typical attitudes and/or behavior, see Coverman
(D-6). For a more detailed listing of the sources
of social values that impact on changing compensation policy, than that provided by Remick, see the
article by R. Fredlund in the Special Issue of PUB-
LIC PERSONNEL MANAGEMENT (Vol. 12, pp. 461-466).
For further general thinking on social values and
the development of comparable worth policy, see:
W. Wolf and N. Fligstein, "Sexual Stratification:
Differences in Power in the Work Setting." SOCIAL
FORCES 58(1979):94-107.

RESOURCE GUIDE

RESOURCE GUIDE

Major Legislation and Court Cases

The primary federal legislation that has bearing on pay equity administration is represented by: The Equal Pay Act of 1963, amendment to the Fair Labor Standards Act of 1938; and, the Civil Rights Act, Title VII, as amended by the Equal Employment Opportunity Act of 1972. Some major court cases on pay equity include:

Schultz v. Wheaton Glass, 1970, 421 F. 2d 259.

Hodgeson v. Brookhaven General Hospital, 1970, 436 F. 2d 719.

Corning Glass Works v. Brennan, 1974, 417 U.S. 188.

Brennan v. Prince William Hospital, 1974, 417 U.S. 188.

DiSalvo v. Chamber of Commerce, 1976, 416 F. Supp. 844.

Angelo v. Bacharach Instrument Company, 1977, 555 F. 2d 1164.

Christensen v. State of Iowa, 1977, 563 F. 2d 353.

Lemons v. City and County of Denver, 1980, 620 F. 2d 228.

IUE v. Westinghouse, 1980, 620 F. 2d 228.

Gunther v. County of Washington, 1981, U.S. Supreme Court, 451 U.S. 161.

Briggs v. City of Madison, 1982, W.D. Wisc., 436 F. Supp. 435.

Kouba and EEOC v. Allstate Insurance Company, 1982, 691 F. 2d 873.

continued next page

Spaulding v. University of Washington,
1984, 740 F. 2d 686.
AFSCME v. State of Washington, 1983,
578 F. Supp. 846.
AFSCME v. State of Washington, 1985,
770 F. 2d 1401.

The case of AFSCME v. State of Washington, although heard in 1983, was reversed in September
1985 by the Ninth Circuit Court of Appeals. Prior
to the court reversal, the parties to this particular case entered into negotiations on an out-of-
court settlement. Such an agreement was reached
on December 31, 1985. Summaries of the settlement's
content can be found in two issues of the PUBLIC
ADMINISTRATION TIMES (Vol. 9, 1986). The issues
are: #2 (January 15); #8 (April 15). In this reversal, the court stated that, although an employer might become aware of an inequitable wage structure, through a comparable worth study, that employer is not obligated to eliminate the inequity
if there was no "intent" to create it. As this book
goes to press, an even more recent ruling has been
handed down by the Seventh Circuit Court of Appeals
that is similar to the Ninth Circuit ruling. The
suit had been filed by the American Nurses' Association, the Illinois Nurses' Association, and others
against the State of Illinois. The ruling is summarized in the PUBLIC ADMINISTRATION TIMES (Vol. 9,
#13--July 1, 1986).
    Major legislation and court decisions are sum-
marized in any number of legal and administrative
journal articles (for examples, see Remick, E-8,
notes #1 and #2), as well as in general textbooks
on personnel/labor law, personnel administration,
labor relations, and compensation administration/
law. The new researcher in the area will, for example, find an excellent introductory review and
commentary in M. Wallace and C. Fay, COMPENSATION
THEORY AND PRACTICE (Boston: Kent Publishing Co.,
1983). More advanced discussion, in book form, can
be found in such sources as: D. Treiman and H. Hartman, WOMEN, WORK, AND WAGES: EQUAL PAY FOR JOBS OF
EQUAL VALUE (Washington, DC: National Academy Press,
1981); E.R. Livernash, COMPARABLE WORTH: ISSUES AND
ALTERNATIVES (Washington, DC: Equal Employment Advisory Council, 1980).

There also exist certain published bibliogra-
phies, which list a number of titles from the legal
literature. Examples include the following, which
are available through the Vance Bibliographies PUB-
LIC ADMINISTRATION SERIES (Monticello, IL): E. Cook,
"Comparable Worth" (Document P-1321, November, 1983);
A. White, "Comparable Work and Equal Pay" (Document
P-1650, March, 1985).

Organizations

What follows is a list of 50 organizations that
demonstrate some interest in compensation issues.
The list is compiled based, in part, on this writer's knowledge of the organizational interests,
as well as from existing organization directories.
The organizations are listed in alphabetical
order, with addresses and telephone numbers provided. Listed by the descriptor, "interests," is
information on the type interests primarily served
by each organization: activist; academic; government
and/or business researcher (GBR); government and/or
business practitioner (GBP). Most of the organizations are quite large; so, it is probable that,
in many cases, several categories of interests are
served. Also identified are any particular sections
or divisions of an organization which appear to take
a special interest in pay equity issues.

[1] ACADEMY OF MANAGEMENT

Interests: Academic.

Headquarters: P.O. Drawer KZ
               Mississippi State, MS 39762
               (601) 325-3928

Divisions: Personnel/Human Resources;
Organizational Behavior; Social Issues in
in Management; Women in Management; Public
Sector; Organization and Management Theory.

[2] ACADEMY OF POLITICAL SCIENCE

Interests: Academic.

Headquarters: 2852 Broadway
               New York, NY 10025
               (212) 866-6752

[3] ADMINISTRATIVE MANAGEMENT SOCIETY

Interests: GBP, GBR.

Headquarters: Maryland Rd.
               Willow Grove, PA 19090
               (215) 659-4300

[4] ADVOCATES FOR WOMEN

Interests: Activist.

Headquarters: 414 Mason St.
               San Francisco, CA 94102
               (415) 391-4870

[5] AMERICAN ANTHROPOLOGICAL ASSOCIATION

Interests: Academic.

Headquarters: 1703 Hampshire Ave., NW
               Washington, DC 20009
               (202) 232-8800

[6] AMERICAN ASSOCIATION FOR COUNSELING AND
     DEVELOPMENT

Interests: Academic, GBP, GBR.

Headquarters: 5999 Stevenson Ave.
               Alexandria, VA 22304
               (703) 823-9800

Division: Association for Non-white Concerns.

[7] AMERICAN ASSOCIATION OF UNIVERSITY PROFESSORS

Interests: Academic, Activist.

Headquarters: 1012 14th St., Suite 500
Washington, DC 20005
(202) 737-5900

[8] AMERICAN ASSOCIATION OF UNIVERSITY WOMEN

Interests: Academic, Activist.

Headquarters: 2401 Virginia Ave., NW
Washington, DC 20037
(202) 785-7700

[9] AMERICAN BAR ASSOCIATION

Interests: The major professional association
of practicing attorneys. Available information, through the ABA Information Service,
serves the interests of all four categories.

Headquarters: 750 N. Lake Shore Dr.
Chicago, IL 60611
(312) 988-5000

[10] AMERICAN CIVIL LIBERTIES UNION

Interests: Activist.

Headquarters: 132 W. 43rd St.
New York, NY 10036
(212) 944-9800

[11] AMERICAN COMPENSATION ASSOCIATION

Interests: GBP, Academic.

Headquarters: P.O. Box 1176
Scottsdale, AZ 85252
(602) 951-9191

[12] AMERICAN ECONOMIC ASSOCIATION

   Interests: Academic, GBP, GBR.

   Headquarters: 1313 21st Ave., S.
                  Nashville, TN 37212
                  (615) 322-2595

[13] AMERICAN EDUCATIONAL RESEARCH ASSOCIATION

   Interests: Academic.

   Headquarters: 1230 17th St., NW
                  Washington, DC 20036
                  (202) 223-9485

[14] AMERICAN FEDERATION OF GOVERNMENT EMPLOYEES

   Interests: Activist.

   Headquarters: 1325 Massachusetts Ave., NW
                  Washington, DC 20005
                  (202) 737-8700

[15] AMERICAN FEDERATION OF LABOR AND CONGRESS OF
     INDUSTRIAL ORGANIZATIONS

   Interests: As the largest of labor organizations, the membership of the AFL-CIO, is classified as "activist." However, most major unions, maintain information services that also
   benefit persons with other than activist interests. The AFL-CIO, in particular, appears
   to hold an exceptional quantity of information.

   Headquarters: 815 16th St., NW
                  Washington, DC 20006
                  (202) 637-5000

   Pay Equity Information appears to be especially
   available from at least two sources:

   (1) AFL-CIO Library--(202) 293-5297.
   (2) Industrial Union Research--(202) 393-5581.

[16] AMERICAN FEDERATION OF STATE, COUNTY, AND
MUNICIPAL EMPLOYEES (AFSCME)

Interests: Activist.

Headquarters: 1625 L St., NW
               Washington, DC 20036
               (202) 452-4800

[17] AMERICAN FEDERATION OF TEACHERS

Interests: Activist.

Headquarters: 555 New Jersey Ave., NW
               Washington, DC 20001
               202-879-4400

[18] AMERICAN MANAGEMENT ASSOCIATIONS

Interests: GBP, GBR, Academic.

Headquarters: 135 W. 50th St.
               New York, NY 10020
               (212) 586-8100

Divisions: Human Resources; Employee Benefits.

[19] AMERICAN POLITICAL SCIENCE ASSOCIATION

Interests: Academic, GBP, GBR.

Headquarters: 1527 New Hampshire Ave., NW
               Washington, DC 20036
               (202) 387-8585

[20] AMERICAN PSYCHOLOGICAL ASSOCIATION

Interests: Academic.

Headquarters: 1200 17th St., NW
               Washington, DC 20036
               (202) 955-7600

[21] AMERICAN SOCIETY FOR PERSONNEL ADMINISTRATION

Interests: GBP, GBR, Academic.

Headquarters: 606 N. Washington St.
                Alexandria, VA 22314
                (703) 548-3440

[22] AMERICAN SOCIETY FOR PUBLIC ADMINISTRATION

Interests: GBP, GBR, Academic.

Headquarters: 1120 G St., NW
                Washington, DC 20005
                (202) 393-7870

Sections: Personnel Administration and Labor
Relations; Women in Public Administration;
Minority Public Administrators; Government
and Business; Intergovernmental Administration and Management.

[23] AMERICAN SOCIOLOGICAL ASSOCIATION

Interests: Academic, GBR, GBP.

Headquarters: 1722 N St., NW
                Washington, DC 20036
                (202) 833-3410

Sections: Organizations and Occupations; Sex
and Gender; Racial and Ethnic Minorities;
Sociological Practice.

[24] THE ASSOCIATION OF HUMAN RESOURCES MANAGEMENT
AND ORGANIZATIONAL BEHAVIOR (HRMOB)

Interests: Academic, GBR, GBP.

Headquarters: George Washington University
                2109 Cunningham Dr., Suite 100
                Hampton, VA 23666
                (804) 838-8101

[25] ASSOCIATION FOR SOCIAL ECONOMICS

Interests: GBR, Academic.

Headquarters: Box 10318
Louisiana Tech University
Ruston, LA 71272
(318) 257-3701

[26] ATLANTIC ECONOMIC SOCIETY

Interests: Academic, GBP, GBR.

Headquarters: Box 101
Southern Illinois University
Edwardsville, IL 62026
(618) 692-2291

[27] CENTER FOR DEMOCRATIC ALTERNATIVES

Interests: Academic, Activist, GBR.

Headquarters: 853 Broadway, Room 2014
New York, NY 10003
(212-473-3920)

[28] COMPARABLE WORTH PROJECT

Interests: Activist.

Headquarters: 488 41st Street, #5
Oakland, CA 94609
(415) 658-1808

[29] EMPLOYEE BENEFIT RESEARCH INSTITUTE

Interests: GBR, GBP.

Headquarters: 2121 K St., NW, Suite 860
Washington, DC 20037
(202) 659-0670

[30] EMPLOYERS COUNCIL ON FLEXIBLE COMPENSATION

Interests: GBP, Activist.

Headquarters: 1700 Pennsylvania Ave., NW
Washington, DC 20006
(202) 393-1728

[31] EMPLOYMENT MANAGEMENT ASSOCIATION

Interests: GBP, GBR.

Headquarters: 20 William St.
Wellesley, MA 02181
(617) 235-8878

[32] EQUAL EMPLOYMENT OPPORTUNITY COMMISSION

Interests: The EEOC is the agency of the federal government with enforcement responsibility for the Equal Pay Act of 1963. The agency
has certain information services of potential
benefit to all four interest categories. The
EEOC publishes, among other things, digests of
legal opinions.

Headquarters: 1800 G St., NW
Washington, DC 20506
(202) 343-5621

[33] HUMAN RESOURCE PLANNING SOCIETY

Interests: GBP.

Headquarters: P.O. Box 2553
Grand Central Station
New York, NY 10163
(617) 837-0630

[34] INTERNATIONAL PERSONNEL MANAGEMENT ASSOCIATION

Interests: GBP, GBR, Academic.

Headquarters: 1617 Duke St.
                Alexandria, VA 22314
                (703) 549-7100

[35] NATIONAL ASSOCIATION OF UNIVERSITY WOMEN

Interests: Academic.

Headquarters: 6453 Belfield Ave.
                Philadelphia, PA 19119
                (215) 438-3119

[36] NATIONAL EMPLOYEE BENEFITS INSTITUTE

Interests: Activist.

Headquarters: 2550 M St., NW, Suite 785
                Washington, DC 20037
                (800) 558-7258

[37] NATIONAL EDUCATION ASSOCIATION

Interests: Academic, Activist.

Headquarters: 1201 16th St., NW
                Washington, DC 20036
                (202) 833-4000

Divisions: Human and Civil Rights; Political
Affairs; Research.

[38] NATIONAL ORGANIZATION FOR WOMEN

Interests: Activist.

Headquarters: 1401 New York Ave., NW
                Suite 800
                Washington, DC 20005
                (202) 347-2279

[39] NATIONAL SOCIAL SCIENCE AND LAW CENTER

Interests: GBR.

Headquarters: 1825 Connecticut Ave., NW
                 Suite 401
                 Washington, DC 20009
                 (202) 797-1100

[40] NATIONAL WOMEN'S LAW CENTER

Interests: Activist, GBR.

Headquarters: 1751 N St., NW
                 Washington, DC 20036
                 (202) 872-0676

[41] PANEL ON PAY EQUITY RESEARCH

Interests: This organization primarily acts
to fund and facilitate research on pay equity
issues. It, therefore, provides services that
are of particular benefit to the Academic and
GBR categories.

Headquarters: NRC/National Academy of Sciences
                 2101 Constitution Ave., NW
                 Room JH852
                 Washington, DC 20418
                 (202) 334-3590

[42] POLICY STUDIES ORGANIZATION

Interests: Academic, GBP, GBR.

Headquarters: 361 Lincoln Hall
                 Univ. of Illinois
                 Urbana, IL 61801
                 (217) 359-8541

[43] SOCIETY FOR THE ADVANCEMENT OF MANAGEMENT

Interests: GBP, GBR, Academic.

Headquarters: 2331 Victory Parkway
               Cincinnati, OH 45206
               (513) 751-4566

[44] SOCIETY FOR APPLIED ANTHROPOLOGY

Interests: Academic.

Headquarters: 1001 Connecticut Ave., NW
               Washington, DC 20036
               (202) 466-8518

[45] SOCIETY FOR THE PSYCHOLOGICAL STUDY OF SOCIAL
ISSUES

Interests: Academic, GBP.

Headquarters: P.O. Box 1248
               Ann Arbor, MI 48106
               (313) 662-9130

[46] SOCIETY FOR THE STUDY OF SOCIAL PROBLEMS

Interests: Academic.

Headquarters: SUNY-Buffalo
               1300 Elmwood Ave.
               Buffalo, NY 14222
               (716) 878-6935

[47] THE WOMAN ACTIVIST

Interests: Activist.

Headquarters: 2310 Barbour Rd.
               Falls Church, VA 22043
               (703) 513-8716

[48] WOMEN IN MANAGEMENT

Interests: GBP.

Headquarters: P.O. Box 11268
                 Chicago, IL 60611
                 (312) 963-0134

[49] WOMEN'S EQUITY PROGRAM

Interests: Academic, GBP.

Headquarters: Nelson House
                 University of Massachusetts
                 Amherst, MA 01003
                 (413) 545-1558

[50] WOMEN'S RESEARCH AND EDUCATION INSTITUTE

Interests: GBR, GBP.

Headquarters: 204 Fourth St., SE
                 Washington, DC 20003
                 (202) 546-1010

AUTHOR INDEX

AUTHOR INDEX